Presented

By

Mr. & Mrs. Earl W. Spangler

In Memory Of

Virgil McIntyre

OUR SOUTHERN HIGHLANDERS

Our Southern Highlanders

*A Narrative of Adventure
in the Southern Appalachians
and a Study of Life among
the Mountaineers*

BY HORACE KEPHART

WITH AN INTRODUCTION BY
GEORGE ELLISON

.

THE UNIVERSITY OF TENNESSEE PRESS
Knoxville

Frontispiece: Horace Kephart, about 1930.
Photograph by George Masa, Asheville, North Carolina

Library of Congress Cataloging in Publication Data

Kephart, Horace, 1862–1931.
  Our southern highlanders.
  Includes bibliographical references.
    1. Mountain whites (Southern States)—Social life and
customs. 2. Appalachian Mountains, Southern—Social
life and customs. I. Title.
F217.A65K46 1976   975   76-18903
ISBN 0-87049-197-0

CONTENTS

ILLUSTRATIONS

INTRODUCTION

No book devoted to the Southern Appalachians is more
widely known, read, and respected than Horace Kephart's
Our Southern Highlanders. It is the classic study of the
Southern mountains, and the authors of virtually every
book written about the region since the publication of
Kephart's volume owe and usually acknowledge a debt
to him. A more lofty tribute, perhaps, to the book's ulti-
mate worth is that among the people of the region, most
especially the native mountaineers of eastern Tennessee,
northern Georgia, and western North Carolina, it is the
most sought after and praised study of the Southern Appalachians. Yet despite the fact that the first edition of
Our Southern Highlanders appeared more than sixty years
ago, very little indeed is known concerning either the
events or motivations behind Kephart's writing of the
book or the methods he utilized in putting it together.

Kephart's life can be divided into three distinct periods. The years from his birth in 1862 to the time of his
arrival in the Great Smoky Mountains in 1904 were ones
of education, travel and work abroad, family life, and
employment as a professional librarian in the Northeast
and St. Louis. The years from 1904 to 1913 were those of
seclusion in the Smokies, travel in other portions of the
Southern Appalachians, and initial establishment of what
became a permanent residence in Bryson City, North
Carolina. It was in this middle period that he produced
his two significant books, *Camping and Woodcraft* (1906)
and *Our Southern Highlanders* (1913). From 1913 until
his death in an automobile accident in 1931, Kephart
lived a comparatively settled life in Bryson City marked

by modest fame and relative security as a writer. Those final years, during which he emerged as one of the leading spokesmen for the movement that led to the establishment of the Great Smoky Mountains National Park, were among his most satisfying and fruitful. However, this introduction, despite the fact that it provides the first substantive account of Kephart's life, necessarily focuses upon the events that culminated in the publication of *Our Southern Highlanders*.

Kephart was forty-two when he left his profession and family and came to the Great Smokies. No real understanding of the peculiar mix of motivations, insights, techniques, and materials which shaped *Our Southern Highlanders* and make it a delight can be had without recourse to those first forty-two years and the history of his forebears. No enduring book is ever created by mere whim or chance.

Horace Kephart's great-great-grandfather, Nicholas Kephart, immigrated to this country in 1747 from Switzerland. At the turn of the century, with his wife and son, he was among the first to settle the Allegheny Mountain region in the central Pennsylvania wilderness. In 1803 the son, Henry Kephart, settled with his wife on a farm several miles north of Osceola Mills in Clearfield County, Pennsylvania. Their third child, Henry Kephart, Jr., and his wife, Sarah Goss, established themselves in the mid 1820s in a cabin on a hundred-acre tract near the senior Kephart. Their family eventually numbered thirteen. Horace Kephart's father, Isaiah Lafayette Kephart, the fourth child and first son, was born in 1832. The backwoods experiences of Isaiah Kephart and his brothers and sisters became the core of the family's frontier traditions that Horace Kephart heard about in his own time. The Kepharts partook in full of a strenuous, do-without, log-rolling, shooting-and-fishing, camp-meeting, wagoneering, lumber-rafting type of existence—a lifestyle which Isaiah Kephart himself fondly recreated in later life in a series of newspaper articles entitled "Pioneer Life in the Alleghenies."[1]

After attending Dickinson Seminary and Mount Pleasant College (which transferred its interests to Otterbein University in Ohio while he was enrolled there), Isaiah Kephart joined the Allegheny Conference of the United Brethren in Christ as a minister and served several circuits in central Pennsylvania. In 1861 he married Mary Elizabeth Sowers of Mechanicsville, Pennsylvania, and on September 8, 1862, Horace Sowers Kephart was born in East Salem, Pennsylvania.

When Lee's Confederate troops invaded Pennsylvania in 1863, Isaiah Kephart joined the Union forces and served with considerable distinction throughout the remainder of the conflict as a chaplain of the Twenty-first Pennsylvania Cavalry. In 1867 he decided to move with his wife and son to Jefferson, Iowa, a village about fifty miles northwest of Des Moines. After farming for awhile he became principal of schools in Jefferson.

Central Iowa in the years following the close of the Civil War was still very much a segment of the American frontier. Hamlin Garland, also a boy in Iowa during that period, evokes in his writings mostly the crudities of the time and place. But for Horace Kephart life on the Iowa

---

[1] Originally published from Jan. 4, 1893–Feb. 8, 1893, in the *Religious Telescope*, Dayton, Ohio, of which Isaiah Kephart was editor. Substantial portions of this remembrance are reproduced in the biographies of Isaiah and Ezekiel Kephart cited below. Rev. Cyrus J. Kephart, Rev. William R. Funk, and [Horace Kephart], *Life of Rev. Isaiah L. Kephart, D.D.* (Dayton, Ohio: United Brethren Publishing House, 1909) is the basis of all statements concerning Horace Kephart's father and the Kephart family except where otherwise documented. A useful source for mid-nineteenth-century family affairs is Lewis Franklin John, *The Life of Ezekiel Boring Kephart: Statesman, Educator, Preacher* (Dayton, Ohio: Press of the United Brethren Publishing House, 1907).

frontier, at least as he remembered it more than half a century later, was comprised more of adventure than deprivation.

It was before the day of fences, and for a year or so there was little to be seen from our front door but a sea of grass waving to the horizon. Behind the house was one of the few groves of trees in all that region. . . . [F]or a couple of years, I was actually in the heart of a region where game birds of every description swarmed in myriads, as they never will again, and I soon became a good shot with real guns. The elk and buffalo had left, but their bleached antlers and skulls were strewn everywhere over the prairie. Wild Indians often passed our house, and one time, had it not been for the timely arrival of my father, I, a little boy, would have killed with Dad's rifle a squaw who, with others, was robbing our house while her band stood agrin at my mother's panic of fear.[2]

Kephart was to seek and find in full some elements of this pioneer experience paradoxically enough in the mountains back east rather than in those farther west. And even at this early age Kephart comported himself as the solitary adventurer.

I had no playmates. My mother taught me to read. When I was seven, and could read anything, she gave me my first book, dear old *Robinson Crusoe*. . . . I used to take *Robinson* out to the old boat amid the trees. . . . I made wooden guns, pistols, hatchet, and a thing I called a cutlass. A fur cap was easily contrived, shaped like the one Crusoe wears in the pictures in my book. Then I built a cave out of prairie sod, and stocked it with all sorts of booty from the sloughs and prairie. The old boat was my wrecked ship, to which I made frequent trips, swimming out in my imagination, returning on an imaginary raft laden with imaginary seamen's chests, bottles of

[2] Horace Kephart, "Horace Kephart *By* Himself," *North Carolina Library Bulletin* 5 (June 1922), 49, 50. This autobiographical sketch, hereinafter cited as "Horace Kephart," was also issued as a separate publication.

rack and cordials, kits of tools, barrels of powder and bags of shot.[3]

The somewhat romantic, yet also manly, earnest, isolated, and self-sufficient figure of Robinson Crusoe had an obvious appeal for Kephart. When he wrote this remembrance of his early years at the age of sixty, the copy of Defoe's book which his mother had given him as a child had "been saved through the vicissitudes of a somewhat venturesome life, and lies before me now, coverless and stained with age, but more precious than all the thousands of other books that I afterwards acquired."[4] Kephart's vision of life was to become sufficiently complex as the result of an eventful and demanding life, as well as through varied and perceptive reading (in Shakespeare, Wordsworth, Shelley, Ruskin, Goethe, Turgenev, Emerson, Thoreau, Whitman, the Bible, among others), but no single prototype had a greater direct appeal to his imagination than Crusoe—that obligated and forlorn adventurer.

In 1871 Isaiah Kephart accepted the chair of natural sciences and history at Western College, about ten miles south of Cedar Rapids, Iowa. As a schoolboy Horace Kephart took the preparatory college course, and in 1875 at the age of thirteen he entered Western College. After the school year ended his father returned with the family to Pennsylvania, having resigned the teaching job to accept a dual position as actuary of the United Brethren Mutual Aid Society and the editorship of the *Mutual Aid Journal*.[5] In the fall of 1876 Kephart enrolled at Lebanon Valley College. No official records pertaining to his academic progress at the institution survive,[6] but Kephart

[3] *Ibid.*
[4] *Ibid.*, 49.
[5] The Kepharts' second and last child, Elizabeth Belle, had been born in 1871; she died in 1892.
[6] William D. Hough, III, Chief Librarian at Lebanon Valley

himself noted that he "was graduated, A.B., . . . in 1879, not without misgivings on the part of the faculty as to my orthodoxy and sundry other qualifications."[7] That fall he enrolled as a senior in the College of Liberal Arts at Boston University. In addition to studying under Alpheus Hyatt, one of the most distinguished zoologists and paleontologists ever produced in this country, Kephart enjoyed "the blessed privilege of studying whatever I pleased in the Boston Public Library." Thus evolved the profession he was to follow for the next twenty years. "The absolute academic freedom of the Library was such a relief to one who had suffered from set curriculums that I resolved to help others find it: I chose librarianship for a career."[8]

After the school year of 1880 at Boston University he went to Cornell University, in upstate New York, and assumed supervision of cataloging the library's holdings. He also enrolled in graduate studies, taking courses in history and political science. At the library Kephart worked for Cornell's first librarian, Willard Fiske, who became a personal friend and benefactor. A successful man, Fiske had engineered a number of careers before coming to Cornell in 1868. Upon the death of his wife in 1881 he inherited a sizable fortune that made him financially independent. Because of a suit against the university involving his wife's bequest, he decided to resign from Cornell and live in Italy. From 1883 to 1886 his residence was the Villa Forini in the eastern quarter of Florence. There, in leisure, Fiske pursued his various interests. For the greater part of his life he had been one of the most indefatigable book collectors in America. His collections, which were augmented to the time of his

College, in a letter to this writer, Feb. 15, 1973, advised a fire in 1904 destroyed data at the school.

[7] "Horace Kephart," 50.

[8] *Ibid.*

death in 1904, included some of the world's very finest holdings on Dante and Petrarch, Icelandic history and literature, and the Rhaeto-Romanic language.[9]

Kephart became engaged to Laura Mack of Ithaca, New York, after Fiske's departure and consequently focused his concern on financial security. A salary dispute with university officials ensued, following which Kephart accepted an offer of employment from Fiske in Italy. Early in 1885 he arrived in Florence, where he lived with Fiske and worked in the elaborately appointed library of the Villa Forini. His primary task was to prepare a card catalog of Fiske's enormous collection of titles by and about the fourteenth-century Italian poet Francis Petrarch. While compiling this catalog Kephart worked in the major libraries of Italy and the Royal Library at Munich. He also assisted Fiske by purchasing manuscript and printed items, seeing to the rebinding of books, and corresponding with book dealers. During Fiske's absences from Florence he supervised the sizable household of the Villa Forini.[10]

Despite his loneliness for his fiancée Kephart found the Fiske villa a lively place. A steady flow of visitors, many of them writers and scholars, came to Florence and enjoyed the unstinted hospitality of the Fiske household. Kephart, as always, was active in pursuing his personal interests. He took a vacation tour in Austria. After acquiring some facility in the Italian language, he

[9] For Fiske consult Mary Fowler, "Willard Fiske as Bibliographer," *Papers of the Bibliographical Society of America* 12 (July–Oct. 1918), 89–95, and the series of publications by Horatio S. White: "Daniel Willard Fiske," *DAB*, 1937, VI, 417; "A Sketch of the Life and Labors of Professor Willard Fiske," *Papers of the Bibliographical Society of America* 12 (July–Oct. 1918), 69–88; *Memorials of Willard Fiske*, 3 vols. (New York: Oxford Univ. Press, 1920–22); and *Life and Correspondence of Willard Fiske* (New York: Oxford Univ. Press, 1925).

[10] Letters from Kephart to Fiske, 1884–86.

attended lectures at the Institute di Studii Superiori under Paolo Mantegazza, an eminent Italian physiologist
and anthropologist. And, displaying a penchant for an
activity that was in later life to become an obsession, he
went on walking trips in the Apennines and Alps.[11]

By late 1885 Kephart was preoccupied with finishing
his work and returning to the United States and Laura
Mack. After completing the Petrarch catalog in mid-
January 1886, he embarked for New York from Antwerp
late in the month, hoping to apply his skills in careful research and recording of data as a professional librarian.
In March he found temporary employment at Rutgers
College in New Jersey, where he completed the card
catalog of that institution's library. In July he attended
the American Library Association meeting in Milwaukee
and came away with two job offers: as the head of a new
library in East Saginaw, Michigan, and as an assistant
at Yale College in New Haven, Connecticut. William
Frederick Poole, librarian of the Chicago Public Library,
had recommended him to the Yale librarian, and it was
the Yale job that Kephart wanted. By the last week in
July he was in New Haven, where "after due sizing and
hefting" his appointment was approved.[12]

During the Christmas holidays of 1886 Kephart, now a
settled man of modest means and some expectations, returned to Ithaca. At that time the wedding was definitely
set for the coming spring. On April 12, 1887, the marriage
took place in Ithaca, after which he and Laura returned
to New Haven, where they lived in a cottage a short distance from the campus.[13]

Kephart at first found both his work and the univer-

[11] "Horace Kephart," 50; and letter from Kephart to Augus-
tus Frank of Rome, Italy, July 19, 1919, wcu.
[12] Letters from Kephart to Fiske and Poole, 1886.
[13] Letters from Kephart to Fiske, 1886–87.

sity milieu congenial. "New Haven," he advised Fiske, "isn't a bad sort of a place. . . . There is an *atmosphere* about New Haven that stimulates a man to use his mental powers profitably . . . ."[14] In Boston, Ithaca, and Florence he had found the time and energy to study under Hyatt and Mantegazza and pursue his interests in history and political science. While in New Haven he broadened the scope of his interests. It was during this period that he began writing for publication. Almost all his early writings are related to professional library and bibliographical matters; however, in 1888, he made his "first legitimate literary earnings" ($3.00) for a piece in the *Nation* about a Pennsylvania Dutch "magic-book."[15] No records survive of exactly which courses he attended at Yale, but he recalled years later studying under William Graham Sumner, who taught political and social science.[16] Kephart had a keen interest in foreign languages and literature as a result of his work with Fiske. He had continued his study of Italian since his return from Florence so that by 1887 he was able to make a careful translation and study of Dante's *Vita nuova*. But his concerns were not always strictly pedantic: he had a knack for introducing a more human and personal dimension into his endeavors—an ability, perhaps even a need, which came into full flower during the preparation of *Our Southern Highlanders*. In this instance he associated himself amicably with the sizable population of Italian immigrants then living in New Haven. In the late 1880s he developed an avid interest in Finnish literature, particularly the *Kalevala* (the Finnish national epic

[14] Letter from Kephart to Fiske, Jan. 15, 1887.

[15] Unsigned, untitled note on the copyright problem as illustrated by a Pennsylvania Dutch "magic-book," *Nation* 46 (Feb. 2, 1888), 96; attribution on the basis of a letter from Kephart to Willard Fiske, March 4, 1888.

[16] "Horace Kephart," 50.

that relates the folklore and traditions of the primeval Finnish race), but because he could not locate either a grammar or English dictionary of the language, he set about learning "Swedish in order to get at the Finnish . . . ."[17] He translated a French treatise on Finnish phonetics to use as a textbook and took lessons three evenings a week from a Norwegian linguist in the Divinity School at Yale. Within two years he was reading the *Kalevala* in a Finnish text. And again, he was able to humanize his pursuit: this time his association was with "a little colony of Finns" he had discovered down the coast from New Haven.[18] Kephart's methods of coming to terms with the problems of this particular interest serve to illustrate not only one aspect of his learning, but also the time and effort he was willing to expend in order to realize fully a personal concern from which he had little or nothing to gain materially—an approach to life that became more and more typical of the man in the ensuing years.

When Willard Fiske visited the Kephart family in New Haven in September 1888, he learned of Kephart's growing dissatisfaction with the library position at Yale. His place was secure but there was little hope for elevation in either salary or rank because of the library's depleted finances. Kephart felt a need to better his situation because there had been an addition to the family— a daughter, Cornelia, born in August 1888—and there can be no doubt that he was ambitious to have a higher position at Yale or, even better, a library directorship of his own. By the time of Fiske's visit he had already contacted a friend in St. Louis, where the librarian of the St. Louis Mercantile Library had recently died. William Frederick Poole had named Kephart his first choice for the newly vacated librarianship of Princeton University, and there was an offer, which he temporarily accepted, to

[17] Letter from Kephart to Fiske, July 27, 1887.
[18] *Ibid.*, Aug. 11, 1888.

be an assistant at the Cornell library. But when the St. Louis position became available in the spring of 1890, he accepted.[19]

Founded in 1846, the St. Louis Mercantile Library Association was "the oldest library west of the Mississippi" and "not merely the old-fashioned subscription library that its name implies; it was also the chief collection of scholarly books in the Mississippi Valley." While Kephart was in New Haven, his historical interests and research had begun to develop "chiefly along the line of American frontier history . . . ."[20] The Mercantile Library in St. Louis, long the gateway to the West, was the natural place for Kephart to situate himself.

He arrived in St. Louis in September 1890 and plunged with his usual intensity into the library activities. For over a decade he ran an exceptionally efficient institution. The most intimate view of the man during these years has been recorded by Clarence Miller, whom Kephart hired in the 1890s as an assistant and who subsequently became the librarian of the Mercantile Library himself. More than half a century later he thought Kephart "was the most brilliant man I have known, and, almost as a matter of course, the least assuming." Miller's perceptive description of Kephart is worth quoting at length.

My first meeting with Horace Kephart . . . came as the result of a letter of application. He hired me after perhaps the briefest interview on record, more, I felt, in order to get rid of me than through any intuitive enthusiasm. I still remember, however, the searching glance he flashed before turning me over to the assistant librarian. Meanwhile, my own glance was as searching as time permitted.

I saw a man of medium height and build, with quick decisive movements that bespoke muscular strength and coordination. His eyes were dark . . . . His bristling black mustache

[19] Letters from Kephart to Fiske and Poole, 1888–90.
[20] "Horace Kephart," 50–51.

seemed to me to contrast violently with his finely modeled features. . . . All in all, though, I felt assured that here was a man in his thirties from whom a youth of eighteen could learn a lot once that obvious barrier of reserve could be hurdled.

It soon became evident that my personal contacts would be with the assistant librarian and my fellow workers at the issue desk, not with the chief. Kephart lived almost exclusively in a world of his own, guarded most securely by his constant activity. He had no secretary and spent most of his day beating a two-fingered tattoo on a Smith-Premier typewriter. He did his own research in the card catalogue, consulting it many times a day, and when he needed a book from the stacks he got it himself. I never saw him on one of those errands without the hopeful feeling that he was about to break into a trot. Late in the afternoon he made his exit, always with a Boston bag gorged with books. A brief but friendly farewell to the assistant nearest him somehow inspired us all.

Kephart was never introverted nor austere, as I fear my words so far suggest. He was always accessible to the staff or the public. Any legitimate question got either a direct answer or concise information as to where the answer could be found. The range of his information seemed incredible to us who drew on it daily. All of his answers revealed a broad basis of understanding as well as a photographic memory.

There were occasions when a venturesome member of the staff would repeat the current intramural joke to Kephart, whereupon he would laugh in an almost boyish manner and add a delightful comment, but for the most part he remained a withdrawn and baffling man.[21]

Laura Kephart did not arrive in St. Louis until late in 1890, having remained in Ithaca after the birth of their second daughter, Margaret. In 1891 she returned to Ithaca for the birth of their first son, Leonard, and the family therefore did not set up a permanent household in St. Louis until early 1892. The couple's last three

[21] Clarence E. Miller, "Horace Kephart, A Personal Glimpse," *Missouri Historical Society Bulletin* 16 (July 1959), 305–306.

children—Lucy, George, and Barbara—were born in
1893, 1894, and 1897. The Kepharts settled into a style
of life that Horace Kephart described to Fiske in the
following terms: "Our little family is getting along nice-
ly. . . . We have a pleasant home and are laying by a little something every pay-day. In short, I am in a blessed
rut."[22] Kephart in the mid-1890s was deliberately settling himself into a pattern of respectable family life,
industrious professional responsibilities, and amiable social activities that most Americans of the late nineteenth
century—indeed, of almost any period—sought with
great earnestness.

Kephart originally came to St. Louis, in part at least,
because of his interest in American frontier history. His
first years as head of the Mercantile Library had been
spent in building a general collection. Later in the 1890s,
he was ready to assemble as large a collection of "material relating to the West as the library's budget would
permit. With all the loving labor of an artist creating a
mosaic he added a few volumes a week in his chosen
field."[23] He also spent years tracking down original "di-
aries or other records of actual participants in the stirring events of the Old West . . . ."[24] By the early years of
the twentieth century he had put together one of the
finest collections of Western Americana then in existence.
But despite his keen appreciation of these materials as
historical documents, he was disappointed in their literary quality. "As a rule," he lamented, "their records
were as dry as a ship's log book . . . 'with scarce any dialogue or characterization. The men themselves figure in
such stories as little more than lay figures in a historical
museum.' " For him, but one writer, Francis Parkman,
in his *Oregon Trail*, had been able to "clothe the bones

[22] Letter from Kephart to Fiske, March 12, 1894.
[23] Miller, 307.
[24] "Horace Kephart," 51.

with flesh and blood.''[25] Kephart, who quickly became a respected authority in the field, took considerable interest in the writers of his own generation who were trying to depict the exploration and settlement of the West in a more vivid fashion. "All the writers on the early West consulted Kephart," Clarence Miller recalled. "I remember best Hiram Chittenden . . . and Emerson Hough . . . . To hear them in discussion was like a trip over the mountains with Frémont, or a voyage up the far reaches of the Missouri with Lewis and Clark.''[26]

Kephart's own plans for writing at this time were far more expansive than those of either Hough or Chittenden, indeed, more so than almost any other American writer of the period. He was "ambitious to take up the story of 'The Winning of the West' where Roosevelt had left it, and continue it to the last frontier . . . .''[27] The fourth and final volume of Theodore Roosevelt's *The Winning of the West*, a depiction of the exploration and settlement of the trans-Appalachian West from the early 1760s to the Louisiana Purchase and the initial explorations of the trans-Mississippi frontier during the first decade of the nineteenth century, had appeared in 1896. It was dedicated to Francis Parkman. In his sequel Kephart planned to open his account of the trans-Mississippi frontier with the French settlements of the eighteenth century, then devote his attention to the explorers and early settlers of the Far West from the time of the Louisiana Purchase in 1803 to the settlement of the Pacific coast in the late 1830s. As it turned out, the closest he came to fulfilling the project was a modest, carefully composed pamphlet published in 1902 under the title *Pennsylvania's Part in the Winning of the West.*[28] Before

[25] *Ibid.*
[26] Miller, 307
[27] "Horace Kephart," 51.
[28] (St. Louis: Published by the Bureau of Publicity of the Louisiana Purchase Exposition, 1902). This nineteen-page pam-

he was able to begin the actual composition of the history, his life underwent drastic transition both in style and locale. His plan to publish a volume on the frontier experience had necessarily to be postponed for over a decade, when, in 1913, he would be able to produce a study of one aspect of that experience: not the Far West of the first half of the nineteenth century but the southern mountains during the first years of the twentieth, a phase which he was able to observe and take part in himself.

At the turn of the century Kephart's outlook upon life underwent a fundamental change. In his work he was apparently, to at least one colleague, the same competent, industrious professional librarian who had come to St. Louis in 1890: an "indefatigable worker devouring dealers' catalogues and keeping the now aging typewriter rattling away."[29] And there can be no doubt that he was working away at the library's collection of Western Americana and doing the research for his proposed study of the Far West. But these endeavors had become more personal than professional in nature. The focus of the writing he was producing also shifted. His last article on librarianship was published in 1897 in *The Library Journal*; thereafter he wrote exclusively on outdoor life, firearms, and American history.

The transformation of his personal life was more evident. He became disenchanted with the basic context of his home life. A serious drinking problem arose and could but complicate that situation. Although he never

phlet originally was delivered as an address before the Pennsylvania Society of St. Louis on Dec. 12, 1901. See also the card-catalog type listing of about five hundred and fifty entries Kephart compiled in the course of his research for his proposed study of the Far West, wcu, as well as the two volumes he devoted to the early American frontier in the Kephart Journals, xii–xiii.

[29] Miller, 307.

saw it happen, Clarence Miller was told "that Kephart
. . . could alter his personality by taking a single drink
. . . ."[30] He drifted away from former friends. What little
companionship he now required was provided by William
Marion Reedy, editor of the St. Louis weekly, *Reedy's
Mirror*, and his coterie of "intellectual bohemians."[31] But
to the greatest extent companionship was exactly what
Kephart did not need or seek. During 1902 and 1903 a
facet of his personality that Miller called "Kephart's
aura of loneliness"[32] (which might also be thought of as a
capacity for being alone) increased. Since the early 1890s
he had taken an intense interest in outdoor life and belonged to a sporting club that had grounds some miles out
in the country from St. Louis. There he went with friends
to hunt, fish, and practice his marksmanship. As time
passed, however, his main pleasure came from solitary
excursions into the Ozark Mountains and Arkansas
swamps. By the turn of the century these trips were becoming more frequent and extended. In making them
Kephart seems to have been consciously putting into
practice a theory of the value of—the need for—personal
isolation that he was privately evolving.

A small, bound notebook that he compiled is gilt-
stamped on the cover *Songs of Barbarism*. Its lettered
title-page reads: "*The Joys of Barbarism* / Compiled by
H.K. / St. Louis 1901." Into its hundred pages Kephart
copied excerpts from writers of every persuasion. Standard authors like Bryant, Longfellow, Wordsworth, By-
ron, George Eliot, and Shakespeare are represented, but
the majority of the excerpts come from authors of adventure, exploration, and sport: George Ruxton, Lewis and
Clark, Parkman, W. H. Hudson, George Catlin, Richard

[30] *Ibid.*
[31] *Ibid.* See also Clarence E. Miller, "William Marion Reedy:
A Patchwork Portrait," *Missouri Historical Society* 17 (Oct.
1960), 45.
[32] *Ibid.*

Jefferies, "Nessmuk" (G. W. Sears), Roosevelt, and others. The common theme is the decadence of an overly civilized, material, urban life and the corresponding virtue of a more or less primitive style of existence. Emphasized throughout is the integrity inherent in the modes of living exhibited by the frontier explorers and the American Indian, as well as the cleansing possibilities of an isolated life. The title-page epigraph Kephart composed for the volume pretty well sums up its intent and substance: "I love the wilderness because there are no shams in it."[33]

It seems clear enough that Kephart's difficulties at home, the excessive drinking, the narrowing of his social life, and the solitary trips into the mountains and swamps were not the causes of his eventual exchange of one kind of life (an urban, settled, institutional world that included a wife and six children) for another (an isolated existence in the Southern Appalachians) but rather were symptoms of a consciously articulated desire and need to be alone in the wilderness. If the events of this period of his life were not inevitable, they came very close to being self-willed.

The wilderness trips "began to alienate the library's directors,"[34] and late in 1903 he was forced to resign from the Mercantile Library. A notice in the December issue of *The Library Journal* stated that he had resigned "owing to ill health, and will devote himself to literary work that will enable him to travel and be out of doors."[35] The family was without money, and before Christmas, Laura Kephart took the children to her family's home in Ithaca. There may have been some agreement between Kephart and his wife that the separation was temporary. This was not to be the case. But certainly there

[33] This notebook is among the Kephart holdings, PML.
[34] Miller, 307.
[35] *The Library Journal* 28 (Dec. 1903), 858.

was an understanding of real substance between them that was maintained for the remainder of their lives. Laura Kephart understood better than anyone besides Kephart himself the motivations which prompted his actions.[36]

When the new head of the Mercantile Library arrived, Clarence Miller attempted to aid his former boss by appealing to his father, the associate editor of the St. Louis *Globe-Democrat,* who "admired Kephart's literary style and thought the paper might use him on the corps of correspondents covering the Russo-Japanese war . . . but early in April 1904 he suffered a complete nervous collapse and was taken to a hospital."[37] Isaiah Kephart came to St. Louis and took his son with him back to Dayton, Ohio, where since 1889 he had been the editor of the *Religious Telescope.* Kephart's collapse was apparently not severe and certainly not extended. In May he asked *The Library Journal* to note that he had "entirely recovered from his recent illness, newspaper reports of which were much exaggerated, and is now in good health and engaged in literary work."[38]

In Dayton, Kephart was preoccupied with three interrelated concerns. First, there was his desire to live a wilderness existence. Also he wanted, if possible, to forge for himself some kind of a literary career. To this point his writings had been of two kinds: scholarly contributions on the technicalities of librarianship and pieces for magazines and newspapers—primarily the sporting journals of the day—on American frontier life, firearms, hunting, fishing, and camping. Only the latter category

[36] Kephart's youngest son, George Kephart, in a letter to Michael Frome, July 26, 1966, wcu, recalled that his "parents understood each other, and the reasons which made their separation necessary. None the less, the affection, one for the other, continued throughout their lifetimes."
[37] Miller, 308.
[38] *The Library Journal* 29 (May 1904), 270.

was still of vital interest to him, and only through this kind of writing could he hope to earn enough to support himself. Finally there was his concern with the early American frontier experience, which was closely connected in his own mind with the history of his ancestors, who had migrated first to the America of the mid-eighteenth century, then to the mountain wilderness of central Pennsylvania, and eventually, in his own time, to the prairie frontier of Iowa after the Civil War. In the early summer of 1904, attempting to sort out the direction his life should take, he journeyed to the graveyard in the central Pennsylvania mountains where his ancestors were buried. He located the headstones for each member of the Kephart family buried there and carefully recorded the inscriptions.[39] Nine years later, in *Our Southern Highlanders*, Kephart offered a brief explanation of the solution that he hit upon that summer.

When I went south into the mountains I was seeking a Back of Beyond. This for more reasons than one. With an inborn taste for the wild and romantic, I yearned for a strange land and a people that had the charm of originality. Again, I had a passion for early American history; and, in Far Appalachia, it seemed that I might realize the past in the present, seeing with my own eyes what life must have been to my pioneer ancestors of a century or two ago. Besides, I wanted to enjoy a free life in the open air, the thrill of exploring new ground, the joys of the chase, and the man's game of matching my woodcraft against the forces of nature, with no help from servants or hired guides.[40]

In 1926 he explained his decision in somewhat different terms to F. H. Behymer, a reporter for the St. Louis *Post-Dispatch* he had probably known in St. Louis in the

[39] Kephart's notes on this visit are among the papers he prepared on his family ancestry, Kephart Journals, VIII, 3a–68, WCU.

[40] *Our Southern Highlanders*, 29–30.

1890s. Behymer wrote that while resting at his father's home in 1904 Kephart

took a map and a compass and with Dayton as the center drew circles, seeking the nearest wilderness, in any direction, where he might cast himself away. The region of the Big Smoky Mountains in Western North Carolina seemed to meet the requirements. A topographical map showed him, by means of the contour lines and blank spaces, where nature was wildest and where there were no settlements. These were the highest mountains east of the Rockies. It was a primitive hinterland without a history. Great areas were uninhabited. It would be a great place to begin again, he thought.[41]

Since the mid-1880s, for nearly twenty years, Kephart had sought to apply his ability for careful research and recording of data as a professional librarian. But professional and institutional life had gone sour; his personal life had gone awry. He still had the original talents. Indeed they had been sharpened through the years. He now sought an entirely new and more personal field upon which to focus them: wilderness woodcraft and such vestiges of the American frontier experience as he might be able to locate in the first decade of the twentieth century. And these were his consuming interests for the rest of his life.

Kephart left Dayton for Asheville, North Carolina, in late July or early August 1904, traveling light. He intended to establish a temporary camp in the mountains and then have a few possessions from his former life shipped on from Dayton. While in Asheville he consulted a physician, Dr. C. D. W. Colby, who found him "a physical wreck," but an individual who "revealed a de-

[41] F. A. Behymer, "Horace Kephart, Driven from Library by Broken Health, Reborn in Woods," as reprinted in the *Asheville Citizen*, Dec. 12, 1926, section C, p. 8, from the St. Louis *Post-Dispatch*.

termination and willingness to cooperate that promised recovery."[42] During the first week of August he moved on to Dillsboro, North Carolina, a hamlet on the Tuckasee-gee River in the valley between the Balsam and Cowee mountain ranges. Located about forty-five miles west of Asheville on the railway, Dillsboro seemed to Kephart like "a good place to take off from . . . ." He made it his "scouting base."[43] Several miles northwest of Dillsboro, near where Dick's Creek empties into the Tuckaseegee from the north, he set up at a site he called Camp Toco (or "'Dak-waw-i' in Cherokee, which means 'fish-monster place'"). Here in a Baker tent (a small canvas-covered lean-to) he lived from August 7 to October 30th. From the moment of his arrival he began to observe and re-cord the mountains, the native inhabitants, and their way of life. He made notes and photographs that delineate his interest in weaving; the making of buttermilk, cider, and sorghum; trout fishing; a mountain pistol match; the native attitude toward Negroes; the flora and fauna of the region; and the Cherokees on the Qualla Reservation a few miles to the northwest. He also began at this early date to gather detailed data on a subject that fascinated him for the rest of his life and which he covered in detail in *Our Southern Highlanders*—moonshining.[44]

But the Dick's Creek campsite was an interim base that he intended to occupy only until he could locate the ideal place from which to pursue his interests. In October he made an excursion by railway to Bryson City and the Snowbird Mountains farther west. On this trip Kephart would have seen for the first time the Great

[42] "Kephart's Friends Voice Tributes for His Work," *Asheville Citizen*, April 4, 1931, p. 4.
[43] Kephart Photograph Album, p. 1.
[44] *Ibid.*, pp. 1–11; and references in the Kephart Journals, I–IV, *passim*.

Smokies looming along the North Carolina-Tennessee line. At this time he perhaps also visited, or at least heard about for the first time, the rugged, backwoods settlements along Hazel Creek "far up under the lee of those Smoky Mountains."[45] On the basis of what he learned Kephart decided to locate in the Hazel Creek watershed. He secured permission to use a cabin near the Everett Mines, an abandoned copper mine, two miles from Medlin, a tiny settlement situated where the Sugar Fork enters Hazel Creek from the west about ten miles up Hazel Creek from its confluence with the Little Tennessee.

On October 30 Kephart left Dick's Creek for Bushnell, the railhead nearest Hazel Creek. At Bushnell he was met by Granville Calhoun, who ran one of the stores, which also served as the post office, at Medlin. Calhoun, a considerable figure of a man then and a legend on the North Carolina side of the Smokies today, had been requested by "a friend, a mining official . . . to show the newcomer around."[46] Kephart was incapacitated (maybe ill, maybe inebriated) when he arrived at Bushnell and had to be assisted to Calhoun's home at Medlin, where he apparently stayed for a short while.[47] By November 2,

[45] *Our Southern Highlanders*, 30.

[46] Michael Frome, *Strangers in High Places: The Story of the Great Smoky Mountains* (Garden City, N.Y.: Doubleday & Co., Inc., 1966), 146.

[47] Frome, 146–47, builds his 1966 account of a drunken Kephart arriving at Bushnell and Hazel Creek around an interview he had conducted with the then eighty-seven-year-old Granville Calhoun, who was recalling events that had transpired more than half a century earlier. This presentation conflicts with available sources. First, Frome shows no knowledge of the fact that Kephart was not coming directly from St. Louis to Hazel Creek although the information is significant since the nearly two-month period at the campsite on

however, he was at the Everett Mines cabin.[48] It was a small two-room structure, half of logs and half of rough planking, which Kephart refurbished, adding his few belongings, including some books, once they arrived by rail at Bushnell and were hauled up to him. The cabin was situated at the base of a ridge and overlooked a small stream called the Little Fork and the deserted workings of the copper mine. His only neighbors on the Little Fork were the Barnett family. Bob Barnett and his wife, whom Kephart called "Mistress Bob," became close friends. Their pungent observations and dialect witticisms intrigued Kephart and found their way into his journals and *Our Southern Highlanders.*

From this vantage point on the Little Fork of the Sugar Fork of Hazel Creek he was able to realize the long-nurtured desire to live in a wilderness area where such civilization as existed was more nearly on the order of the early American experience than the twentieth century. The Smokies he found to be "one of the finest primeval forests in the world." The intimate relationship he found between the isolated settlements and farmsteads and the surrounding wilderness made him

---

Dick's Creek clearly reveals a man going earnestly about his intended business, not someone suffering from or about to suffer from "torpor and tremens, the long hangover"—to use his phrasing. Next, the "Index to Diary" and notes preserved in the Kephart Journals reveal that just before, during, and after the period Frome describes Kephart was behaving as anything but a drunk.

[48] A photograph of his cabin on the Little Fork is captioned by Kephart, "Lived here alone, Nov. 2, 1904, to Jan., 1906" (Kephart Photograph Album, p. 21); therefore he was residing at the cabin within two days of the time he broke camp at Dick's Creek. There was clearly no three-week interval of "torpor and tremens" and "spoon-feeding" as described by Frome.

feel that he "had been carried back, asleep, upon the wings of time, and had awakened in the eighteenth century . . . ."[49] The people themselves

were unlike any people I had ever met elsewhere. They were like figures taken from the old frontier histories and legends that I had been so fond of, only they were living flesh and blood instead of mere characters in books. I seemed to be actually living among the pioneer farmers and herdsmen and hunters, the trappers and traders, the teachers and preachers, the outlaws and the Indians (we had these, too) of a hundred and fifty years ago. They interested me more than the ultra-civilized folk of the cities.[50]

There can be no doubt that Kephart came to the Smokies fully armed with the intention not only of living in but also of writing about this wilderness land and its peoples. From this dual and interrelated interest arose his two major works: *Camping and Woodcraft* (about how to live in the wilderness) and *Our Southern Highlanders* (about the land and the people). At first, he was interested not in the native mountaineers

but in the mountains themselves—in that mysterious beckoning hinterland which rose right back of my chimney and spread upward, outward, almost to the three cardinal points of the compass, mile after mile, hour after hour of lusty climbing—an Eden still unpeopled and unspoiled.[51]

He became preoccupied with the simple and direct challenge of living efficiently in this environment. Most of his neighbors were born backswoodsmen, living in cabins, cooking over open fireplaces, skilled with the rifle, axe, and loom. Despite his previous experiences in the outdoors, Kephart now

[49] *Camping and Woodcraft* (New York: Outing Publishing Co., 1917), 11, 13, 14.

[50] "Horace Kephart," 52.

[51] *Our Southern Highlanders*, 50.

had to make shift in a different way, and fashion many appliances from the materials found on the spot. The forest itself was not only my hunting-ground but my workshop and my garden.

Into this novel and fascinating game I entered with the keenest zest, and soon was going even "further back" than the native woodsmen themselves. I gathered, cooked, and ate (with certain qualms, be it confessed, but never with serious mishap) a great variety of wild plants that country folk in general do not know to be edible. I learned better ways of dressing and keeping game and fish, and worked out odd makeshifts in cooking with rude utensils, or with none at all. I tested the fuel values and other qualities of a great many kinds of wood and bark, made leather and rawhide from game that fell to my rifle, and became more or less adept in other backwoods handicrafts, seeking not novelties but practical results.[52]

These "practical results" he published in the popular outdoor magazines of the day—*Sports Afield, Field and Stream, Forest and Stream, Outing Magazine,* and others. From the modest fees paid for these articles Kephart was able to support himself. By 1906 he had compiled enough material on how to live in the wilderness to put together the first edition of *Camping and Woodcraft,* a storehouse of practical advice, lore, anecdote, and adventure which in its subsequent expanded and revised editions became the standard work in its field. And, despite the fact that it is dated in terms of the recent revolution in camping equipment, *Camping and Woodcraft* is still in print today, still supremely applicable as is no other book in regard to basic technique and philosophy: one of the classics— along with *Woodcraft* by "Nessmuk" (George Washington Sears) and *Camp and Trail* by Stewart Edward White—from an earlier "Go-light" and "Throw-it-away-if-you-don't-need-it" era in American outdoor life.[53]

[52] *Camping and Woodcraft,* II, 14.
[53] The Outing Publishing Company first edition of *Camping*

Kephart soon became engrossed in the inhabitants of the Hazel Creek watershed as well. There were two small settlements—Medlin, on the Sugar Fork, and Proctor, about five miles down the creek. For the most part the families lived in secluded "log cabins of one or two rooms, roofed with clapboards riven with a froe, and heated by hardwood logs in wide stone fireplaces."[54] Their cabins were spread along Hazel Creek, its major tributaries (Shehan Branch, Sugar Fork and its tributary, Haw Creek, and Bone Valley Creek), and the myriad branches that seemingly spread in every direction. There were people with names like Walker, Cable, Crisp, Bradshaw and Buchannon, Calhoun and Cope, Laney and Proctor, Gunter, Hyde, and Flowers. Kephart also became familiar with the residents of Eagle Creek, a more sparsely settled watershed over Jenkins Ridge to the west, where the indomitable hunter, fiddle-player, story-teller, and moonshiner Quill Rose, already a legend, lived with his part-Indian wife, Aunt Vice. He became a neighbor and, in some instances, a friend of these mountain people. There was no doctor close by, and since his services were immediate and free, he became their physician as well, insofar as his "first-aid kit and limited knowledge" would allow.[55] He even became their cartographer. His interest in the Hazel Creek region and its people was such that for his own pleasure and informa-

---

and Woodcraft was revised and expanded at least six times in this country and once in Great Britain. The same company published the greatly expanded two-volume edition 1916–17, which was reprinted by the Macmillan Company in 1921 in a two-volume format, and then by the same company to date in a format of two volumes in one. The 1972 Macmillan printing was noted as being number "twenty-eight." No other outdoors or sporting volume written by an American has enjoyed such acceptance and enduring popularity.

[54] *Camping and Woodcraft*, ii, 13.
[55] *Our Southern Highlanders*, 298.

tion he drew general maps as well as key and section maps, all to scale, which delineate the ridges, peaks, valleys, and watercourses, along with the specific locations of the trails, roads, bridges, mills, schools, stores, and homesites that the settlers had established.[56]

But most importantly Kephart became their chronicler. From 1904 until his departure from Hazel Creek in 1907 he studied their ways of life and how they felt and expressed themselves about that life. The copious notes he made while living on the Little Fork of the Sugar Fork of Hazel Creek record every imaginable aspect of that culture. These notes were subsequently the foundation upon which he constructed *Our Southern Highlanders*, a book about the Southern Appalachians as a whole, but one which utilized Hazel Creek and the years Kephart had resided there as its constant touchstone and point of focus.

During the spring of 1906 he left Hazel Creek for a short while to see to the publication of *Camping and Woodcraft*.[57] He was back in the Smokies by late spring. It was probably at this time that Isaiah Kephart visited with his son in the Southern mountains. Both father and son had an equally keen interest in their family's pioneer heritage and the various aspects of mountain culture. Photographs Kephart took show his father inspecting a mill site on Shehan Branch and riding horseback near the high divide. Kephart spent the summer months of 1907 with J. B. ("Andy") Anderson, a friend from the North, at the Hall cabin situated high on the main divide of the Smokies about ten miles west of Clingman's Dome. This was a two-room herder's hut, one room in Tennessee, the other in North Carolina.[58]

[56] Kephart Maps, wcu.

[57] Kephart spent some time in Dayton, Ohio, with his parents, and may have gone to New York.

[58] Kephart Photograph Album, pp. 33, 39–40. In *Our Southern Highlanders*, 62, this three-month stay at the Hall Cabin is

By this time Kephart was far along in his compilation of materials for a book on the Southern highlanders. But, like most writers at some point in the composition of a large piece of work, he hit snags. Upon first coming to the mountains of western North Carolina he had felt that after a short while he would be able to "deal with all aspects of their lives and culture." His "first impressions" had been reassuring in this regard. The highlanders seemed at first so "picturesque"; and after living with them intimately for a few months—"cheek by jowl . . . back to back and toe to toe"—Kephart began to assume that he knew them well. "What," he thought during those early months in the Smokies, "could be easier than to sketch so directly from nature itself?" But as time passed and his knowledge of the native mountaineers deepened, his perspective changed.

Well, the six months passed, and I was not sure. *Did* I understand this strange race, after all? A year, two years, three. I was among them as one of themselves, participating in all their ways, studying them at guarded and unguarded moments, under all sorts of strain. Their hardships were my hardships; their pleasures were mine too. Yet was I more than dubious as to my ability, my right, to portray their character.[59]

By 1907, then, Kephart knew too much to be satisfied with merely a picturesque book that would not do justice to the mountaineers as he now saw and understood them. At the same time, as he points out in his autobiographical sketch, he was concerned that his observations in the Great Smokies region—primarily in the rugged and in many ways primitive Hazel Creek watershed—might not have general application to the whole

---

apparently dated incorrectly as 1906; the evidence of the Kephart Photograph Album and Journals is that it was actually the following summer.

[59] Letter from Kephart to Albert Britt, editor, *Outing Magazine*, Aug. 26, 1912, WCU.

Southern Appalachian region. So, late in 1907, Kephart left Hazel Creek unsure of the wider applicability of his study there and uncertain about how to present his materials should he decide to do so. In order to verify his findings he

traveled in other parts of the Appalachians, in eastern Kentucky and Tennessee, in northern Georgia, comparing what I found there with what I knew in the Smokies, and I found the southern mountaineers everywhere one people. To make sure that I was not generalizing too hastily from my own limited observations, I studied in detail the mountain counties of the South, tabulating them painstakingly from the complete Federal census reports, and here I verified beyond question my conclusion that the typical southern highlanders were not the relatively few townsmen and prosperous valley farmers of the Appalachian region, but the great multitude of little farmers living up the branches and on the steep hillsides, back from the main highways, and generally far from the railroads. These, the real mountaineers, were what interested me; and so I wrote them up.[60]

Kephart returned to the Great Smokies early in 1910. This time he chose not to settle on Hazel Creek. The W. M. Ritter Lumber Company had begun operations there in 1909 and was in the process of running a railway spur, the Smoky Mountain Railroad, up the watershed. It would not be the same. Instead he settled in Bryson City, a small village situated on the Tuckaseegee River at the mouth of Deep Creek, which, like Hazel Creek, is a watershed of the North Carolina side of the Smokies. It was an excellent choice. Here he had access to a different style of mountain life than he had pursued from 1904 to 1907: the leisurely ebb and flow of mountain village life, which quickened only at election time or on certain holidays or during court week, itself a sort of holiday. Bryson City was the congregating point for a

[60] "Horace Kephart," 52. Kephart's carefully compiled and tabulated data are preserved in the Kephart Journals, 1, 90–90g.

variety of mountain men and women—lawyers, law officers, drummers, and lumbermen as well as the small
farmsteaders from the adjacent watersheds like Alarka
Creek, Cooper Creek, Deep Creek, Noland Creek, Forney
Creek, and Hazel Creek, and, on occasion, Cherokees
from the nearby Qualla Reservation—all of whom fascinated Kephart and found their way into his notes and
writings. It was a style and pace that, for the most part,
Kephart found congenial and satisfying; he lived in Bryson City for the rest of his life.[61]

The Cooper House, a boarding house on Main Street
just west of the courthouse square, was from 1910 his
permanent residence. He also rented a small office above
Bennett's Drug Store, overlooking the river, where he
did much of his writing. During the summer months,
however, he was inclined to leave town and live in the
backwoods. The first summer, 1910, he boarded with his
old neighbors from Hazel Creek, the Bob Barnett family, in the last house up Deep Creek. Afterwards he
camped, mostly by himself, at various sites in the Smokies. Bryson Place, about ten miles up Deep Creek, was
the spot he liked best. Here he would set up camp for the
entire summer, hauling in by wagon or on horseback the
supplies and equipment he required, which included a
small folding desk and writing materials.

During his first two years in Bryson City, Kephart
continued to write for the sporting journals, and he also
published two volumes on subjects in which he delighted
and upon which he was an authority: *Camp Cookery* and
Sporting Firearms. His major efforts, however, were directed toward his study of the Southern Appalachians.
He now earnestly settled down to the writing of *Our
Southern Highlanders*, no longer concerned about the
general relevance and application of what he had ob-

[61] For Bryson City consult Lillian Franklin Thomasson,
Swain County: Early History and Educational Development
(Bryson City, N.C.: n.p., 1965).

served and recorded during the years on Hazel Creek or of the data he was now gathering in Bryson City.

The writing of the book was actually a process of distillation rather than an enlargement upon the materials he had already accumulated and continued to gather. Fortunately the bulk of the materials Kephart used has been preserved in the twenty-seven notebooks he compiled and utilized as a source for all of his writings. Volumes I-IV of the Kephart Journals—comprising well over a thousand pages of material—are devoted exclusively to his study of the Hazel Creek and Bryson City areas in particular and the Southern Appalachians as a whole. Systematically arranged and frequently cross-referenced, these volumes are a mine of information which Kephart labored over with real care. In them one sees reflected the mind of a peculiar and original historian.

The four volumes are divided into about five hundred categories covering virtually every topic relevant to the Southern mountains. Under each heading can be found a variety of information bearing on the subject: newspaper and magazine clippings, references to relevant sources, extended extracts from printed sources, charts and tables along with countless dialect words, expressions, and snatches of dialogue Kephart collected relevant to the subject at hand. Also included are his own observations and notations of things to verify. In writing *Our Southern Highlanders* Kephart carefully used selected material from this mass of data. One of the first pages of the journals contains his brief outline for the book. His method was to be descriptive, but not in a cut-and-dried manner. In order to "clothe the bones in flesh and blood" he used a variety of information ranging from his own first-hand observations to topics he had carefully researched. To give additional depth and perspective he would use maps and photographs. And, to elicit human interest, he planned to employ anecdotes and incidents, native comments and dialect, and comparison with familiar standards. At the foot of his outline Kephart made a final note: "To each section apply touchstone of characters known." On a following page he reminded himself, "Aim at the truth. Don't blink. Don't flinch."

The first edition of *Our Southern Highlanders* was published by the Outing Publishing Company of New York in 1913. It was widely read and praised by people across the country, including those of Southern Appalachia. The Outing Publishing Company sold 10,000 copies of the book in the next eight years.[62] In 1921 the Macmillan Company of New York secured publishing rights to the book and reprinted the Outing text. The following year, because of the book's popularity, the firm brought out an expanded edition containing three new chapters, a new map, and additional illustrations. By 1967 Macmillan had reprinted the book eight times, with and without the illustrations. Copies of the last printing were remaindered, and *Our Southern Highlanders* has since 1967 been out of print, becoming more and more difficult to locate except on library shelves and bringing increasingly higher prices in the rare-book market.

The material Kephart added to the 1922 edition appears there as Chapters IX, X, and XI: "The Snake-Stick Man," "A Raid into the Sugarlands," and "The Killing of Hol Rose," chapters based on events which he had taken part in himself or followed closely in the Bryson City area. These rounded out and gave the humanizing touch Kephart liked to the long middle portion of the book dealing with the history, craft, and detection of moonshining.[63] The Macmillan Company was justified in

[62] Frome, 153.

[63] Kephart does not reveal to the reader of *Our Southern Highlanders* the identity of "The Snake-Stick Man," the central figure of Chapters IX and X. A newspaper clipping from the *Hugo* (Okla.) *Daily News* which Kephart pasted into his Journals, III, 951.53, is entitled "W. W. Thomason is Subject

adding a subtitle to the volume; the title-page now read *Our Southern Highlanders; A Narrative of Adventure in the Southern Appalachians and a Study of Life Among the Mountaineers.*

Kephart was understandably pleased by the book's wide acceptance. More than anything else, however, he was moved by the way the mountain people themselves responded to his account of their land and life. In June 1919 Paul Fink of Jonesboro, Tennessee—an authority on the Southern Appalachians and Great Smokies who became a friend of Kephart's during the 1920s—was spending the night at a ranger's cabin at the junction of Alum Cave Creek and the West Prong of the Little Pigeon River on the Tennessee side of the Smokies. The ranger there was a native mountaineer, Davis Bracken (the "Jasper Finn" of Chapter X of *Our Southern Highlanders*), and during the course of the evening Fink chanced to mention Kephart's book.

Davis said, "I've read it. A woman at the school down in the settlement let me have it." After a little more talk, I [Fink] asked what he thought of it as a true delineation of mountain people and mountain ways. After a little thought, he answered, "I don't guess any body could'a writ it bette."

When Fink told Kephart of Bracken's statement, Kephart responded:

Davis Bracken's opinion of my "Southern Highlanders" is a compliment that I prize far above those from professional critics. While I was writing the book I was little concerned about how the public at large would take it; but I did care for what the mountain people themselves would think of it. One or two of my most intimate friends among them read a few

---

of Two Chapters in New Edition of Book on Mountain People." The article, accompanied by a picture of Thomason, summarizes the chapters in which he appears and states that he was a "special federal officer, well known throughout this section on account of his work in liquor law enforcement."

chapters in Ms. (or I read them to the men) and they gravely advised me to leave the country before publication. It did not suit me to do so; for I wanted to see exactly what effect it would have; so I stayed here. Well, to my great surprise and delight, not one of the real mountaineers has ever said anything but good of it, to my knowledge. The only people who have denied its truth and accuracy are *town* folks, some of whom think it slurs the country. The blockaders and bear hunters and farmers who figure in the book, under thin disguise or none at all, are proud of it. There could be no better testimony to its truth, and that is all I cared for—to get both the letter and the spirit of real mountain life, and then portray them.[64]

Using the lively, crisp style he had developed over the years writing for the sporting journals and composing his own volumes on campcraft and sport, Kephart produced a literary work that is at once historical, sociological, and autobiographical. This blend of method and materials makes *Our Southern Highlanders* quite different in texture and final effect from any other volume about the Southern Appalachians. Marjorie Kinnan Rawlings' *Cross Creek* (1942), an account of her life among the Florida crackers in the 1930s, is the only regional study written in this century that bears much similarity to Kephart's book. Instead *Our Southern Highlanders* has its closest affinity with an earlier tradition of writing that had its roots in the antebellum period of American literature. It is a direct descendant of the humorous-descriptive-realistic accounts of life in the rural settlements and backwoods of the Old South and Southwest produced by writers like A. B. Longstreet in his *Georgia Scenes* (1835), or by Henry Clay Lewis ("Madison Tensas") in *Odd Leaves from the Life of a Louisiana "Swamp Doctor"* (1850), or T. B. Thorpe, author of *The Hive of "The Bee-Hunter:" A Repository of Sketches, In-*

[64] Letter from Kephart to Paul Fink, Oct. 14, 1919, annotated by Mr. Fink.

cluding Peculiar American Character, Scenery, and Rural Sports (1854). It is also in the tradition of the closely related genre of travel-sporting-descriptive writing that Kephart knew so well from his researches in St. Louis, books such as those by Parkman, Ruxton, and Roosevelt. Like those nineteenth-century sporting and humorous works, Kephart's volume is in a sense "sketchy, fragmentary";[65] yet, like most of them, it is unified by an overall purpose: to give the reader not only a valid description of the land and people but also the feeling of how it was to have been there, to have heard them speak and laugh. By casting *Our Southern Highlanders* in this mold of adventurous and anecdotal but ultimately realistic writing, Kephart avoided producing the folksy, sentimental, local color treatment so typical of books past and present about the Southern Appalachians.

After this productive middle period of his life, from 1903-1913, Kephart continued to write, mainly for the sporting and outdoor periodicals. Two other volumes, *Camping* and *The Camper's Manual,* appeared in 1916 and 1923. He saw to the expanded and revised editions of *Camping and Woodcraft* (1916-1917) and *Our Southern Highlanders* (1922). He edited a series of eleven volumes of adventure and exploration that appeared as part of the "Outing Adventure Library" (1915-1917). All during the 1920s he labored on a novel entitled *Smoky Mountain Magic,* which never got out of typescript—it had a barely adequate title, but Kephart's talent was for factual delineation, not fiction.

His most important writing during the 1920s was done on behalf of the movement that eventually culminated in the establishment of the Great Smoky Mountains National Park. Kephart's role in the movement was considerable. He wrote articles for periodicals and newspapers advocating the establishment of a park in the

[65] "Horace Kephart," 52.

Smokies, carefully explaining time and again why the area should be preserved. Many of his pieces were accompanied by the excellent photographs of his Japanese friend George Masa, who spent as much time in the Smokies with Kephart as he did in his Asheville studio. Together they caught the spirit of the high mountains and watersheds in words and pictures. Kephart did not live to see the park become an actuality, but he died knowing it was assured. In the November following his death in the spring of 1931, when representatives of North Carolina and Tennessee went to Washington to present the deed for the lands to be included in the park, Secretary of the Interior Ray Lyman Wilbur recognized Kephart's part in the park movement:

I wish that I could name every one of the men and women who have worked devotedly to see this new national park come into being, but I am sure you will join me in appreciation of the persistent and idealistic interest of Mr. Kephart, who not only knew these mountains and loved the people, but saw in them a great national treasure.[66]

Kephart's own explanation of the motivation behind his considerable expenditure of time and energy on the park movement was concise: "I owe my life to these mountains and I want them preserved that others may profit by them as I have."[67] His personal feelings about the changes that were taking place in the Smokies, even the coming of the park itself, are reflected in a letter he wrote to his son, George Kephart:

The long and difficult task of surveying, examining titles, estimating values, etc., of the Smoky Mt. Nat'l Park lands is finished. And now, at last, the actual purchase or condemnation of the whole area will proceed to a finish. It was a big undertaking, and beset with discouragements of all sorts; but

[66] Frome, 160.
[67] "Authors Die Instantly In Wreck Near Bryson City," *Asheville Citizen*, April 3, 1931, p. 1.

we've won! . . . Within two years we will have good roads into the Smokies, and then—well, then I'll get out.[68]

During the late 1920s and early 1930s Kephart also took an active part in the establishment of the Appalachian Trail. He was instrumental in plotting the route the trail followed through the Smokies and on into north Georgia.[69] And two months before his death Kephart was honored by a decision of the United States Geographic Board designating that a peak on the high divide of the Smokies, about eight miles northeast of Clingman's Dome, be named in his honor.[70]

On April 2, 1931, at the age of sixty-eight, Horace Kephart was killed in an automobile accident near Bryson City. A friend, the Georgia writer Fiswoode Tarleton, who was staying with Kephart for a few weeks, was also killed. They had hired a taxi to take them to a bootlegger's and were on the way back to Bryson City when the driver lost control of the car in a curve.[71] Kephart was buried in Bryson City on April 5. His wife, two sons, and a grandson were in attendance. The services were held in the high school auditorium, which was filled. Hundreds stood outside.[72]

There are several places you can go today to try to get a feeling for the Smokies as Kephart knew them during

[68] Letter from George Kephart to Michael Frome, July 26, 1966, wcu.

[69] See Kephart's correspondence with Appalachian Trail officials and interested parties, pml, wcu, and in possession of Paul Fink.

[70] *Decisions of the United States Geographic Board, No. 5— Decisions Rendered by the Board March 4, 1931* (Washington, D.C.: U.S. Government Printing Office, 1931), 3.

[71] Mercedith Leatherwood, unpublished paper, "'The Father of the Great Smoky Mountains National Park,' Horace Kephart," March 3, 1971, p. 12.

[72] "Kephart Laid to Last Long Rest in Hills," *Asheville Citizen*, April 6, 1931, pp. 1–2.

the early years of the century, before they changed. There's Bryson City, still a lovely town. Kephart's grave, marked by a boulder, is in the hilltop cemetery overlooking the town and the mountains beyond. There's Bryson Place up Deep Creek in the park; a tablet there marks his "last permanent camp." Or you can go to Hazel Creek. To get there you will have to travel by boat, across Lake Fontana, or pack in by one of the wilderness trails. The old homesteads no longer stand along Hazel Creek or up the branches, but you can spot the clearings, which, in season, are marked by the roses the settlers favored for their dooryards. Camp at the primitive campsite at the junction of the Sugar Fork and Hazel Creek. You can find the ruins of Medlin nearby if you try hard enough. In the morning walk west along the Sugar Fork trail. At 1.6 miles you'll see on the right a clearing marking an old homesite. Just beyond, the Little Fork enters the Sugar Fork from the north. Farther on uptrail there's a road leading to the Everett Mines that was cut long after Kephart left. It's tough going, but the best way to go in is to follow the old wagon-ruts through the laurel on the east bank of the Little Fork. When you come to the second mine shaft along the creek, cross the Little Fork and go high up on the west bank. Kephart's cabin was situated in the leveled area you'll find at the foot of the steep draw that runs up the ridge. It's still very quiet there as it was in his time.

But the best place to go for the man and the land and the people as he understood them is to *Our Southern Highlanders*, the finest regional study yet written by an American.

—George Ellison

Bryson City, North Carolina
June 1976

NOTE ON LOCATION OF KEPHART MATERIALS

The major Kephart holdings are in the North Carolina Room of the Pack Memorial Library, Asheville, North Carolina, and the University Archives, Hunter Library, Western Carolina University, Cullowhee, North Carolina. At Pack Memorial Library (cited PML in footnotes) are several boxes of material, containing some of Kephart's personal effects, notebooks, correspondence, photographs, and clippings, as well as typescripts for some of his stories and part of the typescript for his unpublished novel, *Smoky Mountain Magic*. Also, there are letters from Laura Kephart and other members of the Kephart family written to I. K. Stearns and others in Bryson City after Kephart's death. The provenance of these holdings is not clear, except that they were obtained by F. A. Sondley for the Sondley Reference Library at Pack Memorial in the 1940s or 1950s. The most significant holdings are housed at Western Carolina University (cited as WCU in footnotes). These consist, in part, of over three hundred personal letters, the twenty-seven volume set of the Kephart Journals, various notebooks and catalogs, the Kephart Photograph Album, Kephart's maps of the Hazel Creek and Eagle Creek watersheds made in 1905, part of the typescript for *Smoky Mountain Magic*, his library, and most of the personal items and artifacts he possessed at the time of his death. The provenance of these holdings, once in the keeping of the Great Smoky Mountains National Park, is complicated; see the unpublished paper by Terri Pritchard, "Horace Kephart—The Distribution of the Kephart Collection," Nov. 20, 1973, which may be consulted in the archives.

A diary kept by Kephart during his early years in the Smokies has not been located. Fortunately an "Index to Diary" and extracts Kephart made himself from the diary do survive and may be consulted in the Kephart Journals, I, ix-x, and 39.

Additional Kephart correspondence cited in the footnotes may be located as follows: correspondence to Willard Fiske, George Burr, and Ettore Sordi (Cornell University Libraries, Departments of Manuscripts and University Archives, John M. Olin Library, Ithaca, New York); correspondence to William Frederick Poole (The Newberry Library, Chicago, Illinois); and the correspondence to and from Paul Fink, Jonesboro, Tennessee. I wish to thank these institutions, as well as Mr. Fink, for permission to use these materials.

—G. E.

OUR SOUTHERN HIGHLANDERS

Photo by S. H. Essary

In the Great Smoky Mountains.

PREFACE TO THE REVISED EDITION

Nine years have passed since this book first came from the press. My log cabin on the Little Fork of Sugar Fork has fallen in ruin. The great forest wherein it nestled is falling, too, before the loggers' steel. A railroad has pierced the wilderness. A graded highway crosses the county. There are mill towns where newcomers dwell. An aeroplane has passed over the county seat. Mountain boys are listening, through instruments of their own construction, to concerts played a thousand miles away.

We have had the war. We are having an attempt at prohibition. Even in farthest Appalachia people realize that the world has been upset, and that old ways, old notions, old convictions perhaps, must give place to new ones.

And yet, if one strolling along our new Asheville-to-Atlanta highway should step aside at the first brook crossing, turn "up the branch," and follow the rough by-road that steeply ascends the glen, he would come presently to a log cabin where time still lingers a century be-lated. The old-fashioned hospitality would be offered him with right good will. And if he tarried (who would not?) he would observe something of the pioneer life this book de-scribes. They die hard, those old ways, in the mountains. Some of them were good ways, too. They were picturesque, at least.

I have tried to give a true picture of life among the southern mountaineers, as I have found it during eighteen years of intimate as-sociation with them. This book deals with the *mass* of the mountain people. It is not con-cerned with the relatively few townsmen, and prosperous valley farmers, who owe to outside influences all that distinguishes them from their back-country kinsmen. The real mountaineers are the multitude of little farmers living up the branches and on the steep hillsides, away from the main-traveled roads, who have been shaped by their own environment. They are the ones who interest the reading public; and this is as it should be; for they are original, they are "characters."

No one book can give a complete survey of mountain life in all its aspects. Much must be left out. I have chosen to write about those features that seemed to me most picturesque.

PREFACE TO THE REVISED EDITION

The narrative is to be taken literally. There is not a line of fiction or exaggeration in it.

Our Southern Highlanders was first published in 1913. It has had several printings in the original form. In the present edition I have corrected errors of the press, and one or two of my own, but otherwise no alteration has been made of the text. I have continued the story of moonshining to the present day, and have added three new chapters: The Snake-Stick Man, A Raid into the Sugarlands, and The Killing of Hol Rose.

Most of the illustrations in this edition are new, some of them taken by myself, others by friends who generously let me select specimens of their work with the camera here in the Great Smoky Mountains. I am particularly indebted, for such courtesies, to Francis B. Laney, of the U. S. Geological Survey; Professor S. H. Essary, of the University of Tennessee; Paul M. Fink, of Jonesboro, Tenn.; and John Ogden Morrell, of Knoxville.

Some parts of this book originally appeared in *Outing* and *All Outdoors.*

Bryson City, N. C.   HORACE KEPHART.
    April, 1922.

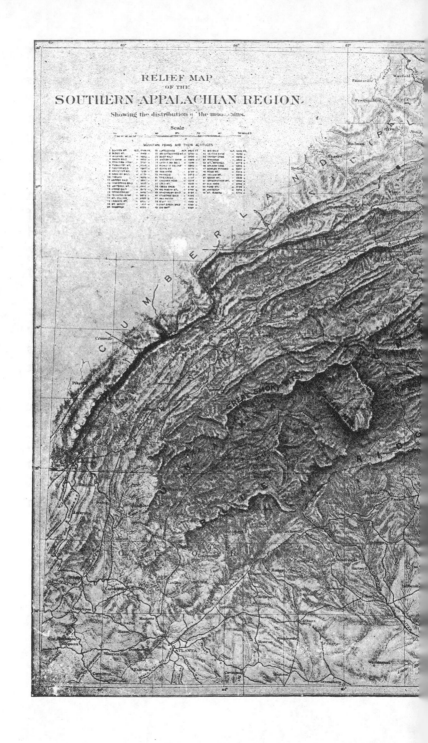

CHAPTER I

"SOMETHING HIDDEN; GO AND FIND IT"

IN one of Poe's minor tales, written in 1845, there is a vague allusion to wild mountains in western Virginia "tenanted by fierce and uncouth races of men." This, so far as I know, was the first reference in literature to our Southern mountaineers, and it stood as their only characterization until Miss Murfree ("Charles Egbert Craddock") began her stories of the Cumberland hills.

Time and retouching have done little to soften our Highlander's portrait. Among reading people generally, South as well as North, to name him is to conjure up a tall, slouching figure in homespun, who carries a rifle as habitually as he does his hat, and who may tilt its muzzle toward a stranger before addressing him, the form of salutation being:

" Stop thar! Whut's you-unses name? Whar's you-uns a-goin' ter? "

Let us admit that there is just enough truth in this caricature to give it a point that will stick. Our typical mountaineer is lank, he is always unkempt, he is fond of toting a gun on his shoulder, and his curiosity about a stranger's name and business is promptly, though politely, out· spoken. For the rest, he is a man of mystery. The great world outside his mountains knows almost as little about him as he does of it; and that is little indeed. News in order to reach him must be of such widespread interest as fairly to fall from heaven; correspondingly, scarce any, incidents of mountain life will leak out unless they be of sensational nature, such as the shooting of a revenue officer in Carolina, the massacre of a Virginia court, or the outbreak of another feud in " bloody Breathitt." And so, from the grim sameness of such reports, the world infers that battle, murder, and sudden death are commonplaces in Appalachia.

To be sure, in Miss Murfree's novels, as in those of John Fox, Jr., and of Alice MacGowan, we do meet characters more genial than feudists and illicit distillers; none the less, when we have closed the book, who is it that stands out clearest as type and pattern of the mountaineer? Is it not he of the long rifle and peremptory challenge? And whether this be because he gets most of the limelight, or because we have a furtive liking for that sort of thing (on paper), or whether the armed outlaw be indeed a genuine protagonist—in any case, the Appalachian people remain in public estimation to-day, as Poe judged them, an uncouth and fierce race of men, inhabiting a wild mountain region little known.

The Southern highlands themselves are a mysterious realm. When I prepared, in 1904, for my first sojourn in the Great Smoky Mountains, which form the master chain of the Appalachian system, I could find in no library a guide to that region. The most diligent research failed to discover so much as a magazine article, written within this generation, that described the land and its people. Nay, there was not even a novel or a story that showed intimate local knowledge. Had I been going to Teneriffe or Timbuctu, the libraries would have furnished information a-plenty; but about this housetop of eastern America they were strangely silent; it was *terra incognita.*

On the map I could see that the Southern Appalachians cover an area much larger than New England, and that they are nearer the

center of our population than any other mountains that deserve the name. Why, then, so little
known? Quaintly there came to mind those
lines familiar to my boyhood: " Get you up
this way southward, and go up into the mountain; and see the land, what it is; and the people
that dwelleth therein, whether they be strong or
weak, few or many; and what the land is that
they dwell in, whether it be good or bad; and
what cities they be that they dwell in, whether
in tents, or in strongholds; and what the land
is, whether it be fat or lean, whether there be
wood therein or not."

In that dustiest room of a great library where
" pub. docs." are stored, I unearthed a government report on forestry that gave, at last, a clear
idea of the lay of the land. And here was news.
We are wont to think of the South as a low
country with sultry climate; yet its mountain
chains stretch uninterruptedly southwestward
from Virginia to Alabama, 650 miles in an air
line. They spread over parts of eight contiguous States, and cover an area somewhat larger
than England and Scotland, or about the same
as that of the Alps. In short, the greatest mountain system of eastern America is massed in our
Southland. In its upper zone one sleeps under
blankets the year round.

In all the region north of Virginia and east of the Black Hills of Dakota there is but one summit (Mount Washington, in New Hampshire) that reaches 6,000 feet above sea level, and there are only a dozen others that exceed 5,000 feet. By contrast, south of the Potomac there are forty-six peaks, and forty-one miles of dividing ridges, that rise above 6,000 feet, besides 288 mountains and some 300 miles of divide that stand more than 5,000 feet above the sea. In North Carolina alone the mountains cover 6,000 square miles, with an *average* elevation of 2,700 feet, and with twenty-one peaks that overtop Mount Washington.

I repeated to myself: "Why, then, so little known?" The Alps and the Rockies, the Pyrennees and the Harz are more familiar to the American people, in print and picture, if not by actual visit, than are the Black, the Balsam, and the Great Smoky Mountains. It is true that summer tourists flock to Asheville and Toxaway, Linville and Highlands, passing their time at modern hotels and motoring along a few macadamed roads, but what do they see of the billowy wilderness that conceals most of the native homes? Glimpses from afar. What do they learn of the real mountaineer? Hearsay. For, mark you, nine-tenths of the Appalachian population are a sequestered folk. The typical, the average mountain man prefers his native hills and his primitive ancient ways.

We read more and talk more about the Filipinos, see more of the Chinese and the Syrians, than of these three million next-door Americans who are of colonial ancestry and mostly of British stock. New York, we say, is a cosmopolitan city; more Irish than in Dublin, more Germans than in Munich, more Italians than in Rome, more Jews than in nine Jerusalems; but how many New Yorkers ever saw a Southern mountaineer? I am sure that a party of hillsmen fresh from the back settlements of the Unakas, if dropped on the streets of any large city in the Union, and left to their own guidance, would stir up more comment (and probably more trouble) than would a similar body of whites from any other quarter of the earth; and yet this same odd people is more purely bred from old American stock than any other element of our population that occupies, by itself, so great a territory.

The mountaineers of the South are marked apart from all other folks by dialect, by customs, by character, by self-conscious isolation. So true is this that they call all outsiders "furriners." It matters not whether your descent

The Author's First Camp in the Smokies.

be from Puritan or Cavalier, whether you come from Boston or Chicago, Savannah or New Orleans, in the mountains you are a "furriner." A traveler, puzzled and scandalized at this, asked a native of the Cumberlands what he would call a "Dutchman or a Dago." The fellow studied a bit and then replied: "Them's the outlandish."

Foreigner, outlander, it is all one; we are "different," we are "quar," to the mountaineer. He knows he is an American; but his conception of the metes and bounds of America is vague to the vanishing point. As for countries over-sea—well, when a celebrated Nebraskan returned from his trip around the globe, one of my backwoods neighbors proudly informed me: "I see they give Bryan a lot of receptions when he kem back from the other world."

No one can understand the attitude of our highlanders toward the rest of the earth until he realizes their amazing isolation from all that lies beyond the blue, hazy skyline of their mountains. Conceive a shipload of emigrants cast away on some unknown island, far from the regular track of vessels, and left there for five or six generations, unaided and untroubled by the growth of civilization. Among the descendants of such a company we would expect to find

customs and ideas unaltered from the time of
their forefathers.   And that is just what we do
find to-day among our castaways in the sea of
mountains.   Time has lingered in Appalachia.
The mountain folk still live in the eighteenth
century.   The progress of mankind from that
age to this is no heritage of theirs.

Our backwoodsmen of the Blue Ridge and
the Unakas, of their connecting chains, and of
the outlying Cumberlands, are still thinking essentially the same thoughts, still living in much
the same fashion, as did their ancestors in the
days of Daniel Boone.   Nor is this their fault.
They are a people of keen intelligence and
strong initiative when they can see anything to
win.   But, as President Frost says, they have
been " beleaguered by nature."   They are be-
lated—ghettoed in the midst of a civilization
that is as aloof from them as if it existed only
on another planet.   And so, in order to be fair
and just with these, our backward kinsmen, we
must, for the time, decivilize ourselves to the extent of *going back* and getting an eighteenth century point of view.

But, first, how comes it that the mountain
folk have been so long detached from the life
and movement of their times?   Why are they
so foreign to present-day Americanism that they

innocently call all the rest of us foreigners?

The answer lies on the map. They are creatures of environment, enmeshed in a labyrinth that has deflected and repelled the march of our nation for three hundred years.

In 1728, when Colonel William Byrd, of Westover, was running the boundary line between Virginia and North Carolina, he finally was repulsed by parallel chains of savage, unpeopled mountains that rose tier beyond tier to the westward, everywhere densely forested, and matted into jungle by laurel and other undergrowth. In his *Journal,* writing in the quaint, old-fashioned way, he said: "Our country has now been inhabited more than 130 years by the English, and still we hardly know anything of the Appalachian Mountains, that are nowhere above 250 miles from the sea. Whereas the French, who are later comers, have rang'd from Quebec Southward as far as the Mouth of Mississippi, in the bay of Mexico, and to the West almost as far as California, which is either way above 2,000 miles."

A hundred and thirty years later, the same thing could have been said of these same mountains; for the " fierce and uncouth races of men " that Poe faintly heard of remained practically undiscovered until they startled the nation on the scene of our Civil War, by sending 180,000 of their riflemen into the Union Army.

If a corps of surveyors to-day should be engaged to run a line due west from eastern Virginia to the Blue Grass of Kentucky, they would have an arduous task. Let us suppose that they start from near Richmond and proceed along the line of 37° 50′. The Blue Ridge is not especially difficult: only eight transverse ridges to climb up and down in fourteen miles, and none of them more than 2,000 feet high from bottom to top. Then, thirteen miles across the lower end of The Valley, a curious formation begins.

As a foretaste, in the three and a half miles crossing Little House and Big House mountains, one ascends 2,200 feet, descends 1,400, climbs again 1,600, and goes down 2,000 feet on the far side. Beyond lie steep and narrow ridges athwart the way, paralleling each other like waves at sea. Ten distinct mountain chains are scaled and descended in the next forty miles. There are few " leads " rising gradually to their crests. Each and every one of these ridges is a Chinese wall magnified to altitudes of from a thousand to two thousand feet, and covered with thicket. The hollows between them are merely deep troughs.

In the next thirty miles we come upon novel

topography. Instead of wave following wave in orderly procession, we find here a choppy sea of small mountains, with hollows running toward all points of the compass. Instead of Chinese walls, we now have Chinese puzzles. The innate perversity of such configuration grows more and more exasperating as we toil westward. In the two hundred miles from the Greenbrier to the Kentucky River, the ridges are all but unscalable, and the streams sprangle in every direction like branches of mountain laurel.

The only roads follow the beds of tortuous and rock-strewn water courses, which may be nearly dry when you start out in the morning, but within an hour may be raging torrents. There are no bridges. One may ford a dozen times in a mile. A spring " tide " will stop all travel, even from neighbor to neighbor, for a day or two at a time. Buggies and carriages are unheard of. In many districts the only means of transportation is with saddlebags on horseback, or with a " tow sack " afoot. If the pedestrian tries a short-cut he will learn what the natives mean when they say: " Goin' up, you can might' nigh stand up straight and bite the ground; goin' down, a man wants hobnails in the seat of his pants."

James Lane Allen was not writing fiction

when he said of the far-famed Wilderness Road
into Kentucky: "Despite all that has been
done to civilize it since Boone traced its course
in 1790, this honored historic thoroughfare remains to-day as it was in the beginning, with all
its sloughs and sands, its mud and holes, and jutting ledges of rock and loose boulders, and
twists and turns, and general total depravity. . . .
One such road was enough. They are said to
have been notorious for profanity, those who
came into Kentucky from this side. Naturally.
Many were infidels—there are roads that make
a man lose faith. It is known that the more
pious companies of them, as they traveled along,
would now and then give up in despair, sit
down, raise a hymn, and have prayers before
they could go further. Perhaps one of the pro-
vocations to homicide among the mountain
people should be reckoned this road. I have
seen two of the mildest of men, after riding over
it for a few hours, lose their temper and begin
to fight—fight their horses, fight the flies, fight
the cobwebs on their noses."

Such difficulties of intercommunication are
enough to explain the isolation of the mountaineers. In the more remote regions this loneliness
reaches a degree almost unbelievable. Miss El-
len Semple, in a fine monograph published in

the *Geographical Journal,* of London, in 1901, gave us some examples:

"These Kentucky mountaineers are not only cut off from the outside world, but they are separated from each other. Each is confined to his own locality, and finds his little world within a radius of a few miles from his cabin. There are many men in these mountains who have never seen a town, or even the poor village that constitutes their county-seat. . . . The women . . . are almost as rooted as the trees. We met one woman who, during the twelve years of her married life, had lived only ten miles across the mountain from her own home, but had never in this time been back home to visit her father and mother. Another back in Perry county told me she had never been farther from home than Hazard, the county-seat, which is only six miles distant. Another had never been to the post-office, four miles away; and another had never seen the ford of the Rockcastle River, only two miles from her home, and marked, moreover, by the country store of the district."

When I first went into the Smokies, I stopped one night in a single-room log cabin, and soon had the good people absorbed in my tales of travel beyond the seas. Finally the housewife said to me, with pathetic resignation: "Bushnell's the furdest ever I've been." Bushnell, at that time, was a hamlet of thirty people, only seven miles from where we sat. When I lived alone on "the Little Fork of Sugar Fork of

Hazel Creek," there were women in the neighborhood, young and old, who had never seen a railroad, and men who had never boarded a train, although the Murphy branch ran within sixteen miles of our post-office. The first time that a party of these people went to the railroad, they were uneasy and suspicious. Nearing the way-station, a girl in advance came upon the first negro she ever saw in her life, and ran screaming back: " My goddamighty, Mam, thar's the boogerman—I done seed him! "

But before discussing the mountain people and their problems, let us take an imaginary balloon voyage over their vast domain. South of the Potomac the Blue Ridge is a narrow rampart rising abruptly from the east, one or two thousand feet above its base, and descending sharply to the Shenandoah Valley on the west. Across the Valley begin the Alleghanies. These mountains, from the Potomac through to the northern Tennessee border, consist of a multitude of narrow ridges with steep escarpment on both sides, running southwesterly in parallel chains, and each chain separated from its neighbors by deep, slender dales. Wherever one goes westward from the Valley he will encounter tier after tier of these ridges, as I have already described.

The Old Copper Mine.

As a rule, the links in each chain can be passed by following small gaps; but often one must make very wide detours. For example, Pine Mountain (every link has its own distinct name) is practically impassable for nearly 150 miles, except for two water gaps and five difficult crossings. Although it averages only a mile thick, the people on its north side, generally, know less about those on the south than a Maine Yankee does about Pennsylvania Dutchmen.

The Alleghanies together have a width of from forty to sixty miles. Westward of them, for a couple of hundred miles, are the labyrinthine roughs of West Virginia and eastern Kentucky.

In southwestern Virginia the Blue Ridge and the Alleghanies coalesce, but soon spread apart again, the Blue Ridge retaining its name, as well as its general character, although much loftier and more massive than in the north. The southeast front of the Blue Ridge is a steep escarpment, rising abruptly from the Piedmont Plateau of Carolina. Not one river cuts through the Ridge, notwithstanding that the mountains to the westward are higher and much more massive. It is the watershed of this whole mountain region. The streams rising on its northwestern front flow down into central plateaus, and thence cut their way through the Unakas in deep and precipitous gorges, draining finally into the Gulf of Mexico, through the Tennessee, Ohio and Mississippi rivers.

The northwestern range, which corresponds to the Alleghanies of Virginia, now assumes a character entirely different from them. Instead of parallel chains of low ridges, we have here, on the border of North Carolina and Tennessee, a single chain that dwarfs all others in the Appalachian system. It is cut into segments by the rivers (Nolichucky, French Broad, Pigeon, Little Tennessee, Hiwassee) that drain the interior plateaus, and each segment has a distinct name of its own (Iron, Northern Unaka, Bald, Great Smoky, Southern Unaka or Unicoi mountains). The Carolina mountaineers still call this system collectively the Alleghanies, but the U. S. Geological Survey has given it a more distinctive name, the Unakas. While the Blue Ridge has only seven peaks that rise above 5,000 feet, the Unakas have 125 summits exceeding 5,000, and ten that are over 6,000 feet.

Connecting the Unaka chain with the Blue Ridge are several transverse ranges, the Stone, Beech, Roan, Yellow, Black, Newfound, Pisgah, Balsam, Cowee, Nantahala, Tusquitee, and a few minor mountains, which as a whole are much higher than the Blue Ridge, 156 summits rising over 5,000 feet, and thirty-six over 6,000 feet above sea-level.

In northern Georgia the Unakas and the Blue Ridge gradually fade away into straggling ridges and foothills, which extend into small parts of South Carolina and Alabama.

The Cumberland Plateau is not attached to either of these mountain systems, but is rather a prolongation of the roughs of eastern Kentucky. It is separated from the Unakas by the broad valley of the Tennessee River. The Plateau rises very abruptly from the surrounding plains. It consists mainly of tableland gashed by streams that have cut their way down in deep narrow gulches with precipitous sides.

Most of the literature about our Southern mountaineers refers only to the inhabitants of the comparatively meagre hills of eastern Kentucky, or to the Cumberlands of Tennessee. Little has been written about the real mountaineers of southwestern Virginia, western North Carolina, and the extreme north of Georgia. The great mountain masses still await their annalist, their artist, and, in some places, even their explorer.

CHAPTER II

"THE BACK OF BEYOND"

OF certain remote parts of Erin, Jane Barlow says: "In Bogland, if you inquire the address of such or such person, you will hear not very infrequently that he or she lives ' off away at the Back of Beyond.' . . . A traveler to the Back of Beyond may consider himself rather exceptionally fortunate, should he find that he is able to arrive at his destination by any mode of conveyance other than ' the two standin' feet of him.' Often enough the last stage of his journey proceeds down some boggy *boreen,* or up some craggy hill-track, inaccessible to any wheel or hoof that ever was shod."

So in Appalachia, one steps shortly from the railway into the primitive. Most of the river valleys are narrow. In their bottoms the soil is rich, the farms well kept and generous, the owners comfortable and urbane. But from the valleys directly spring the mountains, with slopes rising twenty to forty degrees or more. These mountains cover nine-tenths of western North Carolina, and among them dwell a majority of the native people.

The back country is rough. No boat nor canoe can stem its brawling waters. No bicycle nor automobile can enter it. No coach can endure its roads. Here is a land of lumber wagons, and saddle-bags, and shackly little sleds that are dragged over the bare ground by harnessed steers. This is the country that ordinary tourists shun. And well for such that they do, since whoso cares more for bodily comfort than for freedom and air and elbow-room should tarry by still waters and pleasant pastures. To him the backwoods could be only what Burns called Argyleshire: "A country where savage streams tumble over savage mountains, thinly overspread with savage flocks, which starvingly support as savage inhabitants."

When I went south into the mountains I was seeking a Back of Beyond. This for more reasons than one. With an inborn taste for the wild and romantic, I yearned for a strange land and a people that had the charm of originality. Again, I had a passion for early American history; and, in Far Appalachia, it seemed that I might realize the past in the present, seeing with my own eyes what life must have been to my pioneer ancestors of a century or two ago. Besides, I wanted to enjoy a free life in the open air, the thrill of exploring new ground, the joys of the chase, and the man's game of matching my woodcraft against the forces of nature, with no help from servants or hired guides.

So, casting about for a biding place that would fill such needs, I picked out the upper settlement of Hazel Creek, far up under the lee of those Smoky Mountains that I had learned so little about. On the edge of this settlement, scant two miles from the post-office of Medlin, there was a copper mine, long disused on account of litigation, and I got permission to occupy one of its abandoned cabins.

A mountain settlement consists of all who get their mail at the same place. Ours was made up of forty-two households (about two hundred souls) scattered over an area eight miles long by two wide. These are air-line measurements. All roads and trails "wiggled and wingled around" so that some families were several miles from a neighbor. Fifteen homes had no wagon road, and could be reached by no vehicle other than a narrow sled. Quill Rose had not even a sledpath, but journeyed full five miles by trail to the nearest wagon road.

Medlin itself comprised two little stores built

of rough planks and bearing no signs, a corn mill, and four dwellings. A mile and a half away was the log schoolhouse, which, once or twice a month, served also as church. Scattered about the settlement were seven tiny tubmills for grinding corn, some of them mere open sheds with a capacity of about a bushel a day. Most of the dwellings were built of logs. Two or three, only, were weatherboarded frame houses and attained the dignity of a story and a half.

All about us was the forest primeval, where roamed some sparse herds of cattle, razorback hogs, and the wild beasts. Speckled trout were in all the streams. Bears sometimes raided the fields, and wildcats were a common nuisance. Our settlement was a mere slash in the vast woodland that encompassed it.

The post-office occupied a space about five feet square, in a corner of one of the stores. There was a daily mail, by rider, serving four other communities along the way. The contractor for this service had to furnish two horses, working turnabout, pay the rider, and squeeze his own profit, out of $499 a year. In Star Route days the mail was carried afoot, two barefooted young men " toting the sacks on their own wethers " over this thirty-two-mile round trip, for forty-eight cents a day; and they boarded themselves!

In the group that gathered at mail time I often was solicited to " back " envelopes, give out the news, or decipher letters for men who could not read. Several times, in the postmaster's absence, I registered letters for myself, or for someone else, the law of the nation being suspended by general consent.

Our stores, as I have said, were small, yet many of their shelves were empty. Oftentimes there was no flour to be had, no meat, cereals, canned goods, coffee, sugar, or oil. It excited no comment at all when Old Pete would lean across his bare counter and lament that " Thar's lots o' folks a-hurtin' around hyur for lard, and I ain't got none."

I have seen the time when our neighborhood could get no salt nor tobacco without making a twenty-four-mile trip over the mountain and back, in the dead of winter. This was due, partly, to the state of the roads, and to the fact that there would be no wagon available for weeks at a time. Wagoning, by the way, was no sinecure. Often it meant to chop a fallen tree out of the road, and then, with handspikes, " man-power the log outen the way." Sometimes an axle would break (far up on the moun-

Cabin on the Little Fork of Sugar Fork of Hazel Creek, where the
author lived alone for three years.

tain, of course) ; then a tree must be felled, and a new axle made on the spot from the green wood, with no tools but axe and jackknife.

Trade was mostly by barter, in which 'coon skins and ginseng had the same rank as in the days of Davy Crockett and Daniel Boone. Long credits were given on anticipated crops; but the risks were great and the market limited by local consumption, as it did not pay to haul bulky commodities to the railroad. Hence it was self-preservation for the storekeepers to carry only a slender stock of essentials and take pains to have little left through unproductive times.

As a rule, credit would not be asked so long as anything at all could be offered in trade. When Bill took the last quart of meal from the house, as rations for a bear hunt, his patient Marg walked five miles to the store with a skinny old chicken, last of the flock, and offered to barter it for "a dustin' o' salt." There was not a bite in her house beyond potatoes, and "'taters don't go good 'thout salt."

In our primitive community there were no trades, no professions. Every man was his own farmer, blacksmith, gunsmith, carpenter, cobbler, miller, tinker. Someone in his family, or a near neighbor, served him as barber and dentist, and would make him a coffin when he died. One farmer was also the wagoner of the district, as well as storekeeper, magistrate, veterinarian, and accoucheur. He also owned the only "tooth-pullers" in the settlement: a pair of universal forceps that he designed, forged, filed out, and wielded with barbaric grit. His wife kept the only boarding-house for leagues around. Truly, an accomplished couple!

About two-thirds of our householders owned their homes. Of the remainder about three-fifths were renters and two-fifths were squatters, in the sense that these last were permitted to occupy ground for the sake of reporting trespass and putting out fires—or, maybe, to prevent them doing both. Nearly all of the wild land belonged to Northern timber companies who had not yet begun operations (they have done so within the past three years).

Titles were confused, owing to careless surveys, or guesswork, in the past. Many boundaries overlapped, and there were bits of no-man's land here and there, covered by no deed and subject to entry by anyone who discovered them. Our old frontier always was notorious for happy-go-lucky surveys and neglect to make legal entry of claims. Thus Boone lost the fairest parts of the Kentucky he founded, and was ejected and sent adrift. In our own time, over-lapping boundaries have led to bitter litigation and murderous feuds.

As our territory was sparsely occupied, there were none of those "perpendicular farms" so noticeable in older settlements near the river valleys, where men plow fields as steep as their own house roofs and till with the hoe many an acre that is steeper still. John Fox tells of a Kentucky farmer who fell out of his own corn-field and broke his neck. I have seen fields in Carolina where this might occur, as where a forty-five degree slope is tilled to the brink of a precipice. A woman told me: " I've hoed corn many a time on my knees—yes, I have;" and another: " Many's the hill o' corn I've propped up with a rock to keep it from fallin' down-hill." *

Even in our new region many of the fields suffered quickly from erosion. When a forest is cleared there is a spongy humus on the ground surface that is extremely rich, but this washes away in a single season. The soil beneath is

---

* A friend of mine on the U. S. Geological Survey tested with his clinometer a mountain cornfield that sloped at an angle of fifty degrees.

good, but thin on the hillsides, and its soluble, fertile ingredients soon leach out and vanish. Without terracing, which I have never seen practiced in the mountains of the South, no field with a surface slope of more than ten degrees (about two feet in ten) will last more than a few years. As one of my neighbors put it: " Thar, I've cl'ared me a patch and grubbed hit out— now I can raise me two or three severe craps!"

" Then what? " I asked.

" When corn won't grow no more I can turn the field into grass a couple o' years."

" Then you'll rotate, and grow corn again? "

" La, no! By that time the land will be so poor hit wouldn't raise a cuss-fight."

" But then you must move, and begin all over again. This continual moving must be a great nuisance."

He rolled his quid and placidly answered: " Huk-uh; when I move, all I haffter do is put out the fire and call the dog."

His apparent indifference was only philosophy expressed with sardonic humor; just as another neighbor would say, " This is good, strong land, or it wouldn't hold up all the rocks there is around hyur."

Right here is the basis for much of what strangers call shiftlessness among the mountaineers. But of that, more anon.

In clearing new ground, everyone followed the ancient custom of girdling the tree trunks and letting them stand in spectral ugliness until they rotted and fell. This is a quick and easy way to get rid of the shade that otherwise would stunt the crops, and it prevents such trees as chestnut, buckeye and basswood from sprouting from the stumps. In the fields stood scores of gigantic hemlocks, deadened, that never would be used even for fuel, save as their bark furnished the women with quick-burning stove-wood in wet weather. No one dreamt that hemlock ever would be marketable. And this was only five years ago!

The tillage was as rude and destructive as anything we read of in pioneer history. The common plow was a " bull-tongue," which has aptly been described as " hardly more than a sharpened stick with a metal rim." The harrows were of wood, throughout, with locust teeth (a friend and I made one from the green trees in half a day, and it lasted three seasons on rocky ground). Sometimes no harrow was used at all, the plowed ground being " drug " with a big evergreen bough. This needed only to be withed directly to a pony's tail, as they used to do in ancient Ireland, and the picture of prehistoric agriculture would have been complete. After the corn was up, all cultivating was done with the hoe. For this the entire family turned out, the toddlers being left to play in the furrows while their mother toiled like a man.

Corn was the staple crop—in fact, the only crop of most farmers. Some rye was raised along the creek, and a little oats, but our settlement grew no wheat—there was no mill that could grind it. Wheat is raised, to some extent, in the river bottoms, and on the plateaus of the interior. I have seen it flailed out on the bare ground, and winnowed by pouring the grain and chaff from basket to basket while the women fluttered aprons or bed-sheets. Corn is topped for the blade-fodder, the ears gathered from the stalk, and the main stalks afterwards used as " roughness " (roughage). The cribs generally are ramshackle pens, and there is much waste from mold and vermin.

The Carolina mountains are, by nature, one of the best fruit regions in eastern America. Apples, grapes, and berries, especially, thrive exceeding well. But our mountaineer is no horticulturist. He lets his fruit trees take care of themselves, and so, everywhere except on select farms near the towns, we see old apple and peach trees that never were pruned, bristling with shoots, and often bearing wizened fruit, dry and bitter, or half rotted on the stem.

So, too, the gardens are slighted. Late in the season our average garden is a miniature jungle, chiefly of weeds that stand high as one's head. Cabbage and field beans survive and figure mightily in the diet of the mountaineer. Potatoes generally do well, but few farmers raise enough to see them through the winter. Generally some tobacco is grown for family consumption, the strong "twist" being smoked or chewed indifferently.

An interesting crop in our neighborhood was ginseng, of which there were several patches in cultivation. This curious plant is native throughout the Appalachians, but has been exterminated in all but the wildest regions, on account of the high price that its dried root brings. It has long since passed out of our pharmacopœia, and is marketed only in China, though our own people formerly esteemed it as a panacea for all ills of the flesh. Colonel Byrd, in his " History of the Dividing Line," says of it:

" Though Practice will soon make a man of tolerable Vigour an able Footman, yet, as a help to bear Fatigue I us'd to chew a Root of Ginseng as I Walk't along. This

kept up my Spirits, and made me trip away as nimbly in
my half Jack-Boots as younger men cou'd in their Shoes.
This Plant is in high Esteem in China, where it sells for
its Weight in Silver. . . . Its vertues are, that it gives
an uncommon Warmth and Vigour to the Blood, and frisks
the Spirits, beyond any other Cordial. It chears the Heart,
even of a Man that has a bad Wife, and makes him look
down with great Composure on the crosses of the World.
It promotes insensible Perspiration, dissolves all Phlegmatick
and Viscous Humours, that are apt to obstruct the Narrow
channels of the Nerves. It helps the Memory and would
quicken even Helvetian dullness. 'Tis friendly to the
Lungs, much more than Scolding itself. It comforts the
Stomach, and Strengthens the Bowels, preventing all Colicks
and Fluxes. In one Word, it will make a Man live a great
while, and very well while he does live. And what is more,
it will even make Old Age amiable, by rendering it lively,
chearful, and good-humour'd."

Alas that only Chinamen and eighteenth-century Cavaliers could absorb the virtues of this
sovereign herb!

A successful ginseng grower of our settlement
told me that two acres of the plant will bring
an income of $2,500 to $5,000 a year, planting
100,000 to the acre. The roots take eight years
to mature. They weigh from one and a half to
four ounces each, when fresh, and one-third of
this dried. Two acres produce 25,000 roots a
year, by progression. The dried root, at that
time, brought five dollars a pound. At present,

At the Post-Office. (Sheriff Collecting Taxes.)

I believe, it is higher.   Another friend of mine, who is in this business extensively, tried exporting for himself, but got only $6.50 a pound in Amoy, when the U. S. consul at that port assured him that the real market price was from $12.60 to $24.40.   The local trader, knowing American prices, pocketed the difference.

In times of scarcity many of our people took to the woods and gathered commoner medicinal roots, such as bloodroot and wild ginger (there are scores of others growing wild in great profusion), but made only a pittance at it, as synthetic drugs have mostly taken the place of herbal simples in modern medicine.   Women and children did better, in the days before Christmas, by gathering galax, "hemlock" (*leucothoe*), and mistletoe, selling to the dealers at the railroad, who ship them North for holiday decorations.   One bright lad from town informed me, with evident pride of geography, that "Some of this goes to London, England." Nearly everywhere in our woods the beautiful ruddy-bronze galax is abundant.   Along the water-courses, *leucothoe,* which similarly turns bronze in autumn, and lasts throughout the winter, is so prolific as to be a nuisance to travelers, being hard to push through.

Most of our farmers had neither horse nor

mule. For the rough work of cultivating the hillsides a single steer hitched to the "bull-tongue" was better adapted, and the same steer patiently dragged a little sled to the trading post. On steep declivities the sled is more practical than a cart or wagon, because it can go where wheels cannot, it does not require so wide a track, and it "brakes" automatically in going downhill. Nearly all the farmer's hauling is downhill to his home, or down farther to the village. A sled can be made quite easily by one man, out of wood growing on the spot, and with few iron fittings, or none at all. The runners are usually made of natural sourwood crooks, this timber being chosen because it wears very smooth and does not fur up nor splinter.

The hinterland is naturally adapted to grazing, rather than to agriculture. As it stands, the best pasturage is high up in the mountains, where there are "balds" covered with succulent wild grass that resembles Kentucky bluegrass. Clearing and sowing would extend such areas indefinitely. The cattle forage for themselves through eight or nine months of the year, running wild like the razorbacks, and the only attention given them is when the herdsmen go out to salt them or to mark the calves. Nearly all the beasts are scrub stock. Jerseys, and other blooded cattle thrive in the valleys, where there are no free ranges, but the backwoodsman does not want "critters that haffter be gentled and hand-fed." The result is that many families go without milk a great part of the year, and seldom indeed taste butter or beef.

The truth is that mountain beef, being fed nothing but grass and browse, with barely enough corn and roughage to keep the animal alive through winter, is blue-fleshed, watery, and tough. If properly reared, the quality would be as good as any. Almost any of our farmers could have had a pasture near home and could have grown hay, but not one in ten would take the trouble. His cattle were only for export—let the buyer fatten them! It should be understood that nobody had any provision for taking care of fresh meat when the weather was not frosty.

On those rare occasions when somebody killed a beef, he had to travel all over the neighborhood to dispose of it in small portions. The carcass was cut up in the same way as a hog, and all parts except the cheap "bilin' pieces" were sold at the same price: ten cents a pound, or whatever they would bring on the spot. The butchering was done with an axe and a jackknife. The meat was either sliced thin and fried to a crackling, or cut in chunks and boiled furiously just long enough to fit it for boot-heels. What the butcher mangled, the cook damned.

Few sheep were raised in our settlement, and these only for their wool. The untamed Smokies were no place for such defenseless creatures. Sheep will not, cannot, run wild. They are wholly dependent on the fostering hand of man and perish without his shepherd-ing. Curiously enough, our mountaineer knows little or nothing about the goat—an animal per-fectly adapted to the free range of the Smokies. I am convinced that goats would be more profit-able to the small farmers of the wild mountains than cattle. Goats do not graze, but browse upon the shrubbery, of which there is a vast superfluity in all the Southern mountains. Un-like the weak, timorous and stupid sheep, a flock of goats can fight their own battles against wild animals. They are hardy in any weather, and thrive from their own pickings where other for-agers would starve.

A good milch goat gives more and richer milk than the average mountain cow. And a kid yields excellent fresh meat in *manageable* quan-tity, at a time when no one would butcher **a** beef because it would spoil. I used to shut my eyes and imagine the transformation that would be wrought in these mountains by a colony of Swiss, who would turn the coves into gardens, the moderate slopes into orchards, the steeper ones into vineyards, by terracing, and who would export the finest of cheese made from the surplus milk of their goats. But our native mountaineers—well, a man who will not eat beef nor drink fresh cow's milk, and who despises butter, cannot be interested in anything of the dairy order.

The chickens ran wild and scratched for a living; hence were thin, tough, and poor layers. Eggs seldom were for sale. It was not of much use to try to raise many chickens where they were unprotected from hawks, minks, foxes, weasels and snakes.

Honey often was procured by spotting wild bees to their hoard and chopping the tree, a mild form of sport in which most settlers are expert. Our local preacher had a hundred hives of tame bees, producing 1,500 pounds of honey a year, for which he got ten cents a pound at the railroad.

The mainstay of every farmer, aside from his cornfield, was his litter of razorback hogs. "Old cornbread and sowbelly" are a menu complete

for the mountaineer. The wild pig, roaming
foot-loose and free over hill and dale, picks up
his own living at all seasons and requires no
attention at all. He is the cheapest possible
source of meat and yields the quickest return:
" no other food animal can increase his own
weight a hundred and fifty fold in the first eight
months of his life." And so he is regarded by
his owner with the same affection that Connemara Paddy bestows upon " the gintleman that
pays the rint."

In physique and mentality, the razorback dif-
fers even more from a domestic hog than a wild
goose does from a tame one. Shaped in front
like a thin wedge, he can go through laurel
thickets like a bear. Armored with tough hide
cushioned by bristles, he despises thorns, bram-
bles, and rattlesnakes, alike. His extravagantly
long snout can scent like a cat's, and yet burrow,
uproot, overturn, as if made of metal. The
long legs, thin flanks, pliant hoofs, fit him to run
like a deer and climb like a goat. In courage
and sagacity he outranks all other beasts. A
warrior born, he is also a strategist of the first
order. Like man, he lives a communal life, and
unites with others of his kind for purposes of
defense.

The pig is the only large mammal I know

of, besides man, whose eyes will not shine by reflected light—they are too bold and crafty, I wit. The razorback has a mind of his own; not instinct, but *mind*—whatever psychologists may say. He thinks. Anybody can see that when he is not rooting or sleeping he is studying devilment. He shows remarkable understanding of human speech, especially profane speech, and even an uncanny gift of reading men's thoughts, whenever those thoughts are directed against the peace and dignity of pigship. He bears grudges, broods over indignities, and plans redresses for the morrow or the week after. If he cannot get even with you, he will lay for your unsuspecting friend. And at the last, when arrested in his crimes and lodged in the pen, he is liable to attacks of mania from sheer helpless rage.

If you camp out in the mountains, nothing will molest you but razorback hogs. Bears will flee and wildcats sneak to their dens, but the moment incense of cooking arises from your camp every pig within two miles will scent it and hasten to call. You may throw your arm out of joint: they will laugh in your face. You may curse in five languages: it is music to their titillating ears.

Throughout summer and autumn I cooked out

of doors, on the woodsman's range of forked stakes and a lug-pole spanning parallel beds of rock. When the pigs came, I fed them red-pepper pie. Then all said good-bye to my hospitality save one slab-sided, tusky old boar—and he planned a campaign. At the first smell of smoke he would start for my premises. Hiding securely in a nearby thicket, he would spy on the operations until my stew got to simmering gently and I would retire to the cabin and get my fists in the dough. Then, charging at speed, he would knock down a stake, trip the lug-pole, and send my dinner flying. Every day he would do this. It got so that I had to sit there facing the fire all through my cooking, or that beast of a hog would ruin me. With this I thought he was outgeneraled. Idle dream! He would slip off to my favorite neighbor's, break through the garden fence, and raise Ned instanter—all because he hated *me,* for that peppery fraud, and knew that Bob and I were cronies.

I dubbed this pig Belial; a name that Bob promptly adapted to his own notion by calling it Be-liar. "That Be-liar," swore he, "would cross hell on a rotten rail to git into my 'tater patch!"

Finally I could stand it no longer, and took

A Tub Mill

down my rifle. It was a nail-driver, and I, through constant practice in beheading squirrels, was in good form. However, in the mountains it is more heinous to kill another man's pig than to shoot the owner. So I took craft for my guide, and guile for my heart's counsel. I stalked Belial as stealthily as ever hunter crept on an antelope against the wind. At last I had him dead right: broadside to me and motionless as if in a daydream. I knew that if I drilled his ear, or shot his tail clean off, it would only make him meaner than ever. He sported an uncommonly fine tail, and was proud to flaunt it. I drew down on that member, purposely a trifle scant, fired, and—away scuttled that boar, with a *broken* tail that would dangle and cling to him disgracefully through life.

Exit Belial! It was equivalent to a broken heart. He emigrated, or committed suicide, I know not which, but the Smoky Mountains knew him no more.

CHAPTER III

THE GREAT SMOKY MOUNTAINS

FOR a long time my chief interest was not in human neighbors, but in the mountains themselves—in that mysterious beckoning hinterland which rose right back of my chimney and spread upward, outward, almost to three cardinal points of the compass, mile after mile, hour after hour of lusty climbing—an Eden still unpeopled and unspoiled.

I loved of a morning to slip on my haversack, pick up my rifle, or maybe a mere staff, and stride forth alone over haphazard routes, to enjoy in my own untutored way the infinite variety of form and color and shade, of plant and tree and animal life, in that superb wilderness that towered there far above all homes of men. (And I love it still, albeit the charm of new discovery is gone from those heights and gulfs that are now so intimate and full of memories).

The Carolina mountains have a character all their own. Rising abruptly from a low base, and then rounding more gradually upward for 2,000 to 5,000 feet above their valleys, their apparent height is more impressive than that of many a loftier summit in the West which forms only a protuberance on an elevated plateau. Nearly all of them are clad to their tops in dense forest and thick undergrowth. Here and there is a grassy " bald ": a natural meadow curiously perched on the very top of a mountain. There are no bare, rocky summits rising above timberline, few jutting crags, no ribs and vertebræ of the earth exposed. Seldom does one see even a naked ledge of rock. The very cliffs are sheathed with trees and shrubs, so that one treading their edges has no fear of falling into an abyss.

Pinnacles or serrated ridges are rare. There are few commanding peaks. From almost any summit in Carolina one looks out upon a sea of flowing curves and dome-shaped eminences undulating, with no great disparity of height, unto the horizon. Almost everywhere the contours are similar: steep sides gradually rounding to the tops, smooth-surfaced to the eye because of the endless verdure. Every ridge is separated from its sisters by deep and narrow ravines. Not one of the thousand water courses shows a glint of its dashing stream, save where some far-off river may reveal, through a gap in the mountain, one single shimmering curve. In all this vast prospect, a keen eye, knowing where to look, may detect an occasional farmer's clearing, but to the stranger there is only mountain and forest, mountain and forest, as far as the eye can reach.

Characteristic, too, is the dreamy blue haze, like that of Indian summer intensified, that ever hovers over the mountains, unless they be swathed in cloud, or, for a few minutes, after a sharp rain-storm has cleared the atmosphere. Both the Blue Ridge and the Smoky Mountains owe their names to this tenuous mist. It softens all outlines, and lends a mirage-like effect of great distance to objects that are but a few miles off, while those farther removed grow more and more intangible until finally the sky-line blends with the sky itself.

The foreground of such a landscape, in summer, is warm, soft, dreamy, caressing, habitable; beyond it are gentle and luring solitudes; the remote ranges are inexpressibly lonesome, isolated and mysterious; but everywhere the green forest mantle bespeaks a vital present; nowhere does cold, bare granite stand as the sepulchre of an immemorial past.

And yet these very mountains of Carolina are among the ancients of the earth. They were old, very old, before the Alps and the Andes, the Rockies and the Himalayas were molded into their primal shapes. Upon them, in after ages, were born the first hardwoods of America—perhaps those of Europe, too—and upon them to-day the last great hardwood forests of our country stand in primeval majesty, mutely awaiting their imminent doom.

The richness of the Great Smoky forest has been the wonder and the admiration of everyone who has traversed it. As one climbs from the river to one of the main peaks, he passes successively through the same floral zones he would encounter in traveling from mid-Georgia to southern Canada.

Starting amid sycamores, elms, gums, willows, persimmons, chinquapins, he soon enters a region of beech, birch, basswood, magnolia, cucumber, butternut, holly, sourwood, box elder, ash, maple, buckeye, poplar, hemlock, and a great number of other growths along the creeks and branches. On the lower slopes are many species of oaks, with hickory, hemlock, pitch pine, locust, dogwood, chestnut. In this region nearly all trees attain their fullest development. On north fronts of hills the oaks reach a diameter of five to six feet. In cool, rich coves, chestnut trees grow from six to nine feet across the stump; and tulip poplars up to ten or eleven feet, their straight trunks towering like gigantic columns, with scarcely a noticeable taper, seventy or eighty feet to the nearest limb.

Ascending above the zone of 3,000 feet, white oak is replaced by the no less valuable "mountain oak." Beech, birch, buckeye, and chestnut persist to 5,000 feet. Then, where the beeches dwindle until adult trees are only knee-high, there begins a sub-arctic zone of black spruce, balsam, striped maple, aspen and the "Peruvian" or red cherry.

I have named only a few of the prevailing growths. Nowhere else in the temperate zone is there such a variety of merchantable timber as in western Carolina and the Tennessee front of the Unaka system. About a hundred and twenty species of native trees grow in the Smoky forest itself. When Asa Gray visited the North Carolina mountains he identified, in a thirty-mile trip, a greater variety of indigenous trees than could be observed in crossing Europe from England to Turkey, or in a trip from Boston to the Rocky Mountain plateau. As John Muir has said, our forests, "however slighted by man, must have been a great delight to God; for they were the best He ever planted."

The undergrowth is of almost tropical luxuriance and variety. Botanists say that this is the richest collecting ground in the United States. Whether one be seeking ferns or fungi or orchids or almost anything else vegetal, each hour will bring him some new delight. In summer the upper mountains are one vast flower garden: the white and pink of rhododendron, the blaze of azalea, conspicuous above all else, in settings of every imaginable shade of green.

It was the botanist who discovered this Eden for us. Far back in the eighteenth century, when this was still " Cherokee Country," inhabited by no whites but a few Indian-traders, William Bartram of Philadelphia came plant-hunting into the mountains of western Carolina, and spread their fame to the world. One of his choicest finds was the fiery azalea, of which he recorded: "The epithet fiery I annex to this most celebrated species of azalea, as being expressive of the appearance of its flowers; which are in general of the color of the finest red-lead, orange, and bright gold, as well as yellow and cream-color. These various splendid colors are not only in separate plants, but frequently all the varieties and shades are seen in separate branches on the same plant; and the clusters of the blossoms cover the shrubs in such incredible profusion on the hillsides that, suddenly opening to view from dark shades, we are alarmed with apprehension of the woods being set on fire. This is certainly the most gay and brilliant flowering shrub yet known."

And we of a later age, seeing the same wild gardens still unspoiled, can appreciate the almost religious fervor of those early botanists, as of Michaux, for example, who, in 1794, ascending the peak of Grandfather, broke out in song: *"Monté au sommet de la plus haut montagne de tout l'Amérique Septentrionale, chante avec mon compagnon-guide l'hymn de Marsellois, et crié, 'Vive la Liberté et la République Française!'"*

Of course Michaux was wildly mistaken in thinking Grandfather " the highest mountain in all North America." It is far from being even the highest of the Appalachians. Yet we scarcely know to-day, to a downright certainty, which peak is supreme among our Southern highlands. The honor is conceded to Mount Mitchell in the Black Mountains, northeast of Asheville. Still, the heights of the Carolina peaks have been taken (with but one exception, so far as I know) only by barometric measurements, and these, even when official, may vary as much as a hundred feet for the same mountain. Since the highest ten or a dozen of our

A Family of Pioneers in the Twentieth Century

Carolina peaks differ in altitude only one or two hundred feet, their actual rank has not yet been determined.

For a long time there was controversy as to whether Mount Mitchell or Clingman Dome was the crowning summit of eastern America. The Coast and Geodetic Survey gave the height of Mount Mitchell as 6,688 feet; but later figures of the U. S. Geological Survey are 6,711 and 6,712. In 1859 Buckley claimed for Clingman Dome of the Smokies an altitude of 6,941 feet. In recent government reports the Dome appears variously as 6,619 and 6,660. In 1911 I was told by Mr. H. M. Ramseur that when he laid out the route of the railroad from Asheville to Murphy he ran a line of levels from a known datum on this road to the top of Clingman, and that the result was "four sixes" (6,666 feet above sea-level). It is probable that second place among the peaks of Appalachia may belong either to Clingman Dome or Guyot or LeConte, of the Smokies, or to Balsam Cone of the Black Mountains.

In any case, the Great Smoky mountains are the master chain of the Appalachian system, the greatest mass of highland east of the Rockies. This segment of the Unakas forms the boundary between North Carolina and

Tennessee from the Big Pigeon River to the McDaniel Bald.

Although some parts of the Smokies are very rugged, with sharp changes of elevation, yet the range as a whole has no one dominating peak. Mount Guyot (pronounced *Gee*-o, with *g* as in get), Mount LeConte, and Clingman Dome all are over 6,600 feet and under 6,700, according to the most trustworthy measurements. Many miles of the divide rise 6,000 feet above sea-level, with only small undulations like ocean swells.

*   *   *   *   *

The most rugged and difficult part of the Smokies (and of the United States east of Colorado) is in the sawtooth mountains between Collins and Guyot, at the headwaters of the Okona Lufty River. I know but few men who have ever followed this part of the divide, although during the present year trails have been cut from Clingman to Collins, or near it, and possibly others beyond to the northeastward.

In August and September, 1900, Mr. James H. Ferriss and wife, naturalists from Joliet, Illinois, explored the Smokies to the Lufty Gap northeast of Clingman, collecting rare species of snails and ferns. No doubt Mrs. Ferriss is the only white woman who ever went beyond

Clingman or even ascended the Dome itself. She stayed at the Lufty Gap while her husband and a Carolina mountaineer of my acquaintance struggled through to Guyot and returned. Of this trip Mr. Ferriss sent me the following account:

"We bought another axe of a moonshiner, and, with a week's provisions on our backs, one of the guides and I took the Consolidated American Black Bear and Ruffed Grouse Line for Mount Guyot, twenty miles farther by map measurement. The bears were in full possession of the property, and we could get no information in the settlements, as the settlers do not travel this line. They did not know the names of the peaks other than as tops of the Great Smokies—knew nothing of the character of the country except that it was rough. The Tennesseans seem afraid of the mountains, and the Cherokees of the North Carolina side equally so; for, two miles from camp, all traces of man, except surveyors' marks, had disappeared. In the first two days we routed eight bears out of their nests and mud wallows, and they seemed to stay routed, for upon our return we found the blackberry crop unharvested and had a bag pudding—'duff'—or what you call it.

"A surveyor had run part of the line this

year, which helped us greatly, and the bears had made well-beaten trails part of the way. In places they had mussed up the ground as much as a barnyard. We tried to follow the boundary line between the two States, which is exactly upon the top of the Smokies, but often missed it. The government [state] surveyor many years ago made two hacks upon the trees, but sometimes the linemen neglected to use their axes for half a mile or so. It took us three and one-half days to go, and two and one-half to return, and we arose with the morning star and worked hard all day. The last day and a half, going, there was nothing to guide us but the old hacks.

"Equipped with government maps, a good compass, and a little conceit, I thought I could follow the boundary-line. In fact, at one time we intended to go through without a guide. A trail that runs through blackberry bushes two miles out of three is hard to follow. Then there was a huckleberry bush reaching to our waists growing thickly upon the ground as tomato vines, curled hard, and stubborn; and laurel much like a field of lilac bushes, crooked and strong as iron. In one place we walked fully a quarter of a mile over the tops of laurel bushes and these were ten or twelve feet in height, but blown over one way by the wind. Much of the trail was along rocky edges, sometimes but six inches or so wide, but almost straight down on both sides for hundreds of feet. One night, delayed by lack of water, we did not camp till dark, and, finding a smooth spot, lay down with a small log on each side to hold us from rolling out of bed. When daylight came we found that, had we rolled over the logs, my partner would have dropped 500 feet into Tennessee and I would have dropped as far into North Carolina, unless some friendly tree top had caught us. Sometimes the mountain forked, and these ridges, concealed by the balsams, would not be seen. Then there were round knobs—and who can tell where the highest ridge lies on a round mountain or a ball? My woolen shirt was torn off to the shoulders, and my partner, who had started out with corduroys, stayed in the brush until I got him a pair of overalls from camp."

Even to the west of Clingman a stranger is likely to find some desperately rough travel if he should stray from the trail that follows the divide. It is easy going for anyone in fair weather, but when cloud settles on the mountain, as it often does without warning, it may be so thick that one cannot see a tree ten feet away. Under such circumstances I have myself floundered from daylight till dark through heart-breaking laurel thickets, and without a bite to eat, not knowing whither I was going except that it was toward the Little Tennessee River.

In 1906 I spent the summer in a herders' hut on top of the divide, just west of the Locust Ridge (miscalled Chestnut Ridge on the map), about six miles east of Thunderhead. This time I had a partner, and we had a glorious three months of it, nearly a mile above sea-level, and only half a day's climb from the nearest settlement. One day I was alone, Andy having gone down to Medlin for the mail. It had rained a good deal—in fact, there was a shower nearly every day throughout the summer, the only semblance of a dry season in the Smokies being the autumn and early winter. The nights were cold enough for fires and blankets, even in our well-chinked cabin.

Well, I had finished my lonesome dinner, and was washing up, when I saw a man approaching. This was an event, for we seldom saw other men than our two selves. He was a lame man, wearing an iron extension on one foot, and he hobbled with a cane. He looked played-out and gaunt. I met him outside. He smiled as though I looked good to him, and asked with

some eagerness, " Can I buy something to eat
here? "

" No," I answered, "you can't buy anything
here "—how his face fell!—" but I'll give you
the best we have, and you're welcome."

Then you should have seen that smile!

He seemed to have just enough strength left
to drag himself into the hut. I asked no questions, though wondering what a cripple, evidently a gentleman, though in rather bad repair,
was doing on top of the Smoky Mountains. It
was plain that he had spent more than one night
shelterless in the cold rain, and that he was quite
famished. While I was baking the biscuit and
cooking some meat, he told his story. This is
the short of it:

" I am a Canadian, McGill University man,
electrician. My company sent me to Cincinnati. I got a vacation of a couple of weeks, and
thought I'd take a pedestrian tour. I can walk
better than you'd think," and he tapped the
short leg.

I liked his grit.

" I knew no place to go," he continued; " so
I took a map and looked for what might be
interesting country, not too far from Cincinnati.
I picked out these mountains, got a couple of

government topographical sheets, and, thinking they would serve like European ordnance maps, I had no fear of going astray. It was my plan to walk through to the Balsam Mountains, and so on to the Big Pigeon River. I went to Maryville, Tennessee, and there I was told that I would find a cabin every five or six miles along the summit from Thunderhead to the Balsams."

I broke in abruptly: "Whoever told you that was either an impostor or an ignoramus. There are only four of these shacks on the whole Smoky range. Two of them, the Russell cabin and the Spencer place, you have already passed without knowing it. This is called the Hall cabin. None of these three are occupied save for a week or so in the fall when the cattle are being rounded up, or by chance, as my partner and I happen to be here now. Beyond this there is just one shack, at Siler's Meadow. It is down below the summit, hidden in timber, and you would never have seen it. Even if you had, you would have found it as bare as a last year's mouse nest, for nobody ever goes there except a few bear-hunters. From there onward for forty miles is an uninhabited wilderness so rough that you could not make seven miles a day in it to save your life, even if you knew the course; and there is no trail at all.

The Schoolhouse

Those government maps are good and reliable to show the *approaches* to this wild country, but where you need them most they are good for nothing."

" Then," said he, " if I had missed your cabin I would have starved to death, for I depended on finding a house to the eastward, and would have followed the trail till I dropped. I have been out in the laurel thickets, now, three days and two nights; so nothing could have induced me to leave this trail, once I found it, or until I could see out to a house on one side or other of the mountain."

" You would see no house on either side from here to beyond Guyot, about forty miles. Had you no rations at all? "

" I traveled light, expecting to find entertainment among the natives. Here is what I have left."

He showed me a crumpled buckwheat flapjack, a pinch of tea, and a couple of ounces of brandy.

" I was saving them for the last extremity; have had nothing to eat since yesterday morning. Drink the brandy, please; it came from Montreal."

" No, my boy, that liquor goes down your own throat instanter. You're the chap that needs it. This coffee will boil now in a minute. I won't give you all the food you want, for it wouldn't be prudent; but by and by you shall have a bellyful."

Then, as well as he could, he sketched the route he had followed. Where the trail from Tennessee crosses from Thunderhead to Haw Gap he had swerved off from the divide, and he discovered his error somewhere in the neighborhood of Blockhouse. There, instead of retracing his steps, he sought a short-cut by plunging down to the headwaters of Haw Creek, thus worming deeper and deeper into the devil's nest. One more day would have finished him. When I told him that the trip from Clingman to Guyot would be hard work for a party of experienced mountaineers, and that it would probably take them a week, during which time they would have to pack all supplies on their own backs, he agreed that his best course would be down into Carolina and out to the railroad.

* * * * *

Of animal life in the mountains I was most entertained by the raven. This extraordinary bird was the first creature Noah liberated from the ark—he must have known, even at that early period of nature study, that it was the most sagacious of all winged things. Or perhaps Noah and the raven did not get on well together and he rid himself of the pest at first opportunity. Doubtless there could have been no peace aboard a craft that harbored so inquisitive and talkative a fowl. Anyway, the wild raven has been superlatively shy of man ever since the flood.

Probably there is no place south of Labrador where our raven (*Corvus corax principalis*) is seen so often as in the Smokies; and yet, even here, a man may haunt the tops for weeks without sight or sound of the ebon mystery—then, for a few days, they will be common. On the southeast side of the Locust Ridge, opposite Huggins's Hell, between Bone Valley and the main fork of Hazel Creek, there is a " Raven's Cliff " where they winter and breed, using the same nests year after year. Occasionally one is trapped, with bloody groundhog for bait; but I have yet to meet a man who has succeeded in shooting one.

If the raven's body be elusive his tongue assuredly is not. No other animal save man has anything like his vocal range. The raven croaks, clucks, caws, chuckles, squalls, pleads, " pooh-poohs," grunts, barks, mimics small birds, hectors, cajoles—yes, pulls a cork, whets a scythe, files a saw—with his throat. As is well known, ravens can be taught human speech, like parrots; and I am told they show the same preference for bad words—which, I think, is quite in character with their reputation as thieves and butchers. However, I may be prejudiced, seeing that the raven's favorite dainties for his menu are the eyes of living fawns and lambs.

A stranger in these mountains will be surprised at the apparent scarcity of game animals. It is not unusual for one to hunt all day in an absolute wilderness, where he sees never a fresh track of man, and not get a shot at anything fit to eat. The cover is so dense that one still-hunting (going without dogs) has poor chance of spying the game that lurks about him; and there really is little of it by comparison with such hunting fields as the Adirondacks, Maine, Canada, where game has been conserved for many years. It used to be the same up there. The late W. J. Stillman, writing in 1877 of the Maine woods, said:

"The most striking feature of the forest, after one has become habituated to the gloom, the pathlessness, and the apparent impenetrability of the screen it forms around him, is the absence of animal life. You may wander for hours without seeing a living creature. . . . One thinks of the woods and the wild beasts; yet in all the years of my wilderness living I can catalogue the wild creatures other than squirrels, grouse, and small birds (never plenty, generally very rare) which I have accidentally encountered and seen while wandering for hunting or mere pastime in the wild forest: one deer, one porcupine, one marten (commonly called sable), and maybe half a dozen hares. You may walk hours and not see a living creature larger than a fly, for days together and not see a grouse, a squirrel, or a bird larger than the Canada jay. . . . Lands running with game are like those flowing with milk and honey; and when the sporting books tell you that game is abundant, don't imagine that you are assured from starvation thereby. I have been reduced, in a country where deer were swarming, to live several days together on corn meal."

It is much the same to-day in our Appalachian wilderness, where no protection worthy the name has ever been afforded the game and fish since Indian times. There is a class of woods-loafers, very common here, that ranges the forest at all seasons with single-barrel shotguns or " hog rifles," killing bearing females as well as legitimate game, fishing at night, even using dynamite in the streams; and so, in spite of the fact that there is no better game harborage granted by Nature on our continent than the Carolina mountains, the deer are all but exterminated in most districts, turkeys and even squirrels are rather scarce, and good trout fishing is limited to stocked waters or streams flowing through virgin forest. The only game animal that still holds his own is the black bear, and he endures in few places other than the roughest districts, such as that southwest of the Sugarland Mountains, where laurel and cliffs daunt all but the hardiest of men.

The only venomous snakes in the mountains are rattlers and copperheads, the former common, the latter rare. The chance of being bitten by one is about as remote as that of being struck by lightning—either accident *might* happen, of course. The mountaineers have an absurd notion that the little lizard so common in the hills is rank " pizen." Oddly enough, they call it a " scorpion."

From those two pests of the North Woods, black-flies and mosquitoes, the Smokies are mercifully exempt. At least there are no mosquitoes that bite or sing, except down in the river valleys where they have been introduced by railroad trains—and even there they are but a feeble folk. The reason is that in the mountains there is almost no standing water where they can breed.

On the other hand, the common house-fly is extraordinarily numerous and persistent — a daily curse, even on top of Smoky. I imagine this is due to the wet climate, as in Ireland. Minute gnats (the " punkies " or " no-see-ums " of the North) are also offensively present in trout-fishing time. And every cabin is alive with fleas. A hundred nights I have anointed myself with citronella from head to foot, and outsmelt a cheap barber-shop, to escape their plague. In a tent, and without dogs, one can be immune.

In most years there are very few chiggers, except on pine ridges. They are worse along rivers than in the mountains. The ticks of this country are not numerous, and seldom fasten on man.

The climate of the Carolina mountains is pleasantly cool in summer. Even at low altitudes (1,600 to 2,000 feet) the nights generally are refreshing. It may be hot in the sun, but always cool in the shade. The air is drier (less relative humidity) than in the lowlands, notwithstanding that there is greater rainfall here than elsewhere in the United States outside of Florida and the Puget Sound country. The annual rainfall varies a great deal according to locality, being least at Asheville (42 inches) and greatest on the southeastern slope of the

Blue Ridge, where as much as 105 inches has been recorded in a year. The average rainfall of the whole region is 73 inches a year.*

In general the mornings are apt to be lowery, with fogs hanging low until, say, 9 o'clock, so that one cannot predict weather for the day. Heavy dews remain on the bushes until about the same hour.

The winters are short. What Northerners would call cold weather is not expected until Christmas, and generally it is gone by the end of February. Snow sometimes falls on the higher mountains by the first of October, and the last snow may linger there until April (exceptionally it falls in May). Tornadoes are unknown here, but sometimes a hurricane will sweep the upper ranges. On April 19, 1900, a blizzard from the northwest struck the Smokies. In twenty minutes everything was frozen. At Siler's Meadow seventeen cattle climbed upon each other for warmth and froze to death in a solid hecatomb. A herdsman who was out at the time, and narrowly escaped a similar fate, assured me that " that was the beatenest snow-storm ever I seen." In the valleys there may be a few days in January and February

* Average annual rainfall of New York City, 44 inches; of Glencoe, in the Scotch Highlands, nearly 130 inches.

Scouting in the Laurel.
(The Author.)

when the mercury drops to zero or a few degrees lower. On the high peaks, of course, the winter cold often is intense, and on the sunless north side of Clingman there are overhangs or crevices where a little ice may be found the year around.

Undoubtedly there is vast mineral wealth hidden in the Carolina mountains. A greater variety of minerals has been found here than in any other State save Colorado. But, for the present, it is a hard country to prospect in, owing to the thick covering of the forest floor. Not only is the underbrush very dense, but beneath it there generally is a thick stratum of clay overlaying the rocks, even on steep slopes. Gold has been found in numberless places, but finely disseminated. I do not know a locality in the mountains proper where a working vein has been discovered. At my cabin I did just enough panning to get a notion that if I could stand working in icy water ten hours a day I might average a dollar in yellow dust by it. The adjacent copper mine carries considerable gold. Silver and lead are not common, so far as known, but there are many good copper and iron properties. Gems are mined profitably in several of the western counties. The corundum, mica, talc, and monazite are, I believe, unexcelled in the United States. Building stone is abundant, and there is fine marble in various places. Kaolin is shipped out in considerable quantities. The rocks chiefly are gneisses, granites, metamorphosed marbles, quartzites, and slates, all of them far too old to bear fossils or coal.

CHAPTER IV

A BEAR HUNT IN THE SMOKIES

"GIT up, pup! you've scrouged right in hyur in front of the fire. You Dred! what makes you so blamed contentious?"

Little John shoved both dogs into a corner, and strove to scrape some coals from under a beech forestick that glowed almost hot enough to melt brass.

"This is the wust coggled-up fire I ever seed, to fry by. Bill, hand me some Old Ned from that suggin o' mine."

A bearded hunchback reached his long arm to a sack that hung under our rifles, drew out a chuck of salt pork, and began slicing it with his jackknife. On inquiry I learned that "Old Ned" is merely slang for fat pork, but that "suggin" or "sujjit" (the *u* pronounced like *oo* in look) is true mountain dialect for a pouch, valise, or carryall, its etymology being something to puzzle over.

75

Four dogs growled at each other under a long bunk of poles and hay that spanned one side of our cabin. The fire glared out upon the middle of an unfloored and windowless room. Deep shadows clung to the walls and benches, charitably concealing much dirt and disorder left by previous occupants, much litter of our own contributing.

At last we were on a saddle of the divide, a mile above sea-level, in a hut built years ago for temporary lodgment of cattle-men herding on the grassy " balds " of the Smokies. A sagging clapboard roof covered its two rooms and the open space between them that we called our " entry." The State line between North Carolina and Tennessee ran through this uninclosed hallway. The Carolina room had a puncheon floor and a clapboard table, also better bunks than its mate; but there had risen a stiff southerly gale that made the chimney smoke so abominably that we were forced to take quarters in the neighbor State.

Granville lifted the lid from a big Dutch oven and reported " Bread's done."

There was a flash in the frying-pan, a curse and a puff from Little John. The coffee-pot boiled over. We gathered about the hewn benches that served for tables, and sat *à la Turc* upon the ground. For some time there was no sound but the gale without and the munching of ravenous men.

" If this wind 'll only cease afore mornin', we'll git us a bear to-morrow."

A powerful gust struck the cabin, by way of answer; a great roaring surged up from the gulf of Defeat, from Desolation, and from the other forks of Bone Valley—clamor of ten thousand trees struggling with the blast.

" Hit's gittin' wusser."

" Any danger of this roost being blown off the mountain? " I inquired.

" Hit's stood hyur twenty year through all the storms; I reckon it can stand one more night of it."

"A man couldn't walk upright, outside the cabin," I asserted, thinking of the St. Louis tornado, in which I had lain flat on my belly, clinging to an iron post.

The hunchback turned to me with a grave face. " I've seed hit blow, here on top o' Smoky, till a hoss couldn't stand up agin it. You'll spy, to-morrow, whar several trees has been wind-throwed and busted to kindlin'."

I recalled that several, in the South, means many—" a good many," as our own tongues phrase it.

"Oh, shucks! Bill Cope," put in "Doc" Jones, "whut do you-uns know about wind-storms? Now, *I've* hed some experiencin' up hyur that 'll do to tell about. You remember the big storm three year ago, come grass, when the cattle all huddled up a-top o' each other and friz in one pile, solid."

Bill grunted an affirmative.

"Wal, sir, I was a-herdin', over at the Spencer Place, and was out on Thunderhead when the wind sprung up. Thar come one turrible vyg'-rous blow that jest nacherally lifted the ground. I went up in the sky, my coat ripped off, and I went a-sailin' end-over-end."

"Yes?"

"Yes. About half an hour later, I lit *spang* in the mud, way down yander in Tuckaleechee Cove—yes, sir: ten mile as the crow flies, and a mile deeper 'n trout-fish swim."

There was silence for a moment. Then Little John spoke up: "I mind about that time, Doc; but I disremember which buryin'-ground they-all planted ye in."

"Planted! *Me?* Huh! But I had one tor-mentin' time findin' my hat!"

The cabin shook under a heavier blast, to match Doc's yarn.

"Old Wind-maker's blowin' liars out o'

North Car'lina. Hang on to yer hat, Doc!
Whoop! hear 'em a-comin'!"

"Durn this blow, anyhow! No bear 'll cross
the mountain sich a night as this."

"Can't we hunt down on the Carolina side?"
I asked.

"That's whar we're goin' to drive; but hit's
no use if the bear don't come over."

"How is that? Do they sleep in one State
and eat in the other?"

"Yes: you see, the Tennessee side of the
mountain is powerful steep and laurely, so 't
man nor dog cain't git over it in lots o' places;
that's whar the bears den. But the mast, sich
as acorns and beech and hickory nuts, is mostly
on the Car'lina side; that's whar they hafter
come to feed. So, when it blows like this, they
stay at home and suck their paws till the
weather clars."

"So we'll have to do, at this rate."

"I'll go see whut the el-e-ments looks like."

We arose from our squatting postures. John
opened the little clapboard door, which swung
violently backward as another gust boomed
against the cabin. Dust and hot ashes scattered
in every direction. The dogs sprang up, one
encroached upon another, and they flew at each
other's throats. They were powerful beasts,

dangerous to man as well as to the brutes they
were trained to fight; but John was their master,
and he soon booted them into surly subjection.

"The older dog don't ginerally raise no ruction; hit's the younger one that's ill," by which
he meant vicious. "You, Coaly, you'll git some
o' that meanness shuck outen you if you tackle
an old she-bear to-morrow!"

"Has the young dog ever fought a bear?"

"No; he don't know nothin'; but I reckon
he'll pick up some larnin' in the next two, three
days."

"Have these dogs got the Plott strain? I've
been told that the Plott hounds are the best bear
dogs in the country."

"'Tain't so," snorted John. "The Plott curs
are the best: that is, half hound, half cur—
though what we-uns calls the cur, in this case,
raelly comes from a big furrin dog that I don't
rightly know the breed of. Fellers, you can
talk as you please about a streak o' the cur spilin'
a dog; but I know hit ain't so—not for bear
fightin' in these mountains, whar you cain't foller up on hossback, but hafter do your own
runnin'."

"What is the reason, John?"

"Waal, hit's like this: a plumb cur, of course,
cain't foller a cold track—he just runs by sight;

Photo by S. H. Essary

The Spencer Place, near Thunderhead Mountain.

and he won't hang—he quits. But, t'other way, no hound 'll raelly fight a bear—hit takes a big severe dog to do that. Hounds has the best noses, and they'll run a bear all day and night, and the next day, too; but they won't never tree —they're afeared to close in. Now, look at them dogs o' mine. A cur ain't got no dew-claws—them dogs has. My dogs can foller ary trail, same's a hound; but they'll run right in on the varmint, snappin' and chawin' and wor-ryin' him till he gits so mad you can hear his tushes pop half a mile. He cain't run away— he haster stop every bit, and fight. Finally he gits so tired and het up that he trees to rest hisself. Then we-uns ketches up and finishes him."

"Mebbe you-uns don't know that a dew-clawed dog is snake-proof——"

But somebody, thinking that dog-talk had gone far enough, produced a bottle of soothing-syrup that was too new to have paid tax. Then we discovered that there was musical talent, of a sort, in Little John. He cut a pigeon-wing, twirled around with an imaginary banjo, and sang in a quaint minor:

Did you *ever* see the devil,
With his *pitchfork* and ladle,
And his *old* iron shovel,

And his old gourd head?
    O, I *will* go to meetin',
    And I *will* go to meetin',
    Yes, I *will* go to meetin',
    In an old tin pan.

Other songs followed, with utter irrelevance —mere snatches from "ballets" composed, mainly, by the mountaineers themselves, though some dated back to a long-forgotten age when the British ancestors of these Carolina woodsmen were battling with lance and long-bow. It was one of modern and local origin that John was singing when there came a diversion from without—

    La-a-ay down, boys,
        Le's take a nap:
    Thar's goin' to be trouble
    In the Cumberland Gap—

Our ears were stunned by one sudden thundering crash. The roof rose visibly, as though pushed upward from within. In an instant we were blinded by moss and dried mud — the chinking blown from between the logs of our shabby cabin. Dred and Coaly cowered as though whipped, while "Doc's" little hound slunk away in the keen misery of fear. We men looked at each other with lowered eyelids and the grim smile that denotes readiness, though no special eagerness, for dissolution. Beyond the " gant-lot " we could hear trees and limbs popping like skirmishers in action.

Then that tidal wave of air swept by. The roof settled again with only a few shingles missing. We went to " redding up." Squalls broke against the mountainside, hither and yon, like the hammer of Thor testing the foundations of the earth. But they were below us. Here, on top, there was only the steady drive of a great surge of wind; and speech was possible once more.

" Fellers, you want to mark whut you dream about, to-night: hit'll shore come true to-morrow."

" Yes: but you mustn't tell whut yer dream was till the hunt's over, or it'll spile the charm."

There ensued a grave discussion of dream-lore, in which the illiterates of our party declared solemn faith. If one dreamt of blood, he would surely see blood the next day. Another lucky sign for a hunter was to dream of quarreling with a woman, for that meant a she-bear; it was favorable to dream of clear water, but muddy water meant trouble.

The wind died away. When we went out for

a last observation of the weather we found the
air so clear that the lights of Knoxville were
plainly visible, in the north-northwest, thirty-
two miles in an air line. Not another light was
to be seen on earth, although in some directions
we could scan for nearly a hundred miles. The
moon shone brightly. Things looked rather
favorable for the morrow, after all.

* * * * *

" Brek-k-k-*fust!* "

I awoke to a knowledge that somebody had
built a roaring fire and was stirring about. Between the cabin logs one looked out upon a
starry sky and an almost pitch-dark world.
What did that pottering vagabond mean by
arousing us in the middle of the night? But I
was hungry. Everybody half arose on elbows
and blinked about. Then we got up, each after
his fashion, except one scamp who resumed
snoring.

" Whar's that brekfust you're yellin' about? "

" Hit's for you-uns to help *git!* I knowed I
couldn't roust ye no other way. Here, you, go
down to the spring and fetch water. Rustle out,
boys; we've got to git a soon start if you want
bear brains an' liver for supper."

The " soon start " tickled me into good humor.

Our dogs were curled together under the long bunk, having popped indoors as soon as the way was opened. Somebody trod on Coaly's tail. Coaly snapped Dred. Instantly there was action between the four. It is interesting to observe what two or three hundred pounds of dog can do to a ramshackle berth with a man on top of it. Poles and hay and ragged quilts flew in every direction. Sleepy Matt went down in the midst of the mêlée, swearing valiantly. I went out and hammered ice out of the wash-basin while Granville and John quelled the riot. Presently our frying-pans sputtered and the huge coffee-pot began to get up steam.

"Waal, who dreamt him a good dream?"

"I did," affirmed the writer. "I dreamt that I had an old colored woman by the throat and was choking dollars out of her mouth——"

"Good la!" exclaimed four men in chorus; "you hadn't orter a-told."

"Why? Wasn't that a lovely dream?"

"Hit means a she-bear, shore as a cap-shootin' gun; but you've done spiled it all by tellin'. Mebbe somebody'll git her to-day, but *you* won't—your chanct is ruined."

So the reader will understand why, in this veracious narrative, I cannot relate any heroic

exploits of my own in battling with Ursus
Major. And so you, ambitious one, when you
go into the Smokies after that long-lost bear,
remember these two cardinal points of the
Law:

(1) Dream that you are fighting some poor old colored
woman. (That is easy: the victuals you get will fix up
your dream, all right.) And—

(2) Keep your mouth shut about it.

There was still no sign of rose-color in the
eastern sky when we sallied forth. The ground,
to use a mountaineer's expression, was "all
spewed up with frost." Rime crackled under-
foot and our mustaches soon stiffened in the icy
wind.

It was settled that Little John Cable and the
hunchback Cope should take the dogs far down
into Bone Valley and start the drive, leaving
Granville, "Doc," Matt, and myself to picket
the mountain. I was given a stand about half
a mile east of the cabin, and had but a vague
notion of where the others went.

By jinks, it was cold! I built a little fire between the buttressing roots of a big mountain
oak, but still my toes and fingers were numb.
This was the 25th of November, and we were
at an altitude where sometimes frost forms in

July. The other men were more thinly clad than I, and with not a stitch of wool beyond their stockings; but they seemed to revel in the keen air. I wasted some pity on Cope, who had no underwear worthy of the name; but afterwards I learned that he would not have worn more clothes if they had been given him. Many a night my companions had slept out on the mountain without blanket or shelter, when the ground froze and every twig in the forest was coated with rime from the winter fog.

Away out yonder beyond the mighty bulk of Clingman Dome, which, black with spruce and balsam, looked like a vast bear rising to contemplate the northern world, there streaked the first faint, nebulous hint of dawn. Presently the big bear's head was tipped with a golden crown flashing against the scarlet fires of the firmament, and the earth awoke.

A rustling some hundred yards below me gave signal that the gray squirrels were on their way to water. Out of a tree overhead hopped a mountain "boomer" (red squirrel), and down he came, eyed me, and stopped. Cocking his head to one side he challenged peremptorily: "Who are you? Stump? Stump? Not a stump. What the deuce!"

I moved my hand.

" Lawk—the booger-man! Run, run, run! "

Somewhere from the sky came a strange, half-human note, as of someone chiding: *" Wal*-lace, *Wal*-lace, *Wat!* " I could get no view for the trees. Then the voice flexibly changed to a deep-toned " Co-*logne,* Co-*logne,* Co-*logne,"* that rang like a bell through the forest aisles.

Two names uttered distinctly from the air! Two scenes conjured in a breath, vivid but unrelated as in dreams: Wallace—an iron-bound Scottish coast; Cologne—tall spires, and cliffs along the Rhine! What magic had flashed such pictures upon a remote summit of the Smoky Mountains?

The weird speaker sailed into view—a raven. Forward it swept with great speed of ebon wings, fairly within gunshot for one teasing moment. Then, as if to mock my gaping stupor, it hurtled like a hawk far into the safe distance, whence it flung back loud screams of defiance and chuckles of derision.

As the morning drew on, I let the fire die to ashes and basked lazily in the sun. Not a sound had I heard from the dogs. My hoodoo was working malignly. Well, let it work. I was comfortable now, and that old bear could go to any other doom she preferred. It was pleas-

Skinning a frozen bear

ant enough to lie here alone in the forest and be free! Aye, it was good to be alive, and to be far, far away from the broken bottles and old tin cans of civilization.

For many a league to the southward clouds covered all the valleys in billows of white, from which rose a hundred mountain tops, like islands in a tropic ocean. My fancy sailed among and beyond them, beyond the horizon's rim, even unto those far seas that I had sailed in my youth, to the old times and the old friends that I should never see again.

But a forenoon is long-drawn-out when one has breakfasted before dawn, and has nothing to do but sit motionless in the woods and watch and listen. I got to fingering my rifle trigger impatiently and wishing that a wild Thanksgiving gobbler might blunder into view. Squirrels made ceaseless chatter all around my stand. Large hawks shrilled by me within tempting range, whistling like spent bullets. A groundhog sat up on a log and whistled, too, after a manner of his own. He was so near that I could see his nose wiggle. A skunk waddled around for twenty minutes, and once came so close that I thought he would nibble my boot. I was among old mossy beeches, scaled with polyphori, and twisted into postures of torture by their battles with the storms. Below, among chestnuts and birches, I could hear the *t-wee, t-wee* of " joree-birds " (towhees), which winter in the valleys. Incessantly came the *chip-chip-cluck* of ground squirrels, the saucy bark of the grays, and great chirruping among the " boomers," which had ceased swearing and were hard at work.

Far off on my left a rifle cracked. I pricked up and listened intently, but there was never a yelp from a dog. Since it is a law of the chase to fire at nothing smaller than turkeys, lest big game be scared away, this shot might mean a gobbler. I knew that Matt Hyde could not, to save his soul, sit ten minutes on a stand without calling turkeys (and he *could* call them, with his unassisted mouth, better than anyone I ever heard perform with leaf or wing-bone or any other contrivance).

Thus the slow hours dragged along. I yearned mightily to stretch my legs. Finally, being certain that no drive would approach my stand that day, I ambled back to the hut and did a turn at dinner-getting. Things were smoking, and smelt good, by the time four of our men turned up, all of them dog-tired and disappointed, but stoical.

" That pup Coaly chased off atter a wildcat,"

blurted John. " We held the old dogs together
and let him rip. Then Dred started a deer. It
was that old buck that everybody's shot at, and
missed, this three year back. I'd believe he's
a hant if 't wasn't for his tracks—they're the
biggest I ever seen. He must weigh two hunderd and fifty. But he's a foxy cuss. Tuk right
down the bed o' Desolation, up the left prong
of Roaring Fork, right through the Devil's
Race-path (how a deer can git through thar *I*
don't see!), crossed at the Meadow Gap, went
down Eagle Creek, and by now he's in the Little
Tennessee. That buck, shorely to God, has
wings! "

We were at table in the Carolina room when
Matt Hyde appeared. Sure enough, he bore a
turkey hen.

" I was callin' a gobbler when this fool thing
showed up. I fired a shoot as she riz in the
air, but only bruk her wing. She made off on
her legs like the devil whoppin' out fire. I run,
an' she run. Guess I run her half a mile
through all-fired thickets. She piped ' *Quit—
quit,*' but I said, ' I'll see you in hell afore I
quit! ' and the chase resumed. Finally I
knocked her over with a birch stob, and here
we are."

Matt ruefully surveyed his almost denuded

legs, evidence of his chase. " Boys," said he,
" I'm nigh breechless! "

* * * * *

None but native-born mountaineers could
have stood the strain of another drive that day,
for the country that Cope and Cable had been
through was fearful, especially the laurel up
Roaring Fork and Killpeter Ridge. But the
stamina of these "withey" little men was even
more remarkable than their endurance of cold.
After a small slice of fried pork, a chunk of
half-baked johnny-cake, and a pint or so of
coffee, they were as fresh as ever.

What soldiers these fellows would make,
under leadership of some backwoods Napoleon
who could hold them together!—some man like
Daniel Morgan of the Revolution, who was one
of them, yet greater!

I had made the coffee strong, and it was good
stuff that I had brought from home. After his
first deep draught, Little John exclaimed:

" Hah! boys, that coffee hits whar ye hold it! "

I thought that a neat compliment from a
sharpshooter.

We took new stands; but the afternoon passed
without incident to those of us on the mountain
tops. I returned to camp about five o'clock, and
was surprised to see three of our men lugging

across the " gant-lot " * toward the cabin a small female bear.

" Hyur's yer old nigger woman," shouted John.

The hunters showed no elation—in fact, they looked sheepish—and I suspected a nigger in the woodpile.

" How's this? I didn't hear any drive."

" There wa'n't none."

" Then where did you get your bear?"

" In one of Wit Hensley's traps, dum him! Boys, I wish t' we *hed* roasted the temper outen them trap-springs, like we talked o' doin'."

" Was the bear alive? "

" Live as a hot coal. See the pup's head! "

I examined Coaly, who looked sick. The flesh was torn from his lower jaw and hung down a couple of inches. Two holes in the top of his head showed where the bear's tusks had tried to crack his skull.

" When the other dogs found her, he rushed right in. She hadn't been trapped more'n a few

---

* *Gant-lot:* a fenced enclosure into which cattle are driven after cutting them out from those of other owners. So called because the mountain cattle run wild, feeding only on grass and browse, and " they couldn't travel well to market when filled up on green stuff: so they're penned up to git *gant* and nimble."

hours, and she larned Coaly somethin' about the bear business."

" Won't this spoil him for hunting here-after? "

" Not if he has his daddy's and mammy's grit. We'll know by to-morrow whether he's a shore-enough bear dog; for I've larned now whar they're crossin'—seed sign a-plenty and it's spang fraish. Coaly, old boy! you-uns won't be so feisty and brigaty atter this, will ye!"

" John, what do those two words mean? "

" *Good* la! whar was you fotch up? Them's common. They mean nigh about the same thing, only there's a differ. When I say that Doc Jones thar is brigaty among women-folks, hit means that he's stuck on hisself and wants to show off——"

" And John Cable's sulkin' around with his nose out o' jint," interjected " Doc."

" Feisty," proceeded the interpreter, " feisty means when a feller's allers wigglin' about, wantin' ever'body to see him, like a kid when the preacher comes. You know a feist is one o' them little bitty dogs that ginerally runs on three legs and pretends a whole lot."

All of us were indignant at the setter of the trap. It had been hidden in a trail, with no sign to warn a man from stepping into it. In Tennessee, I was told, it is a penitentiary offense to set out a bear trap. We agreed that a similar law ought to be passed as soon as possible in North Carolina.

"It's only two years ago," said Granville to me, "that Jasper Millington, an old man living on the Tennessee side, started acrost the mountain to get work at the Everett mine, where you live. Not fur from where we are now, he stepped into a bear trap that was hid in the leaves, like this one. It broke his leg, and he starved to death in it."

Despite our indignation meeting, it was decided to carry the trapped bear's hide to Hensley, and for us to use only the meat as recompense for trouble, to say nothing of risk to life and limb. Such is the mountaineers' regard for property rights!

The animal we had ingloriously won was undersized, weighing scant 175 pounds. The average weight of Smoky Mountain bears is not great, but occasionally a very large beast is killed. Matt Hyde told us that he killed one on the Welch Divide in 1901, the meat of which, dressed, without the hide, weighed 434 pounds, and the hide "squared eight feet"

when stretched for drying. "Doc" Jones killed a bear that was "kivered with fat, five
inches thick."

Afterwards I took pains to ask the most famous bear hunters of our region what were the
largest bears they had personally killed. Uncle
Jimmy Crawford, of the Balsam Mountains,
estimated his largest at 500 pounds gross, and
the hide of another that he had killed weighed
forty pounds after three days' drying. Quill
Rose, of Eagle Creek, said that, after stripping
the hide from one of his bears, he took the fresh
skin by the ears and raised it as high as he could
reach above his head, and that four inches of the
butt end of the hide (not legs) trailed on the
ground. " And," he added severely, " thar's no
lie about it." Quill is six feet one and one-half
inches tall. Black Bill Walker, of the middle
prong of Little River (Tennessee side), told
me " The biggest one I ever saw killed had a
hide that measured ten feet from nose to rump,
stretched for drying. The biggest I ever killed
myself measured nine and a half feet, same way,
and weighed a good four hunderd net, which,
allowin' for hide, blood, and entrails, would run
full five hunderd live weight."

Within the past two years two bears of about
500 pounds each have been killed in Swain and
Graham counties, the Cables getting one of

"By and by up they came, carrying the Bear on a trimmed sapling"

them. The veteran hunters that I have named have killed their hundreds of bears and are men superior to silly exaggeration. In the Smoky Mountains the black bear, like most of the trees, attains its fullest development, and that it occasionally reaches a weight of 500 pounds when "hog fat" is beyond reasonable doubt, though the average would not be more than half that weight.

  * * * * *

We spent the evening in debate as to where the next drive should be made. Some favored moving six miles eastward, to the old mining shack at Siler's Meadow, and trying the headwaters of Forney's Creek, around Rip Shin Thicket and the Gunstick Laurel, driving towards Clingman Dome and over into the bleak gulf, southwest of the Sugarland Mountains, that I had named Godforsaken—a title that stuck. We knew there were bears in that region, though it was a desperately rough country to hunt in.

But John and the hunchback had found "sign" in the opposite direction. Bears were crossing from Little River in the neighborhood of Thunderhead and Briar Knob, coming up just west of the Devil's Court House and "using" around Block House, Woolly Ridge,

Bear Pen, and thereabouts. The motion carried, and we adjourned to bed.

We breakfasted on bear meat, the remains of our Thanksgiving turkey, and wheat bread shortened with bear's grease until it was light as a feather; and I made tea. It was the first time that Little John ever saw " store tea." He swallowed some of it as if it had been boneset, under the impression that it was some sort of " yerb " that would be good for his insides. Without praising its flavor, he asked what it had cost, and, when I told him " a dollar a pound," reckoned that it was " rich man's medicine "; said he preferred dittany or sassafras or goldenrod. " Doc " Jones opined that it " looked yaller," and he even affirmed that it " tasted yaller."

" Waal, people," exclaimed Matt, " I 'low I've done growed a bit, atter that mess o' meat. Le's be movin'."

It was a hard pull for me, climbing up the rocky approach to Briar Knob. This was my first trip to the main divide, and my heart was not yet used to mountain climbing.

The boys were anxious for me to get a shot. I was paying them nothing; it was share-and-share alike; but their neighborly kindness moved them to do their best for the outlander.

So they put me on what was probably the best stand for the day. It was above the Fire-scald, a brulé or burnt-over space on the steep southern side of the ridge between Briar Knob and Laurel Top, overlooking the grisly slope of Killpeter. Here I could both see and hear an uncommonly long distance, and if the bear went either east or west I would have timely warning.

This Fire-scald, by the way, is a famous place for wildcats. Once in a blue moon a lynx is killed in the highest zone of the Smokies, up among the balsams and spruces, where both the flora and fauna, as well as the climate, resemble those of the Canadian woods. Our native hunters never heard the word lynx, but call the animal a " catamount." Wolves and panthers used to be common here, but it is a long time since either has been killed in this region, albeit impressionable people see wolf tracks or hear a " pant'er " scream every now and then.

I had shivered on the mountain top for a couple of hours, hearing only an occasional yelp from the dogs, which had been working in the thickets a mile or so below me, when suddenly there burst forth the devil of a racket.

On came the chase, right in my direction. Presently I could distinguish the different notes: the deep bellow of old Dred, the hound-like baying of Rock and Coaly, and little Towse's feisty yelp.

I thought that the bear might chance the com-paratively open space of the Fire-scald, because there were still some ashes on the ground that would dust the dogs' nostrils and throw them off the scent. And such, I believe, was his in-tention. But the dogs caught up with him. They nipped him fore and aft. Time after time he shook them off; but they were true bear dogs, and, like Matt Hyde after the turkey, they knew no such word as quit.

I took a last squint at my rifle sights, made sure there was a cartridge in the chamber, and then felt my ears grow as I listened. Suddenly the chase swerved at a right angle and took straight up the side of Saddle-back. Either the bear would tree, or he would try to smash on through to the low rhododendron of the Devil's Court House, where dogs who followed might break their legs. I girded myself and ran, "wiggling and wingling" along the main di-vide, and then came the steep pull up Briar Knob. As I was grading around the summit with all the lope that was left in me, I heard a rifle crack, half a mile down Saddle-back. Old "Doc" was somewhere in that vicinity. I halted to listen. Creation, what a rumpus! Then another shot. Then the warwhoop of the South, that we read about.

By and by, up they came, John and Cope and " Doc," two at a time, carrying the bear on a trimmed sapling. Presently Hyde joined us, then came Granville, and we filed back to camp, where " Doc " told his story:

" Boys, them dogs' eyes shined like new money. Coaly fit agin, all right, and got his tail bit. The bear div down into a sink-hole with the dogs a-top o' him. Soon's I could shoot without hittin' a dog, I let him have it. Thought I'd shot him through the head, but he fit on. Then I jumped down into the sink and kicked him loose from the dogs, or he'd a-killed Coaly. Waal, sir, he wa'n't hurt a bit—the ball jest glanced off his head. He riz an' knocked me down with his left paw, an' walked right over me, an' lit up the ridge. The dogs treed him in a minute. I went to shoot up at him, but my new hulls [cartridges] fit loose in this old chamber and this one drap [dropped] out, so the gun stuck. Had to git my knife out and fix hit. Then the dad-burned gun wouldn't stand roostered [cocked]; the feather-spring had jumped out o' place. But I held back with my thumb, and killed him anyhow.

" Fellers," he added feelingly, " I wish t' my legs growed hind-side-fust."

" *What* fer? "

" So 's 't I wouldn't bark my shins! "

" Bears," remarked John, " is all left-handed. Ever note that? Hit's the left paw you wanter look out fer. He'd a-knocked somethin' out o' yer head if there'd been much in it, Doc."

" Funny thing, but hit's true," declared Bill, " that a bear allers dies flat on his back, onless he's trapped."

" So do men," said " Doc " grimly; · men who've been shot in battle. You go along a battlefield, right atter the action, and you'll find most o' the dead faces pintin' to the sky."

" Bears is almost human, anyhow. A skinned bear looks like a great big-bodied man with long arms and stumpy legs."

I did not relish this turn of the conversation, for we had two bears to skin immediately. The one that had been hung up over night was frozen solid, so I photographed her standing on her legs, as in life. When it came to skinning this beast the job was a mean one; a fellow had to drop out now and then to warm his fingers.

The mountaineers have an odd way of sharing the spoils of the chase. They call it " stoking the meat," a use of the word *stoke* that I have never heard elsewhere. The hide is sold, and the proceeds divided equally among the hunters, but the meat is cut up into as many pieces as there are partners in the chase; then one man goes indoors or behind a tree, and somebody at the carcass, laying his hand on a portion, calls out: "Whose piece is this?"

"Granville Calhoun's," cries the hidden man, who cannot see it.

"Whose is this?"

"Bill Cope's."

And so on down the line. Everybody gets what chance determines for him, and there can be no charge of unfairness.

*　　*　　*　　*　　*

It turned very cold that night. The last thing I heard was Matt Hyde protesting to the hunchback:

"Durn you, Bill Cope, you're so cussed crooked a man cain't lay cluss enough to you to keep warm!"

Once when I awoke in the night the beech trees were cracking like rifle-shots from the intense frost.

Next morning John announced that we were going to get another bear.

"Night afore last," he said, " Bill dremp that

he seed a lot o' fat meat layin' on the table; an' it done come true. Last night I dremp me one that never was knowed to fail yet. Now you see!"

It did not look like it by evening. We all worked hard and endured much—standers as well as drivers—but not a rifle had spoken up to the time when, from my far-off stand, I yearned for a hot supper.

Away down in the rear I heard the snort of a locomotive, one of those cog-wheel affairs that are specially built for mountain climbing. With a steam-loader and three camps of a hundred men each, it was despoiling the Tennessee forest. Slowly, but inexorably, a leviathan was crawling into the wilderness and was soon to consume it.

"All this," I apostrophized, "shall be swept away, tree and plant, beast and fish. Fire will blacken the earth; flood will swallow and spew forth the soil. The simple-hearted native men and women will scatter and disappear. In their stead will come slaves speaking strange tongues, to toil in the darkness under the rocks. Soot will arise, and foul gases; the streams will run murky death. Let me not see it! No; I will

A Home-made Bear Trap.

" '. . . Get me to some far-off land
Where higher mountains under heaven stand . . .
Where other thunders roll amid the hills,
Some mightier wind a mightier forest fills
With other strains through other-shapen boughs.' "

Wearily I plodded back to camp. No one had arrived but " Doc." The old man had been thumped rather severely in yesterday's scrimmage, but complained only of " a touch o' rheumatiz." Just how this disease had left his clothes in tatters he did not explain.

It was late when Matt and Granville came in. The crimson and yellow of sunset had turned to a faultless turquoise, and this to a violet afterglow; then suddenly night rose from the valleys and enveloped us.

About nine o'clock I went out on the Little Chestnut Bald and fired signals, but there was no answer. The last we had known of the drivers was that they had been beyond Thunderhead, six miles of hard travel to the westward. There was fog on the mountain. We did some uneasy speculating. Then Granville and Matt took the lantern and set out for Briar Knob. " Doc " was too stiff for travel, and I, being at that time a stranger in the Smokies, would be of no use hunting amid clouds and darkness. "Doc" and I passed a dreary three hours. Finally, at midnight, my shots were answered, and soon the dogs came limping in. Dred had been severely bitten in the shoulders and Rock in the head. Coaly was bloody about the mouth, where his first day's wound had reopened. Then came the four men, empty-handed, it seemed, until John slapped a bear's "melt" (spleen) upon the table. He limped from a bruised hip.

"That bear outsharped us and went around all o' you-uns. We follered him clar over to the Spencer Place, and then he doubled and come back on the fur side o' the ridge. He crossed through the laurel on the Devil's Court House and tuk down an almighty steep place. It was plumb night by that time. I fell over a rock clift twenty feet down, and if 't hadn't been for the laurel I'd a-bruk some bones. I landed right in the middle of them, bear and dogs, fightin' like gamecocks. The bear clim a tree. Bill sung out 'Is it fur down thar?' and I said 'Purty fur.' 'Waal, I'm a-comin',' says he; and with that he grabbed a laurel to swing hisself down by, but the stem bruk, and down he come suddent, to jine the music. Hit was so dark I couldn't see my gun barrel, and we wuz

all tangled up in greenbriers as thick as plough-
lines. I had to fire twiste afore he tumbled.
Then Matt an' Granville come. The four of us
tuk turn-about crawlin' up out o' thar with the
bear on our back. Only one man could handle
him at a time—and he'll go a good two hunderd, that bear. We gutted him, and left him
near the top, to fotch in the mornin'. Fellers,
I'm bodaciously tired out. This is the time I'd
give half what I'm worth for a gallon o' liquor
—and I'd promise the rest!"

"You'd orter see what Coaly did to that varmint," said Bill. "He bit a hole under the fore
leg, through hide and ha'r, clar into the holler,
so t' you can stick your hand in and seize the
bear's heart."

"John, what was that dream of yours?"

"I dremp I stole a feller's overcoat. Now
d'ye see? That means a bear's hide."

Coaly, three days ago, had been an inconse-
quential pup; but now he looked up into my
eyes with the calm dignity that no fool or brag-
gart can assume. He had been knighted. As
he licked his wounds he was proud of them.
"Scars of battle, sir. You may have your swag-
ger ribbons and prize collars in the New York
dog show, but *this* for me!"

Poor Coaly! after two more years of valiant

service, he was to meet an evil fortune. In connection with it I will relate a queer coincidence:

Two years after this hunt, a friend and I spent three summer months in this same old cabin on top of Smoky. When Andy had to return North he left with me, for sale, a .30-30 carbine, as he had more guns than he needed. I showed this carbine to Quill Rose, and the old hunter said: "I don't like them power-guns; you could shoot clar through a bear and kill your dog on the other side." The next day I sold the weapon to Granville Calhoun. Within a short time, word came from Granville's father that "Old Reelfoot" was despoiling his orchard. This Reelfoot was a large bear whose cunning had defied our best hunters for five or six years. He got his name from the fact that he "reeled" or twisted his hind feet in walking, as some horses do, leaving a peculiar track. This seems rather common among old bears, for I have known of several "reelfoots" in other, and widely separated, regions.

Cable and his dogs were sent for. A drive was made, and the bear was actually caught within a few rods of old Mr. Calhoun's stable. His teeth were worn to the gums, and, as he could no longer kill hogs, he had come down to an apple diet. He was large-framed, but very poor. The only hunters on the spot were Granville, with the .30-30, and a northern lumberman named Hastings, with a Luger carbine. After two or three shots had wounded the bear, he rose on his hind feet and made for Granville. A .30-30 bullet went clear through the beast at the very instant that Coaly, who was unseen, jumped up on the log behind it, and the missile gave both animals their death wound.

CHAPTER V

MOONSHINE LAND

I WAS hunting alone in the mountains, and exploring ground that was new to me.

About noon, while descending from a high ridge into a creek valley, to get some water, I became enmeshed in a rhododendron "slick," and, to some extent, lost my bearings.

After floundering about for an hour or two, I suddenly came out upon a little clearing. Giant hemlocks, girdled and gaunt, rose from a steep cornfield of five acres, beyond which loomed the primeval forest of the Great Smoky Mountains. Squat in the foreground sat one of the rudest log huts I had ever seen, a tiny one-room shack, without window, cellar, or loft, and without a sawed board showing in its construction. A thin curl of smoke rose from one end of the cabin, not from a chimney, but from a mere semi-circle of stones piled four feet high around a hole cut through the log wall. The stones of this fire-

place were not even plastered together with
mud, nor had the builder ever intended to raise
the pile as high as the roof to guard his premises
against the imminent risk of fire. Two low
doors of riven boards stood wide open, opposite
each other. These, helped by wide crevices between the unchinked logs, served to let in some
sunlight, and quite too much of the raw November air. The surroundings were squalid and
filthy beyond anything I had hitherto witnessed
in the mountains. As I approached, wading
ankle-deep in muck that reached to the door-
sill, two pigs scampered out through the opposite door.

Within the hut I found only a slip of a girl,
rocking a baby almost as big as herself, and
trying to knit a sock at the same time. She
was toasting her bare toes before the fire, and
crooning in a weird minor some mountain ditty
that may have been centuries old.

I shivered as I looked at this midget, comparing her only garment, a torn calico dress,
with my own stout hunter's garb that seemed
none too warm for such a day as this.

Knowing that the sudden appearance of a
stranger would startle the girl, I chose the
quickest way to reassure her by saluting in the
vernacular:

" Howdy? "

" Howdy? " she gasped.

" Who lives here? "

" Tom Kirby."

" Kirby? Oh! yes, I know him—we've been hunting together. Is your father at home? "

" No, he's out somewheres."

" Where is your mother? "

" She's in the field, up yan, gittin' roughness."

I took some pride in not being stumped by this answer. " Roughness," in mountain lingo, is any kind of rough fodder, specifically corn fodder.

" How far is it to the next house? "

" I don't know; maw, she knows."

" All right; I'll find her."

I went up to the field. No one was in sight but a shock of fodder was walking away from me, and I conjectured that " maw's " feet were under it; so I hailed:

" Hello! "

The shock turned around, then tumbled over, and there stood revealed a bare-headed, bare-footed woman, coarse featured but of superb physique—one of those mountain giantesses who think nothing of shouldering a two-bushel sack of corn and carrying it a mile or two without letting it down.

Moonshine Still-House Hidden in the Laurel

She flushed, then paled, staring at me round-eyed—frightened, I thought, by this apparition of a stranger whose approach she had not detected. To these people of the far backwoods everyone from outside their mountains is a doubtful character at best.

However, Mistress Kirby quickly recovered her aplomb. Her mouth straightened to a thin slit. She planted herself squarely across my path, now regarding me with contracted lids and a hard glint, till I felt fairly bayoneted by those steel-gray eyes.

"Good-morning. Is Mr. Kirby about?" I inquired.

There was no answer. Instead, the thin slit opened and let out a yell of almost yodel quality, penetrating as a warwhoop—a yell that would carry near half a mile. I wondered what she meant by this; but she did not enlighten me by so much as a single word. It was puzzling, not to say disconcerting; but, charging it to the custom of a country that still was new to me, I found my tongue again, and started to give credentials.

"My name is Kephart. I am staying at the Everett Mine on Sugar Fork——"

Another yell that set the wild echoes flying.

"I am acquainted with your husband; we've

hunted together. Perhaps he has told you——"

Yell number three, same pitch and vigor as before.

By this time I was quite nonplussed. I waited for her to speak; but never a word did the woman deign. So there we stood and stared at each other in silence—I leaning on my rifle, she with red arms akimbo—till I grew embarrassed, half wondering, too, if the creature were demented.

Suddenly a light flashed upon my groping wits. This amazon was on picket. Her three shrieks had been a signal to someone up the branch. Her attitude showed that there was no thoroughfare in that direction at present. Circumstances, whatever they were, forbade explanation. Clearly, the woman thought that I could not help seeing how matters stood. Not for a moment did she suspect but that her yells, her belligerent attitude, and her refusal to speak, were the conventional way, this world over, of intimating that there was a *contretemps*. She considered that if I was what I claimed to be, an acquaintance of her husband and on friendly footing, I would be gentleman enough to retire. If I was something else—an officer, a spy—well, she was there to stop me until the captain of the guard arrived.

For one silly moment I was tempted to advance and see what this martial spouse would do if I tried to pass her on the trail. But a hunter's instinct made me glance forward to the upper corner of the field. There was thick cover beyond the fence, with a clear range of a hundred and fifty yards between it and me— too far for Tom to recognize me, I thought, but deadly range for his Winchester, I knew. One forward step of mine would put me in the status of an armed intruder. So I concluded that common sense would better become me at this juncture than a bit of fooling that surely would be misinterpreted, and that might end ingloriously.

"Ah, well!" I remarked, "when your husband gets back, tell him, please, that I was sorry to miss him; though I did not call on any special business—just wanted to say ' Howdy?' you know. Good day!"

I turned and went down the valley.

All the way home I speculated on this queer adventure. What was going on " up yan "?

A month before, when I had started for this wildest nook of the Smokies, a friend had intimated that I was venturing into a dubious district—Moonshine Land. It is but frank to confess that this prospect was not unpleasant. My only fear had been that I might not find any moonshiners, or that, having found them, I might not succeed in winning their confidence to the extent of learning their own side of an interesting story. As to how I could do this without getting tarred with the same stick, I was by no means clear; but I hoped that good luck might find a way. And now it seemed as if luck had indeed favored me with an excuse for broaching the topic to some friendly mountaineer, so I could at least see how he would take it.

And it chanced (or was it chance?) that I had no more than finished supper, that evening, when a man called at my lonely cabin. He was the one that I knew best among my scattered neighbors. I gave him a rather humorous account of my reception by Madame Kirby, and asked him what he thought she was yelling about.

There was no answering smile on my visitor's face. He pondered in silence, weighing many contingencies, it seemed, and ventured no more than a helpless " Waal, now I wonder! "

It did not suit me to let the matter go at that; so, on a sudden impulse, I fired the question point-blank at him: " Do you suppose that Tom is running a still up there at the head of that little cove? "

The man's face hardened, and there came a glint into his eyes such as I had noticed in Mistress Kirby's.

"Jedgmatically, I don't know."

"Excuse me! I don't want to know, either. But let me explain just what I am driving at. People up North, and in the lowlands of the South as well, have a notion that there is little or nothing going on in these mountains except feuds and moonshining. They think that a stranger traveling here alone is in danger of being potted by a bullet from almost any laurel thicket that he passes, on mere suspicion that he may be a revenue officer or a spy. Of course, that is nonsense;* but there is one thing that I'm as ignorant about as any novel-reader of them all. You know my habits; I like to explore—I never take a guide—and when I come to a place that's particularly wild and primitive, that's just the place I want to peer into. Now the dubious point is this: Suppose that, one of these days when I'm out hunting, or looking for rare plants, I should stumble upon a moonshine still in full operation—what would happen? What would they do?"

* Pure bluff of mine, at that time; but it was good policy to assume perfect confidence.

"Waal, sir, I'll tell you whut they'd do. They'd fust-place ask you some questions about yourself, and whut you-uns was doin' in that thar neck o' the woods. Then they'd git you to do some triflin' work about the still—feed the furnace, or stir the mash—jest so 's 't they could prove that you took a hand in it your own self."

"What good would that do?"

"Hit would make you one o' them in the eyes of the law.

"I see. But, really, doesn't that seem rather childish? I could easily convince any court that I did it under compulsion; for that's what it would amount to."

"I reckon you-uns would find a United States court purty hard to convince. The judge 'd right up and want to know why you let grass go to seed afore you came and informed on them."

He paused, watched my expression, and then continued quizzically: "I reckon you wouldn't be in no great hurry to do *that.*"

"No! Then, if I stirred the mash and sampled their liquor, nobody would be likely to mistreat me?"

"Shucks! Why, man, whut could they gain by hurtin' you? At the wust, s'posin' they was convicted by your own evidence, they'd only git

a month or two in the pen. So why should they
murder you and get hung for it? Hit's all
'tarnal foolishness, the notions some folks has!"

"I thought so. Now, here! the public has
been fed all sorts of nonsense about this moonshining business. I'd like to learn the plain
truth about it, without bias one way or the
other. I have no curiosity about personal
affairs, and don't want to learn incriminating
details; but I would like to know how the business is conducted, and especially how it is regarded from the mountain people's own point
of view. I have already learned that a stranger's life and property are safer here than they
would be on the streets of Chicago or of St.
Louis. It will do your country good to have
that known. But I can't say that there is no
moonshining going on here; for a man with a
wooden nose could smell it. Now what is your
excuse for defying the law? You don't seem
ashamed of it."

The man's face turned an angry red.

"Mister, we-uns hain't no call to be ashamed
of ourselves, nor of ary thing we do. We're
poor; but we don't ax no favors. We stay 'way
up hyar in these coves, and mind our own business. When a stranger comes along, he's welcome to the best we've got, such as 'tis; but if

he imposes on us, he gits his medicine purty damned quick!"

"And you think the Government tax on whiskey is an imposition."

"Hit is, undʊr some sarcumstances."

My guest stretched his legs, and "jedgmatically" proceeded to enlighten me.

"Thar's plenty o' men and women grown, in these mountains, who don't know that the Government is ary thing but a president in a biled shirt who commands two-three judges and a gang o' revenue officers. They know thar's a president, because the men folks 's voted for him, and the women folks 's seed his pictur. They've heered tell about the judges; and they've seed the revenuers in flesh and blood. They believe in supportin' the Government, because hit's the law. Nobody refuses to pay his taxes, for taxes is fair and squar'. Taxes cost mebbe three cents on the dollar; and that's all right. But revenue costs a dollar and ten cents on twenty cents' worth o' liquor; and that's robbin' the people with a gun to their faces.

"Of course, I ain't so ignorant as all that— I've traveled about the country, been to Asheville wunst, and to Waynesville a heap o' times —and I know the theory. Theory says 't revenue is a tax on luxury. Waal, that's all right—

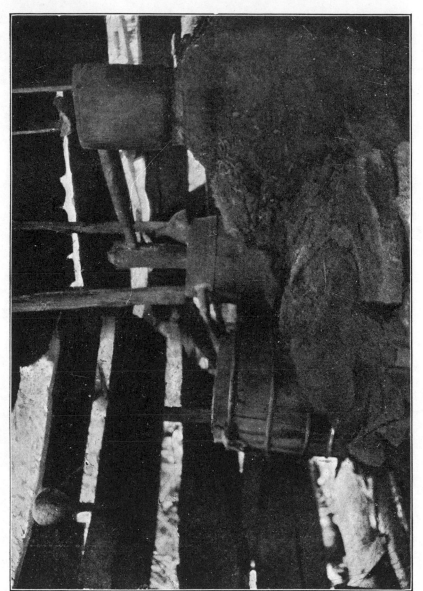

Moonshine Still in Full Operation

anything in reason. The big fellers that makes
lots of money out o' stillin', and lives in luxury,
ought to pay handsome for it. But who ever
seen luxury cavortin' around in these Smoky
Mountains?"

He paused for a reply. Even then, with my
limited experience in the mountains, I could not
help wincing at the idea. Often, in later times,
this man's question came back to me with
peculiar force. Luxury! in a land where the
little stores were often out of coffee, sugar,
kerosene, and even salt; where, in dead of
winter, there was no meal, much less flour, to
be had for love or money. Luxury! where I
had to live on bear-meat (tough old sow bear)
for six weeks, because the only side of pork that
I could find for sale was full of maggots.

My friend continued: "Whiskey means more
to us mountain folks than hit does to folks in
town, whar thar's drug-stores and doctors. Let
ary thing go wrong in the fam'ly—fever, or
snake bite, or somethin'—and we can't git a
doctor up hyar less'n three days; and it costs
scand'lous. The only medicines we-uns has is
yerbs, which customarily ain't no good 'thout
a leetle grain o' whiskey. Now, th'r ain't no
saloons allowed in all these western counties.
The nighest State dispensary, even, is sixty miles

away.* The law wunt let us have liquor shipped
to us from anywhars in the State. If we git it
sent to us from outside the State it has to come
by express—and reg-lar old pop-skull it is, too.
So, to be good law-abiding citizens, we-uns
must travel back and forth at a heap of expense,
or pay express rates on pizened liquor—and we
are too durned poor to do ary one or t'other.

"Now, yan's my field o' corn. I gather the
corn, and shuck hit and grind hit my own self,
and the woman she bakes us a pone o' bread to
eat—and I don't pay no tax, do I? Then why
can't I make some o' my corn into pure whiskey
to drink, without payin' tax? I tell you, *'tain't
fair,* this way the Government does! But, when
all's said and done, the main reason for this
' moonshining,' as you-uns calls it, is bad roads."

" Bad roads? " I exclaimed. " What the——"

" Jest thisaway: From hyar to the railroad is
seventeen miles, with two mountains to cross;
and you've seed that road! I recollect you-uns
said every one o' them miles was a thousand
rods long. Nobody's ever measured them, except by mountain man's foot-rule—big feet, and
a long stride between 'em. Seven hundred

* This was in 1904.

pounds is all the load a good team can haul over that road, when the weather's good. Hit takes three days to make the round trip, less'n you break an axle, and then hit takes four. When you do git to the railroad, th'r ain't no town of a thousand people within fifty mile. Now us folks ain't even got wagons. Thar's only one sarviceable wagon in this whole settlement, and you can't hire it without team and driver, which is two dollars and a half a day. Whar one o' our leetle sleds can't go, we haffter pack on mule-back or tussle it on our own wethers. Look, then! The only farm produce we-uns can sell is corn. You see for yourself that corn can't be shipped outen hyar. We can trade hit for store credit—that's all. Corn *juice* is about all we can tote around over the country and git cash money for. Why, man, that's the only way some folks has o' payin' their taxes!"

"But, aside from the work and the worry," I remarked, "there is the danger of being shot, in this business."

"Oh, we-uns don't lay *that* up agin the Government! Hit's as fair for one as 'tis for t'other. When a revenuer comes sneakin' around, why, whut he gits, or whut we-uns gits, that's a 'fortune of war,' as the old sayin' is."

There is no telegraph, wired or wireless, in the mountains, but there is an efficient substitute. It seemed as though, in one night, the news traveled from valley to cove, and from cove to nook, that I was investigating the moonshining business, and that I was apparently " safe." Each individual interpreted that word to suit himself. Some regarded me askance, others were so confiding that their very frankness threatened at times to become embarrassing.

Thereafter I had many talks and adventures with men who, at one time or other, had been engaged in the moonshining industry. Some of these men had known the inside of the penitentiary; some were not without blood-guilt. I doubt not that more than one of them could, even now, find his way through night and fog and laurel thicket to some " beautiful piece of copper " that has not yet been punched full of holes. They knew that I was on friendly terms with revenue agents. What was worse, they knew that I was a scribbler. More than once I took notes in their presence while interviewing them, and we had the frankest understanding as to what would become of those notes.

My immunity was not due to any promises made or hostages given, for there were none. I did not even pose as an apologist, but merely volunteered to give a fair report of what I heard and saw. They took me at my word. Had I used such representations as a mask and secretly played the spy or informer—well, I would have deserved whatever might have befallen me. As it was, I never met with any but respectful treatment from these gentry, nor, to the best of my belief, did they ever tell me a lie.

CHAPTER VI

WAYS THAT ARE DARK

OUR terms moonshiner and moonshining are not used in the mountains. Here an illicit distiller is called a blockader, his business is blockading, and the product is blockade liquor. Just as the smugglers of old Britain called themselves free-traders, thereby proclaiming that they risked and fought for a principle, so the moonshiner considers himself simply a blockade-runner dealing in contraband. His offense is only *malum prohibitum,* not *malum in se.*

There are two kinds of blockaders, big and little. The big blockader makes unlicensed whiskey on a fairly large scale. He may have several stills, operating alternately in different places, so as to avert suspicion. In any case, the still is large and the output is quite profitable. The owner himself may not actively engage in the work, but may furnish the capital and hire confederates to do the distilling for him, so that personally he shuns the appearance

126

of evil. These big fellows are rare. They are the ones who seek collusion with the small-fry of Government officialdom, or, failing in that, instruct their minions to " kill on sight."

The little moonshiner is a more interesting character, if for no other reason than that he fights fair, according to his code, and single-handed against tremendous odds. He is innocent of graft. There is nothing between him and the whole power of the Federal Government, except his own wits and a well-worn Winchester or muzzle-loader. He is very poor; he is very ignorant; he has no friends at court; his apparatus is crude in the extreme, and his output is miserably small. This man is usually a good enough citizen in other ways, of decent standing in his own community, and a right good fellow toward all the world, save revenue officers. Although a criminal in the eyes of the law, he is soundly convinced that the law is unjust, and that he is only exercising his natural rights. Such a man, as President Frost has pointed out, suffers none of the moral degradation that comes from violating his conscience; his self-respect is whole.

In describing the process of making whiskey in the mountain stills, I shall confine myself to the operations of the little moonshiner, because they illustrate the surprising shiftiness of our backwoodsmen. Every man in the big woods is a jack-of-all-trades. His skill in extemporizing utensils, and even crude machines, out of the trees that grow around him, is of no mean order. As good cider as ever I drank was made in a hollowed log fitted with a press-block and operated by a handspike. It took but half a day's work to make this cider press, and the only tools used in its construction were an ax, a mattock in lieu of adze. an auger, and a jack-knife.

It takes two or three men to run a still. It is possible for one man to do the work, on so small a scale as is usually practiced, but it would be a hard task for him; then, too, there are few mountaineers who could individually furnish the capital, small though it be. So three men, let us say, will " chip in " five or ten dollars apiece, and purchase a second-hand still, if such is procurable, otherwise a new one, and that is all the apparatus they have to pay money for. If they should be too poor even to go to this expense, they will make a retort by inverting a half-barrel or an old wooden churn over a soap-kettle, and then all they have to buy is a piece of copper tubing for the worm.

In choosing a location for their clandestine

work, the first essential is running water. This can be found in almost any gulch; yet, out of a hundred known spring-branches, only one or two may be suitable for the business, most of them being too public. In a country where cattle and hogs run wild, and where a good part of every farmer's time is taken in keeping track of his stock, there is no place so secret but that it is liable to be visited at any time, even though it be in the depths of the great forest, several miles from any human habitation. Moreover, cattle, and especially hogs, are passionately fond of still-slop, and can scent it a great distance, so that no still can long remain unknown to them.* Consequently the still must be placed several miles away from the residence of anyone who might be liable to turn informer. Although nearly all the mountain people are indulgent in the matter of blockading, yet personal rivalries and family jealousies are rife among them, and it is not uncommon for them

---

* It is a curious fact that most horses despise the stuff. A celebrated revenue officer told me that for several years he rode a horse which was in the habit of drinking a mouthful from every stream that he forded; but if there was the least taint of still-slop in the water, he would whisk his nose about and refuse to drink. The officer then had only to follow up the stream, and he would infallibly find a still.

to inform against their enemies in the neighbor-hood.

Of course, it would not do to set up a still near a common trail—at least in the far-back settlements. Our mountaineers habitually notice every track they pass, whether of beast or man, and " read the sign " with Indian-like facility. Often one of my companions would stop, as though shot, and point with his toe to the fresh imprint of a human foot in the dust or mud of a public road, exclaiming: " Now, I wonder who *that* feller was! 'Twa'n't (so-and-so), for he hain't got no squar'-headed hobnails; 'twa'n't (such-a-one), 'cause he wouldn't be hyar at this time o' day "; and so he would go on, figuring by a process of elimination that is extremely cunning, until some such conclusion as this was reached, "That's some stranger goin' over to Little River [across the line in Tennessee], and he's footin' hit as if the devil was atter him— I'll bet he's stobbed somebody and is runnin' from the sheriff! " Nor is the incident closed with that; our mountaineer will inquire of neighbors and passersby until he gets a descrip-tion of the wayfarer, and then he will pass the word along.

Some little side-branch is chosen that runs through a gully so choked with laurel and

briers and rhododendron as to be quite impassable, save by such worming and crawling as
must make a great noise. Doubtless a faint cat-
tle-trail follows the backbone of the ridge above
it, and this is the workers' ordinary highway in
going to and fro; but the descent from ridge
to gully is seldom made twice over the same
course, lest a trail be printed direct to the still-
house.

This house is sometimes inclosed with logs,
but oftener it is no more than a shed, built low,
so as to be well screened by the undergrowth.
A great hemlock tree may be felled in such position as to help the masking, so long as its top
stays green, which will be about a year. Back
far enough from the still-house to remain in
dark shadow when the furnace is going, there
is built a sort of nest for the workmen, barely
high enough to sit up in, roofed with bark and
thatched all over with browse. Here many a
dismal hour of night is passed when there is
nothing to do but to wait on the " cooking."
Now and then a man crawls on all fours to the
furnace and pitches in a few billets of wood,
keeping low at the time, so as to offer as small
a target as possible in the flare of the fire. Such
precaution is especially needed when the number of confederates is too small for efficient

picketing. Around the little plot where the still-shed and lair are hidden, laurel may be cut in such way as to make a *cheval-de-frise,* sharp stubs being entangled with branches, so that a quick charge through them would be out of the question. Two or three days' work, at most, will build the still-house and equip it ready for business, without so much as a shingle being brought from outside.

After the blockaders have established their still, the next thing is to make arrangements with some miller who will jeopardize himself by grinding the sprouted corn; for be it known that corn which has been forced to sprout is a prime essential in the making of moonshine whiskey, and that the unlicensed grinding of such corn is an offense against the law of the United States no less than its distillation. Now, to any one living in a well-settled country, where there is, perhaps, only one mill to every hundred farms, and it is visited daily by men from all over the township, the finding of an accessory in the person of a miller would seem a most hopeless project. But when you travel in our southern mountains, one of the first things that will strike you is that about every fourth or fifth farmer has a tiny tub-mill of his own. Tiny is indeed the word, for there are

few of these mills that can grind more than a
bushel or two of corn in a day; some have a capacity of only half a bushel in ten hours of
steady grinding. Red grains of corn being
harder than white ones, it is a humorous saying
in the mountains that " a red grain in the gryste
[grist] will stop the mill." The appurtenances
of such a mill, even to the very buhr-stones themselves, are fashioned on the spot. How primitive such a meal-grinder may be is shown by the
fact that a neighbor of mine recently offered
a new mill, complete, for sale at six dollars. A
few nails, and a country-made iron rynd and
spindle, were the only things in it that he had
not made himself, from the raw materials.

In making spirits from corn, the first step is
to convert the starch of the grain into sugar.
Regular distillers do this in a few hours by
using malt, but at the little blockade still a
slower process is used, for malt is hard to get.
The unground corn is placed in a vessel that
has a small hole in the bottom, warm water is
poured over the corn and a hot cloth is placed
over the top. As water percolates out through
the hole, the vessel is replenished with more
of the warm fluid. This is continued for two
or three days and nights until the corn has
put forth sprouts a couple of inches long. The

diastase in the germinating seeds has the same chemical effect as malt—the starch is changed to sugar.

The sprouted corn is then dried and ground into meal. This sweet meal is then made into a mush with boiling water, and is let stand two or three days. The "sweet mash" thus made is then broken up, and a little rye malt, similarly prepared in the meantime, is added to it, if rye is procurable. Fermentation begins at once. In large distilleries, yeast is added to hasten fermentation, and the mash can then be used in three or four days; the blockader, however, having no yeast, must let his mash stand for eight or ten days, keeping it all that time at a proper temperature for fermentation. This requires not only constant attention, but some skill as well, for there is no thermometer nor saccharometer in our mountain still-house. When done, the sugar of what is now "sour mash" has been converted into carbonic acid and alcohol. The resulting liquid is technically called the "wash," but blockaders call it "beer." It is intoxicating, of course, but "sour enough to make a pig squeal."

This beer is then placed in the still, a vessel with a closed head, connected with a spiral tube, the worm. The latter is surrounded by a closed jacket through which cold water is constantly passing. A wood fire is built in the rude furnace under the still; the spirit rises in vapor, along with more or less steam; these vapors are condensed in the cold worm and trickle down into the receiver. The product of this first distillation (the " low wines " of the trade, the " singlings " of the blockader) is a weak and impure liquid, which must be redistilled at a lower temperature to rid it of water and rank oils.

In moonshiners' parlance, the liquor of second distillation is called the " doublings." It is in watching and testing the doublings that an accomplished blockader shows his skill, for if distillation be not carried far enough, the resulting spirits will be rank, though weak, and if carried too far, nothing but pure alcohol will result. Regular distillers are assisted at this stage by scientific instruments by which the " proof " is tested; but the maker of " mountain dew " has no other instrument than a small vial, and his testing is done entirely by the " bead " of the liquor, the little iridescent bubbles that rise when the vial is tilted. When a mountain man is shown any brand of whiskey, whether a regular distillery product or not, he invariably tilts the bottle and levels it again, before tasting; if the bead rises and is persistent, well and good; if not, he is prepared to condemn the liquor at once.

It is possible to make an inferior whiskey at one distillation, by running the singlings through a steam-chest, commonly known as a "thumpin'-chist." The advantage claimed is that "Hit allows you to make your whiskey afore the revenue gits it; that's all."

The final process is to run the liquor through a rude charcoal filter, to rid it of most of its fusel oil. This having been done, we have moonshine whiskey, uncolored, limpid as water, and ready for *immediate consumption.*

I fancy that some gentlemen will stare at the words here italicised; but I am stating facts.

It is quite impracticable for a blockader to age his whiskey. In the first place, he is too poor to wait; in the second place, his product is very small, and the local demand is urgent; in the third place, he has enough trouble to conceal, or run away with, a mere copper still, to say nothing of barrels of stored whiskey. Cheerfully he might "waive the quantum o' the sin," but he is quite alive to "the hazard o' concealin'." So, while the stuff is yet warm from the still, it is taken by confederates and quickly disposed of. There is no exaggeration in the answer a moonshiner once made to me when I

Cornmill and Blacksmith Forge

Photo by F. B. Laney

asked him how old the best blockade liquor ever got to be: "If it 'd git to be a month old, it 'd fool me!"

They tell a story on a whilom neighbor of mine, the redoubtable Quill Rose, which, to those who know him, sounds like one of his own: "A slick-faced dude from Knoxville," said Quill, "told me once that all good red-liquor was aged, and that if I'd age my block-ade it would bring a fancy price. Well, sir, I tried it; I kept some for three months—and, by godlings, *it aint so.*"

As for purity, all of the moonshine whiskey used to be pure, and much of it still is; but every blockader knows how to adulterate, and when one of them does stoop to such tricks he will stop at no halfway measures. Some add washing lye, both to increase the yield and to give the liquor an artificial bead, then prime this abominable fluid with pepper, ginger, to-bacco, or anything else that will make it sting. Even buckeyes, which are poisonous themselves, are sometimes used to give the drink a soapy bead. Such decoctions are known in the moun-tains by the expressive terms " pop-skull," " bust head," " bumblings" (" they make a bumbly noise in a feller's head "). Some of them are so toxic that their continued use might be fatal to the drinker. A few drams may turn a normally good-hearted fellow into a raging fiend who will shoot or stab without provocation.

As a rule, the mountain people have no compunctions about drinking, their ideas on this, as on other matters of conduct, being those current everywhere in the eighteenth century. Men, women and children drink whiskey in family concert. I have seen undiluted spirits drunk, a spoonful at a time, by a babe that was still at the breast, and she never batted an eye (when I protested that raw whiskey would ruin the infant's stomach, the mother replied, with widened eyes: " Why, if there's liquor about, and she don't git none, *she jist raars!* "). In spite of this, taking the mountain people by and large, they are an abstemious race. In drinking, as in everything else, this is the Land of Do Without. Comparatively few highlanders see liquor oftener than once or twice a month. The lumberjacks and townspeople get most of the output; for they can pay the price.

Blockade whiskey, until recently, sold to the consumer at from $2.50 to $3.00 a gallon. The average yield is only two gallons to the bushel of corn. Two and a half gallons is all that can be got out of a bushel by blockaders' methods, even with the aid of a " thumpin'-chist," unless lye be added. With corn selling at seventy-five cents to a dollar a bushel, as it did in our settlement, and taking into account that the average sales of a little moonshiner's still probably did not exceed a gallon a day, and that a bootlegger must be rewarded liberally for marketing the stuff, it will be seen that there was no fortune in this mysterious trade, before prohibition raised the price. Let me give you a picture in a few words.—

Here in the laurel-thicketed forest, miles from any wagon road, is a little still, without so much as a roof over it. Hard by is a little mill. There is not a sawed board in that mill— even the hopper is made of clapboards riven on the spot.

Three or four men, haggard from sleepless vigils, strike out into pathless forest through driving rain. Within five minutes the wet underbrush has drenched them to the skin. They climb, climb, climb. There is no trail for a long way; then they reach a faint one that winds, winds, climbs, climbs. Hour after hour the men climb. Then they begin to descend.

They have crossed the divide, a mile above sea-level, and are in another State. Hour after hour they " climb down," as they would say. They visit farmers' homes at dead of night.

Each man shoulders two bushels of shelled corn and starts back again over the highest mountain range in eastern America. It is twenty miles to the little mill. They carry the corn thither on their own backs. They sprout it, grind it, distill it. Two of them then carry the whiskey twenty miles in the opposite direction, and, at the risk of capture and imprisonment, or of death if they resist, peddle it out by dodging, secret methods.

This is no fancy sketch; it is literal truth. It is no story of the olden time, but of our own day. Do you wonder that one of these men should say, with a sigh—should say this? " Blockadin' is the hardest work a man ever done. And hit's wearin' on a feller's narves. Fust chance I git, I'm a-goin' ter quit! "

And it is a fact that nine out of ten of those who try the moonshining game do quit before long, of their own accord.

*   *   *   *   *

One day there came a ripple of excitement in our settlement. A blockader had shot at Jack Coburn, and a posse had arrested the would-be assassin—so flew the rumor, and it proved to be true.

Coburn was a northern man who, years ago, opened a little store on the edge of the wilder-

ness, bought timber land, and finally rose to
affluence. With ready wit he adapted himself
to the ways of the mountaineers and gained ascendancy among them. Once in a while an
emergency would arise in which it was necessary
either to fight or to back down, and in these
contests a certain art that Jack had acquired in
Michigan lumber camps proved the undoing of
more than one mountain tough, at the same time
winning the respect of the spectators. He was
what a mountaineer described to me as " a practiced knocker." This phrase, far from meaning
what it would on the Bowery, was interpreted
to me as denoting "a master hand in a knock-
fight." Pugilism, as distinguished from shooting or stabbing, was an unknown art in the
mountains until Jack introduced it.

Coburn had several tenants, among whom was
a character whom we will call Edwards. In
leasing a farm to Edwards, Jack had expressly
stipulated that there should be no moonshining
on the premises. But, by and by, there was
reason to suspect that Edwards was violating
this part of the contract. Coburn did not send
for a revenue officer; he merely set forth on a
little still-hunt of his own. Before starting, he
picked up a revolver and was about to stick it
in his pocket, but, on second thought, he con-

cluded that no red-headed man should be
trusted with a loaded gun, even in such a case
as this; so he thrust the weapon back into its
drawer, and strode away, with nothing but his
two big fists to enforce a seizure.

Coburn searched long and diligently, but
could find no sign of a still. Finally, when he
was about to give it up, his curiosity was aroused
by the particularly dense browse in the top of
an enormous hemlock that had recently been
felled. Pushing his way forward, he discovered a neat little copper still installed in the treetop itself. He picked up the contraband utensil, and marched away with it.

Meantime, Edwards had not been asleep.
When Jack came in sight of the farmhouse,
humped under his bulky burden, the enraged
moonshiner seized a shotgun and ran toward
him, breathing death and destruction. Jack,
however, trudged along about his business. Edwards, seeing that no bluff would work, fired;
but the range was too great for his birdshot
even to pepper holes through the copper still.

Edwards made a mistake in firing that shot.
It did not hurt Coburn's skin, but it ruffled his
dignity. In this case it was out of the question to pommel the blackguard, for he had
swiftly reloaded his gun. So Jack ran off with

the still, carried it home, sought out our magistrate, Brooks, and forthwith swore out a warrant.

Brooks did not fuss over any law books. Moonshining in itself may be only a peccadillo, a venial sin—let the Government skin its own skunks—but when a man has promised not to moonshine, and then goes and does it, why that, by Jeremy, is a breach of contract! Straightway the magistrate hastened to the post-office, and swore in, as a posse comitatus, the first four men that he met.

Now, when four men are picked up at random in our township, it is safe to assume that at least three of them have been moonshiners themselves, and know how this sort of thing should be done. At any rate, the posse wasted no time in discussion. They went straight after that malefactor, got him, and, within an hour after the shot was fired, he was drummed out of the county for good and forever.

But Edwards had a son who was a trifle brash. This son armed himself, and offered show of battle. He fired two or three shots with his Winchester (wisely over the posse's heads) and then took to the tall timber. Dodging from tree to tree he led the impromptu officers such a dance up the mountainside that by the time they had corralled him they were " plumb overhet."

They set that impetuous young man on a sharp-spined little jackass, strapped his feet under the animal's belly, and their chief (my hunting partner, he was) drove him, that same night, twenty-five miles over a horrible mountain trail, and lodged him in the county jail, on a charge more serious than tuat of moonshining.

In due time, a United States deputy arrived in our midst, bearing a funny-looking hatchet with a pick at one end, which he called a " devil." With the pick end of this instrument he punched numerous holes through the offending copper vessel, until the still looked somewhat like a gigantic horseradish-grater turned inside out. Then he straightened out the worm by ramming a long stick through it, and triumphantly carried away with him the copper-sheathed staff, as legal proof, trophy, and burgeon of office.

The sorry old still itself reposes to this day in old Brooks's backyard, where it is regarded by passersby as an emblem, not so much of Federal omnipotence, as of local efficiency in administering the law with promptitude, and without a pennyworth of cost to anybody, save to the offender.

CHAPTER VII

A LEAF FROM THE PAST

BEFORE prohibition, moonshining was seldom practiced outside the mountains and foothills of the southern Appalachians, and those parts of the southwest (namely, in southern Missouri, Arkansas and Texas), into which the mountaineers have immigrated in considerable numbers.

Here, then, was a conundrum: How does it happen that moonshining is distinctly a foible of the southern mountaineer?

To get to the truth, we must hark back into that eighteenth century wherein, as I have already remarked, our mountain people are lingering to this day. We must leave the South; going, first, to Ireland of 150 or 175 years ago, and then to western Pennsylvania shortly after the Revolution.

The people of Great Britain, irrespective of race, have always been ardent haters of excise laws. As Blackstone has curtly said, " From its original to the present time, the very name of excise has been odious to the people of England." Dr. Johnson, in his dictionary, defined excise as " A hateful tax levied upon commodities, and adjudged not by the common judges of property, but by wretches hired by those to whom excise is paid." In 1659, when the town of Edinburgh placed an additional impost on ale, the Convenanter Nicoll proclaimed it an act so impious that immediately " God frae the heavens declared his anger by sending thunder and unheard tempests and storms." And we still recall Burns' fiery invective:

> Thae curst horse-leeches o' the Excise
> Wha mak the whisky stills their prize!
> Haud up thy han', Deil! ance, twice, thrice!
> There, seize the blinkers! [wretches]
> An bake them up in brunstane pies
> For poor d—n'd drinkers.

Perhaps the chief reason, in England, for this outspoken detestation of the exciseman lay in the fact that the law empowered him to enter private houses and to search at his own discretion. In Scotland and Ireland there was another objection, even more valid in the eyes of the common people; excise struck heaviest at their national drink. Englishmen, at the time of which we are speaking, were content with

their ale, not yet having contracted the habit of
drinking gin; but Scotchmen and Irishmen preferred distilled spirits, manufactured, as a rule,
out of their own barley, in small pot-stills (*poteen* means, literally, a little pot), the process
being a common household art frequently practiced " every man for himself and his neighbor." A tax, then, upon whiskey was as odious
as a tax upon bread baked on the domestic
hearth—if not, indeed, more so.

Now, there came a time when the taxes laid
upon spirituous liquors had increased almost to
the point of prohibition. This was done, not so
much for the sake of revenue, as for the sake
of the public health and morals. Englishmen
had suddenly taken to drinking gin, and the immediate effect was similar to that of introducing
firewater among a race of savages. There was
hue and cry (apparently with good reason), that
the gin habit, spreading like a plague, among a
people unused to strong liquors, would soon exterminate the English race. Parliament,
alarmed at the outlook, then passed an excise
law of extreme severity. As always happens
in such cases, the law promptly defeated its own
purpose by breeding a spirit of defiance and resistance among the great body of the people.

The heavier the tax. the more widespread be-

came the custom of illicit distilling. The law
was evaded in two different ways, the method
depending somewhat upon the relative loyalty
of the people toward the Crown, and somewhat
upon the character of the country, as to whether
it was thickly or thinly settled.

In rich and populous districts, as around London and Edinburgh and Dublin, the common
practice was to bribe government officials. A
historian of that time declares that "Not infrequently the gauger could have laid his hands
upon a dozen stills within as many hours; but
he had cogent reasons for avoiding discoveries
unless absolutely forced to make them. Where
informations were laid, it was by no means uncommon for a trusty messenger to be dispatched
from the residence of the gauger to give due
notice, so that by daybreak next morning 'the
boys,' with all their utensils, might disappear.
Now and then they were required to leave an
old and worn-out still in place of that which
they were to remove, so that a report of actual
seizure might be made. A good understanding
was thus often kept up between the gaugers and
and the distillers; the former not infrequently
received a 'duty' upon every still within his
jurisdiction, and his cellars were never without
'a sup of the best.' . . . . The commerce was car-

ried on to a very great extent, and openly. Poteen was usually preferred, even by the gentry, to 'Parliament' or 'King's' whiskey. It was known to be free from adulteration, and had a smoky flavor (arising from the peat fires) which many liked." Another writer says that "The amount of spirits produced by distillation avowedly illicit vastly exceeded that produced by the licensed distilleries. According to Wakefield, stills were erected even in the kitchens of baronets and in the stables of clergymen."

However, this sort of thing was not moonshining. It was only the beginning of that system of wholesale collusion which, in later times, was perfected in our own country by the "Whiskey Ring."

Moonshining proper was confined to the poorer class of people, especially in Ireland, who lived in wild and sparsely settled regions, who were governed by a clan feeling stronger than their loyalty to the central Government, and who either could not afford to share their profits with the gaugers, or disdained to do so. Such people hid their little pot-stills in inaccessible places, as in the savage mountains and glens of Connemara, where it was impossible, or at least hazardous, for the law to reach them. With arms in hand they defied the officers

"The hatred of the people toward the gauger was for a very long period intense. The very name invariably aroused the worst passions. To kill a gauger was considered anything but a crime; wherever it could be done with comparative safety, he was hunted to the death."

Thus we see that the townsman's weapon against the government was graft, and the mountaineer's weapon was his gun—a hundred and fifty years ago, in Ireland, as they are in America to-day. Whether racial character had much to do with this is a debatable question. But, having spoken of race, a new factor, and a curious one, steps into our story. Let it be noted closely, for it bears directly on a problem that has puzzled many of our own people, namely: What was the origin of our southern mountaineers?

The north of Ireland, at the time of which we have been speaking, was not settled by Irishmen, but by Scotchmen, who had been imported by James I. to take the place of native Hibernians whom he had dispossessed from the three northern counties. These immigrants came to be known as the Scotch-Irish. They learned how to make poteen in little stills, after the Irish fashion, and to defend their stills from intrusive foreigners, also after the Irish fashion. By and

by these Scotch-Irish fell out with the British
Government, and large bodies of them emigrated to America, settling, for the most part, in
western Pennsylvania.

They were a fighting race. Accustomed to
plenty of hard knocks at home, they took to the
rough fare and Indian wars of our border as
naturally as ducks take to water. They brought
with them, too, an undying hatred of excise
laws, and a spirit of unhesitating resistance to
any authority that sought to enforce such laws.

It was these Scotchmen, in the main, assisted
by a good sprinkling of native Irish, and by the
wilder blades among the Pennsylvania-Dutch,
who drove out the Indians from the Alleghany
border, formed our rear-guard in the Revolution, won that rough mountain region for civilization, left it when the game became scarce and
neighbors' houses too frequent, followed the
mountains southward, settled western Virginia
and Carolina, and formed the vanguard westward into Kentucky, Tennessee, Missouri, and
so onward till there was no longer a West to
conquer. Some of their descendants remained
behind in the fastnesses of the Alleghanies, the
Blue Ridge, and the Unakas, and became, in
turn, the progenitors of that singular race which,
by an absurd pleonasm, is now commonly known

as the "mountain whites," but properly southern highlanders.

The first generation of Pennsylvania frontiersmen knew no laws but those of their own making. They were too far away, too scattered, and
too poor, for the Crown to bother with them.
Then came the Revolution. The backwoodsmen were loyal to the new American Government—loyal to a man. They not only fought
off the Indians from the rear, but sent many of
their incomparable riflemen to fight at the front
as well.

They were the first English-speaking people
to use weapons of precision (the rifle, introduced by the Pennsylvania-Dutch about 1700,
was used by our backwoodsmen exclusively
throughout the war). They were the first to
employ open-order formation in civilized warfare. They were the first outside colonists to
assist their New England brethren at the siege
of Boston. They were mustered in as the First
Regiment of Foot of the Continental Army (being the first troops enrolled by our Congress,
and the first to serve under a Federal banner).
They carried the day at Saratoga, the Cowpens,
and King's Mountain. From the beginning to
the end of the war, they were Washington's
favorite troops.

A "Rock House" in Moonshine Land.

And yet these same men were the first rebels against the authority of the United States Government! And it was their old commander-in-chief, Washington himself, who had the ungrateful task of bringing them to order by a show of Federal bayonets.

It happened in this wise:

Up to the year 1791 there had been no excise tax in the United Colonies or the United States. (One that had been tried in Pennsylvania was utterly abortive). Then the country fell upon hard times. A larger revenue had to be raised, and Hamilton suggested an excise. The measure was bitterly opposed by many public men, notably by Jefferson; but it passed. Immediately there was trouble in the tall timber.

Western Pennsylvania, and the mountains southward, had been settled, as we have seen, by the Scotch-Irish; men who had brought with them a certain fondness for whiskey, a certain knack in making it, and an intense hatred of excise, on general as well as special principles. There were few roads across the mountains, and these few were execrable—so bad, indeed, that it was impossible for the backwoodsmen to bring their corn and rye to market, except in a concentrated form. The farmers of the seaboard had grown rich, from the high prices that prevailed during the French Revolution; but the mountain farmers had remained poor, owing partly to difficulties of tillage, but chiefly to difficulties of transportation. As Albert Gallatin said, in defending the western people, " We have no means of bringing the produce of our lands to sale either in grain or in meal. We are therefore distillers through necessity, not choice, that we may comprehend the greatest value in the smallest size and weight. The inhabitants of the eastern side of the mountains can dispose of their grain without the additional labor of distillation at a higher price than we can after we have disposed that labor upon it."

Again, as in all frontier communities, there was a scarcity of cash in the mountains. Commerce was carried on by barter; but there had to be some means of raising enough cash to pay taxes, and to purchase such necessities as sugar, calico, gun powder, etc., from the peddlers who brought them by pack train across the Alleghanies. Consequently a still had been set up on nearly every farm. A horse could carry about sixteen gallons of liquor, which represented eight bushels of grain, in weight and bulk, and double that amount in value. This whiskey, even after it had been transported

across the mountains, could undersell even so
cheap a beverage as New England rum—so
long as no tax was laid upon it.

But when the newly created Congress passed
an excise law, it virtually placed a heavy tax
on the poor mountaineers' grain, and let the
grain of the wealthy eastern farmers pass on to
market without a cent of charge. Naturally
enough, the excitable people of the border regarded such a law as aimed exclusively at themselves. They remonstrated, petitioned, stormed.
" From the passing of the law in January, 1791,
there appeared a marked dissatisfaction in the
western parts of Pennsylvania, Maryland, Virginia, the Carolinas, and Georgia. The legis-
latures of North Carolina, Virginia and Maryland passed resolutions against the law, and that
of Pennsylvania manifested a strong spirit of
opposition to it. As early as 1791, Washington
was informed that throughout this whole region
the people were ready for revolt." " To tax
their stills seemed a blow at the only thing which
obdurate nature had given them—a lot hard indeed, in comparison with that of the people of
the sea-board."

Our western mountains (we call most of them
southern mountains now) resembled somewhat
those wild highlands of Connemara to which

reference has been made—only they were far wilder, far less populous, and inhabited by a people still prouder, more independent, more used to being a law unto themselves than were their ancestors in old Hibernia. When the Federal exciseman came among this border people and sought to levy tribute, they blackened or otherwise disguised themselves and treated him to a coat of tar and feathers, at the same time threatening to burn his house. He resigned. Indignation meetings were held, resolutions were passed calling on all good citizens to *disobey* the law, and whenever anyone ventured to express a contrary opinion, or rented a house to a collector, he, too, was tarred and feathered. If a prudent or ultra-conscientious individual took out a license and sought to observe the law, he was visited by a gang of " Whiskey Boys " who smashed the still and inflicted corporal punishment upon its owner.

Finally, warrants were issued against the lawbreakers. The attempt to serve these writs produced an uprising. On July 16, 1794, a company of mountain militia marched to the house of the inspector, General Neville, to force him to give up his commission. Neville fired upon them, and, in the skirmish that ensued, five of the attacking force were wounded and one was

killed. The next day, a regiment of 500 mountaineers, led by one " Tom the Tinker," burned
Neville's house, and forced him to flee for his
life. His guard of eleven U. S. soldiers surrendered, after losing one killed and several
wounded.

A call was then issued for a meeting of the
mountain militia at the historic Braddock's
Field. On Aug. 1, a large body assembled, of
whom 2,000 were armed. They marched on
Pittsburgh, then a village of 1,200 souls. The
townsmen, eager to conciliate and to ward off
pillage, appointed a committee to meet the mob
half way. The committee, finding that it could
not induce the mountain men to go home, made
a virtue of necessity by escorting 5,400 of them
into Pittsburgh town. As Fisher says, " The
town was warned by messengers, and every preparation was made, not for defense, but to extinguish the fire of the Whiskey Boys' thirst,
which would prevent the necessity of having to
extinguish the fire they might apply to houses.
. . . Then the work began. Every citizen
worked like a slave to carry provisions and buck-
ets of whiskey to that camp." Judge Bracken-
ridge tells us that it was an expensive as well
as laborious day, and cost him personally four
barrels of prime old whiskey. The day ended

in a bloodless, but probably uproarious, joilification.

On this same day (the Governor of Pennsylvania having declined to interfere) Washington issued a proclamation against the rioters, and called for 15,000 militia to quell the insurrection. Meantime he had appointed commissioners to go into the disaffected region and try to persuade the people to submit peacefully before the troops should arrive. Peace was offered on condition that the leaders of the disturbance should submit to arrest.

While negotiations were proceeding, the army advanced. Eighteen ringleaders of the mob were arrested, and the "insurrection" faded away like smoke. When the troops arrived, there was nothing for them to do. The insurgent leaders were tried for treason, and two of them were convicted, but Washington pardoned both of them. The cost of this expedition was more than one-third of the total expenditures of the Government, for that year, for all other purposes. The moral effect upon the nation at large was wholesome, for the Federal Government had demonstrated, on this its first test, that it could enforce its own laws and maintain domestic tranquility. The result upon the mountain people themselves was dubious. Thomas

Jefferson wrote to Madison in December: " The information of our [Virginia's] militia, returned from the westward, is uniform, that though the people there let them pass quietly, they were objects of their laughter, not of their fear; that one thousand men could have cut off their whole force in a thousand places of the Alleghany; that their detestation of the excise law was universal, and has now associated with it a detestation of the Government; and that a separation which was perhaps a very distant and problematical event, is now near and certain, and determined in the mind of every man."

But Jefferson himself came to the presidency within six years, and the excise tax was promptly repealed, never again to be instituted, save as a war measure, until within a time so recent that it is now remembered by men whom we would not call very old.

The moonshiners of our own day know nothing of the story that has here been written. Only once, within my knowledge, has it been told in the mountains, and then the result was so unexpected, that I append the incident as a color contrast to this rather sombre narrative.—

I was calling on a white-bearded patriarch who was a trifle vain of his historical learning. He could not read, but one of his daughters read to him, and he had learned by heart nearly all that lay between the two lids of a " Universal History " such as book agents peddle about. Like one of John Fox's characters, he was fond of the expression " hist'ry says " so-and-so, and he considered it a clincher in all matters of debate.

Our conversation drifted to the topic of moonshining.

" Down to the time of the Civil War," declared the old settler, " nobody paid tax on the whiskey he made. Hit was thataway in my Pa's time, and in Gran'sir's, too. And so 'way back to the time of George Washington. Now, hist'ry says that Washington was the Father of his Country; and I reckon he was the *greatest* man that ever lived—don't you? "

I murmured a complaisant assent.

" Waal, sir, if 't was right to make free whiskey in Washington's day, hit's right *now!* " and the old man brought his fist down on the table.

" But that is where you make a mistake," I replied. "Washington did enforce a whiskey tax." Then I told about the Whiskey Insurrection of 1794.

This was news to Grandpa. He listened with deep attention, his brows lowering as the narrative proceeded. When it was finished he offered no comment, but brooded to himself in silence. My own thoughts wandered far afield, until recalled to the topic by a blunt demand:

"You say Washington done that?"

"He did."

"George Washington?"

"Yes, sir: the Father of his Country."

"Waal, I'm satisfied now that Washington was a leetle-grain cracked."

*   *   *   *   *

The law of 1791, although it imposed a tax on whiskey of only 9 to 11 cents per proof gallon, came near bringing on a civil war, which was only averted by the leniency of the Federal Government in granting wholesale amnesty. The most stubborn malcontents in the mountains moved southward along the Alleghanies into western Virginia and the Carolinas, where no serious attempt was made to collect the excise; so they could practice moonshining to their heart's content, and there their descendants remain to-day.

On the accession of Jefferson, in 1800, the tax on spirits was repealed. The war of 1812 compelled the Government to tax whiskey again, but as this was a war tax, shared by commodities generally, it aroused no opposition. In 1817 the excise was again repealed; and from that time until 1862 no specific tax was levied on liquors. During this period of thirty-five years the average market price of whiskey was 24 cents a gallon, sometimes dropping as low as 14 cents. Spirits were so cheap that a "burning fluid," consisting of one part spirits of turpentine to four or five parts alcohol was used in the lamps of nearly every household. Moonshining, of course, had ceased to exist.

Then came the Civil War. In 1862 a tax of 20 cents a gallon was levied. Early in 1864 it rose to 60 cents. This cut off the industrial use of spirits, but did not affect its use as a beverage. In the latter part of 1864 the tax leaped to $1.50 a gallon, and the next year it reached the prohibitive figure of $2. The result of such excessive taxation was just what it had been in the old times, in Great Britain. In and around the centers of population there was wholesale fraud and collusion. "Efforts made to repress and punish frauds were of absolutely no account whatever. . . . The current price at which distilled spirits were sold in the markets was everywhere recognized and commented on by the press as less than the amount of the tax, allowing nothing whatever for the cost of manufacture."

Seeing that the outcome was disastrous from a fiscal point of view—the revenue from this source was falling to the vanishing point—Congress, in 1868, cut down the tax to 50 cents a gallon. " Illicit distillation practically ceased the very hour that the new law came into operation; . . . the Government collected during the second year of the continuance of the act $3 for every one that was obtained during the last year of the $2 rate."

In 1869 there came a new administration, with frequent removals of revenue officials for political purposes. The revenue fell off. In 1872 the rate was raised to 70 cents, and in 1875 to 90 cents. The result is thus summarized by David A. Wells:

" Investigation carefully conducted showed that on the average the product of illicit distillation costs, through deficient yields, the necessary bribery of attendants, and the expenses of secret and unusual methods of transportation, from two to three times as much as the product of legitimate and legal distillation. So that, calling the average cost of spirits in the United States 20 cents per gallon, the product of the illicit distiller would cost 40 to 60 cents, leaving but 10 cents per gallon as the maximum profit to be realized from fraud under the most favor-

able conditions—an amount not sufficient to offset the possibility of severe penalties of fine,
imprisonment, and confiscation of property.
. . . The rate of 70 cents . . . constituted
a moderate temptation to fraud. Its increase
to 90 cents constituted a temptation altogether
too great for human nature, as employed in
manufacturing and selling whiskey, to resist.
. . . During 1875-6, highwines sold openly in
the Chicago and Cincinnati markets at prices
less than the average cost of production plus
the Government tax. Investigations showed
that the persons mainly concerned in the work
of fraud were the Government officials rather
than the distillers; and that a so-called ' Whiskey Ring ' . . . extended to Washington, and
embraced within its sphere of influence and par-
ticipation, not merely local supervisors, collectors, inspectors, and storekeepers of the revenue,
but even officers of the Internal Revenue Bureau, and probably, also, persons occupying
confidential relations with the Executive of the
Nation."

*   *   *   *   *

Such being the condition of affairs in the
centers of civilization in the latter part of the
nineteenth century, let us now turn to the mountains, and see how matters stood among those

primitive people who were still tarrying in the eighteenth. Their situation at that time is thus briefly sketched by a southern historian *:

" Before the war these simple folks made their apples and peaches into brandy, and their corn into whiskey, and these products, with a few cattle, some dried fruits, honey, beeswax, nuts, wool, hides, fur, herbs, ginseng and other roots, and woolen socks knitted by the women in their long winter evenings, formed the stock in trade which they bartered for their plain necessaries and few luxuries, their homespun and cotton cloths, sugar, coffee, snuff, and fiddles. . . . The raising of a crop of corn in summer, and the getting out of tan-bark and lumber in winter, were almost their only resources. . . . The burden of taxation rested lightly on them. For near two generations no excise duties had been levied. . . . The war came on. They were mostly loyal to the Union. They paid the first moderate tax without a murmur.

" They were willing to pay any tax that they were able to pay. But suddenly the tax jumped to $1.50, and then to $2, a gallon. The people were goaded to open rebellion. Their corn at that time brought only from 25 to 40 cents a

* Ellwood Wilson, Sr., in the *Sewanee Review.*

bushel; apples and peaches, rarely more than 10 cents at the stills. These were the only crops that could be grown in their deep and narrow valleys. Transportation was so difficult, and markets so remote, that there was no way to utilize the surplus except to distill it. Their stills were too small to bear the cost of government supervision. The superior officers of the Revenue Department (collectors, marshals, and district-attorneys or commissioners) were paid only by commissions on collections and by fees. Their subordinate agents, whose income depended upon the number of stills they cut up and upon the arrests made, were, as a class, brutal and desperate characters. Guerrilla warfare was the natural sequence."

CHAPTER VIII

" BLOCKADERS " AND " THE REVENUE "

L ITTLE or no attention seems to have been paid to the moonshining that was going on in the mountains until about 1876, owing, no doubt, to the larger game in registered distilleries. In his report for 1876-7, the new Commissioner of Internal Revenue called attention to the illicit manufacture of whiskey in the mountain counties of the South, and urged vigorous measures for its immediate suppression.

" The extent of these frauds," said he, " would startle belief. I can safely say that during the past year not less than 3,000 illicit stills have been operated in the districts named. Those stills are of a producing capacity of 10 to 50 gallons a day. They are usually located at inaccessible points in the mountains, away from the ordinary lines of travel, and are generally owned by unlettered men of desperate character, armed and ready to resist the officers of the law. Where occasion requires, they come together in

companies of from ten to fifty persons, gun in
hand, to drive the officers out of the country.
They resist as long as resistance is possible, and
when their stills are seized, and they themselves
are arrested, they plead ignorance and poverty,
and at once crave the pardon of the Government.

"These frauds had become so open and notorious . . . that I became satisfied extraordinary measures would be required to break them
up. Collectors were . . . each authorized to
employ from five to ten additional deputies.
. . . Experienced revenue agents of persever-
ance and courage were assigned to duty to co-
operate with the collectors. United States marshals were called upon to co-operate with the
collectors and to arrest all persons known to
have violated the laws, and district-attorneys
were enjoined to prosecute all offenders.

"In certain portions of the country many
citizens not guilty of violating the law themselves were in strong sympathy with those who
did violate, and the officers in many instances
found themselves unsupported in the execution
of the laws by a healthy state of public opinion.
The distillers—ever ready to forcibly resist the
officers—were, I have no doubt, at times treated
with harshness. This occasioned much indigna-

tion on the part of those who sympathized with the lawbreakers. . . ."

The Commissioner recommended, in his report, the passage of a law " expressly providing that where a person is caught in the act of operating an illicit still, he may be arrested without warrant." In conclusion, he said: "At this time not only is the United States defrauded of its revenues, and its officers openly resisted, but when arrests are made it often occurs that prisoners are rescued by mob violence, and officers and witnesses are often at night dragged from their homes and cruelly beaten, or waylaid and assassinated."

*   *   *   *   *

One day I asked a mountain man, " How about the revenue officers? What sort of men are they?"

" Torn down scoundrels, every one."

" Oh, come, now!"

" Yes, they are; plumb onery—lock, stock, barrel and gun-stick."

" Consider what they have to go through," I remarked. " Like other detectives, they cannot secure evidence without practicing deception. Their occupation is hard and dangerous. Here in the mountains, every man's hand is against them."

"Why is it agin them? We ain't all blockaders; yet you can search these mountains
through with a fine-tooth comb and you wunt
find ary critter as has a good word to say for
the revenue. The reason is 't we know them
men from 'way back; we know whut they uster
do afore they jined the sarvice, and why they₁
did it. Most of them were blockaders their own
selves, till they saw how they could make more
money turncoatin'. They use their authority to
abuse people who ain't never done nothin' nohow. Dangerous business? Shucks! There's
Jim Cody, for a sample [I suppress the real
name]; he was principally raised in this county,
and I've knowed him from a boy. He's been
eight years in the Government sarvice, and
hain't never been shot at once. But he's killed
a blockader—oh, yes! He arrested Tom Hay-
ward, a chunk of a boy, that was scared most
fitified and never resisted more'n a mouse. Cody,
who was half drunk his-self, handcuffed Tom,
quarreled with him, and shot the boy dead while
the handcuffs was on him! Tom's relations
sued Cody in the County Court, but he carried
the case to the Federal Court, and they were too
poor to follow it up. I tell you, though, thar's
a settlement less 'n a thousand mile from the
river whar Jim Cody ain't never showed his

nose sence. He knows there'd be another revenue 'murdered.'"

"It must be ticklish business for an officer to
prowl about the headwaters of these mountain
streams, looking for 'sign.'"

"Hell's banjer! they don't go prodjectin'
around looking for stills. They set at home on
their hunkers till some feller comes and in-
forms."

"What class of people does the informing?"

"Oh, sometimes hit's some pizen old bum
who's been refused credit. Sometimes hit's the
wife or mother of some feller who's drinkin' too
much. Then, agin, hit may be some rival blockader who aims to cut off the other feller's trade,
and, same time, divert suspicion from his own
self. But ginerally hit's jest somebody who has
a gredge agin the blockader fer family reasons,
or business reasons, and turns informer to git
even."

It is only fair to present this side of the case,
because there is much truth in it, and because it
goes far to explain the bitter feeling against
revenue agents personally that is almost universal in the mountains, and is shared even by
the mountain preachers. It should be understood, too, in this connection, that the southern
highlander has a long memory. Slights and

injuries suffered by one generation have their scars transmitted to sons and grandsons. There is no denying that there have been officers in the revenue service who, stung by the contempt in which they were held as renegades from their own people, have used their authority in settling private scores, and have inflicted grievous wrongs upon innocent people. This is matter of official record. In his report for 1882, the Commissioner of Internal Revenue himself declared that " Instances have been brought to my attention where numerous prosecutions have been instituted for the most trivial violations of law, and the arrested parties taken long distances and subjected to great inconveniences and expense, not in the interest of the Government, but apparently for no other reason than to make costs."

An ex-United States Commissioner told me that, in the darkest days of this struggle, when he himself was obliged to buckle on a revolver every time he put his head out of doors, he had more trouble with his own deputies than with the moonshiners. "As a rule, none but desperadoes could could be hired for the service," he declared. "For example, one time my deputy in your county wanted some liquor for himself. He and two of his cronies crossed the line into

South Carolina, raided a still, and got beastly drunk. The blockaders bushwhacked them, riddled a mule and its rider with buckshot, and shot my deputy through the brain with a squirrel rifle. We went over there and buried the victims a few days later, during a snow storm, working with our holster flaps unbuttoned. I had all that work and worry simply because that rascal was bent on getting drunk without paying for it. However, it cost him his life.

"They were not all like that, though," continued the Judge. "Now and then there would turn up in the service a man who had entered it from honorable motives, and whose conduct, at all times, was chivalric and clean. There was Hersh Harkins, for example, now United States Collector at Asheville. I had many cases in which Harkins figured."

"Tell me of one," I urged.

"Well, one time there was a man named Jenks [that was not the real name, but it will serve], who was too rich to be suspected of blockading. Jenks had a license to make brandy, but not whiskey. One day Harkins was visiting his still-house, and he noticed something dubious. Thrusting his arm down through the peach pomace, he found mash underneath. It is a penitentiary offense to mix the two. Harkins procured more evidence from Jenk's distiller, and haled the offender before me. The trial was conducted in a hotel room, full of people. We were not very formal in those days —kept our hats on. There was no thought of Jenks trying to run away, for he was well-to-do; so he was given the freedom of the room. He paced nervously back and forth between my desk and the door, growing more restless as the trial proceeded. A clerk sat near me, writing a bond, and Harkins stood behind him dictating its terms. Suddenly Jenks wheeled around, near the door, jerked out a navy revolver, fired and bolted. It is hard to say whom he shot at, for the bullet went through Harkins's coat, through the clerk's hat, and through my hat, too. I ducked under the desk to get my revolver, and Harkins, thinking that I was killed, sprang to pick me up; but I came up firing. It was wonderful how soon that room was emptied! Harkins took after the fugitive, and had a wild chase; but he got him."

* * * * *

It was my good fortune, a few evenings later, to have a long talk with Mr. Harkins himself. He was a fine giant of a man, standing six feet three, and symmetrically proportioned. No one looking into his kindly gray eyes would suspect that they belonged to one who had seen as hard and dangerous service in the Revenue Department as any man then living. In an easy, unassuming way he told me many stories of his own adventures among moonshiners and counterfeiters in the old days when these southern Appalachians fairly swarmed with desperate characters. One grim affair will suffice to give an impression of the man, and of the times in which his spurs were won.

There was a man on South Mountain, South Carolina, whom, for the sake of relatives who may still be living, we will call Lafonte. There was information that Lafonte was running a blind tiger. He got his whiskey from four brothers who were blockading near his father's house, just within the North Carolina line. The Government had sent an officer named Merrill to capture Lafonte, but the latter drove Merrill away with a shotgun. Harkins then received orders to make the arrest. Taking Merrill with him as guide, Harkins rode to the father's house, and found Lafonte himself working near a high fence. As soon as the criminal saw the officers approaching, he ran for the house to get his gun. Harkins galloped along the other side of the fence, and, after a rough-and-tumble fight, captured his man. The officers then carried their prisoner to the house of a man whose name I have forgotten—call him White—who lived about two miles away. Meantime they had heard Lafonte's sister give three piercing screams as a signal to his confederates in the neighborhood, and they knew that trouble would quickly brew.

Breakfast was ready in White's home when the mob arrived. Harkins sent Merrill in to breakfast, and himself went out on the porch, carbine in hand, to stand off the thoroughly angry gang. White also went out, beseeching the mob to disperse. Matters looked squally for a time, but it was finally agreed that Lafonte should give bond, whereupon he was promptly released.

The two officers then finished their breakfast, and shortly set out for the Blue House, an abandoned schoolhouse about forty miles distant, where the trial was to be conducted. They were followed at a distance by Lafonte's half-drunken champions, who were by no means placated, owing to the fact that the Blue House was in a neighborhood friendly to the Government. Harkins and Merrill soon dodged to one side in the forest, until the rioters had passed them, and then proceeded leisurely in the rear. On their way to the Blue House they cut up four stills, destroyed a furnace, and made several arrests.

The next day three United States commissioners opened court in the old schoolhouse. The room was crowded by curious spectators. The trial had not proceeded beyond preliminaries when shots and shouts from the pursuing mob were heard in the distance. Immediately the room was emptied of both crowd and commissioners, who fled in all directions, leaving Harkins and Merrill to fight their battle alone.

There were thirteen men in the moonshiners' mob. They surrounded the house, and immediately began shooting in through the windows. The officers returned the fire, but a hard-pine ceiling in the room caused the bullets of the attacking party to ricochet in all directions and made the place untenable. Harkins and his comrade sprang out through the windows, but from opposite sides of the house. Merrill ran, but Harkins grappled with the men nearest to him, and in a moment the whole force of desperadoes was upon him like a swarm of bees. Unfortunately, the brave fellow had left his carbine at the house where he had spent the night. His only weapon was a revolver that had only three cartridges in the cylinder. Each of these shots dropped a man; but there were ten men left. Nothing but Harkins's gigantic strength saved him, that day, from immediate death. His long arms tackled three or four men at once, and all went down in a bunch. Others fell on top, as in a college cane-rush. There had been swift shooting, hitherto, but now it was mostly knife and pistol-butt. It is almost incredible, but it is true, that this extraordinary battle waged for three-quarters of an hour. At its end only one man faced the now thoroughly exhausted and badly wounded, but indomitable officer. At this fellow, Harkins hurled his pistol; it struck him in the forehead, and the battle was won.

A thick overcoat that Mr. Harkins wore was pierced by twenty-one bullets, seven of which penetrated his body. He received, besides, three or four bad knife-wounds in his back, and he was literally dripping blood from head to foot.

This tragedy had an almost comic sequel. After all danger had passed, a sheriff appeared on the scene, who placed, not the mob-leader, but the Federal officer under arrest. Harkins left a guard over the three men whom he had shot, and submitted to arrest, but demanded that he be taken to the farmhouse where he had left his horse. This the sheriff actually refused to permit, although Harkins was evidently past all possibility of continuing far afoot. Disgusted at such imbecility, the deputy stalked away from the sheriff, leaving the latter with his mouth open, and utterly obsessed.

A short distance up the road, Harkins met a countryman mounted on a sorry old mule. "Loan me that mule for half an hour," he requested; "you see, I can walk no further." But the fellow, scared out of his wits by the spectacle of a man in such desperate plight, refused to accommodate him.

"Get down off that mule, or I'll break your neck!"

The mule changed riders.

When the story was finished, I asked Mr. Harkins if it was true, as the reading public generally believes, that moonshiners prefer death to capture. "Do they shoot a revenue officer at sight?"

The answer was terse:

"They used to shoot; nowadays they run."

*　　*　　*　　*　　*

We have come to the time when our Government began in dead earnest to fight the moonshiners and endeavor to suppress their traffic. It was in 1877. To give a fair picture, from the official standpoint, of the state of affairs at that time, I will quote from the report of the Commissioner of Internal Revenue for the year 1877-78:

"It is with extreme regret," he said, "I find it my duty to report the great difficulties that have been and still are encountered in many of the Southern States in the enforcement of the laws. In the mountain regions of West Virginia, Virginia, Kentucky, Tennessee, North Carolina, Georgia and Alabama, and in some portions of Missouri, Arkansas and Texas, the illicit manufacture of spirits has been carried on for a number of years, and I am satisfied that the annual loss to the Government from this source has been very nearly, if not quite, equal to the annual appropriation for the collection of the internal revenue tax throughout the whole country. In the regions of country named there are known to exist about 5,000 copper stills, many of which at certain times are lawfully used in the production of brandy from apples and peaches, but I am convinced that a large portion of these stills have been and are used in the illicit manufacture of spirits. Part of the spirits thus produced has been consumed in the immediate neighborhood; the balance has been distributed and sold throughout the adjacent districts.

"This nefarious business has been carried on,

as a rule, by a determined set of men, who in their various neighborhoods league together for defense against the officers of the law, and at a given signal are ready to come together with arms in their hands to drive the officers of internal revenue out of the country.

"As illustrating the extraordinary resistance which the officers have had on some occasions to encounter, I refer to occurrences in Overton County, Tennessee, in August last, where a posse of eleven internal revenue officers, who had stopped at a farmer's house for the night, were attacked by a band of armed illicit distillers, who kept up a constant fusillade during the whole night, and whose force was augmented during the following day till it numbered nearly two hundred men. The officers took shelter in a log house, which served them as a fort, returning the fire as best they could, and were there besieged for forty-two hours, three of their party being shot—one through the body, one through the arm, and one in the face. I directed a strong force to go to their relief, but in the meantime, through the intervention of citizens, the besieged officers were permitted to retire, taking their wounded with them, and without surrendering their arms.

"So formidable has been the resistance to the

enforcement of the laws that in the districts of
5th Virginia, 6th North Carolina, South Carolina, 2d and 5th Tennessee, 2d West Virginia.
Arkansas, and Kentucky, I have found it necessary to supply the collectors with breech-loading
carbines. In these districts, and also in the
States of Georgia, Alabama, Mississippi, in the
4th district of North Carolina, and in the 2d
and 5th districts of Missouri, I have authorized
the organization of posses ranging from five to
sixty in number, to aid in making seizures and
arrests, the object being to have a force sufficiently strong to deter resistance if possible, and,
if need be, to overcome it."

The intention of the Revenue Department
was certainly not to inflame the mountain people, but to treat them as considerately as possible. And yet, the policy of " be to their faults
a little blind " had borne no other fruit than to
strengthen the combinations of moonshiners and
their sympathizers to such a degree that they
could set the ordinary force of officers at defiance, and things had come to such a pass that
men of wide experience in the revenue service
had reached the conclusion that " the fraud of
illicit distilling was an evil too firmly established to be uprooted, and that it must be
endured."

The real trouble was that public sentiment in the mountains was almost unanimously in the moonshiners' favor. Leading citizens were either directly interested in the traffic, or were in active sympathy with the distillers. " In some cases," said the Commissioner, " State officers, including judges on the bench, have sided with the illicit distillers and have encouraged the use of the State courts for the prosecution of the officers of the United States upon all sorts of charges, with the evident purpose of obstructing the enforcement of the laws of the United States. . . . I regret to have to record the fact that when the officers of the United States have been shot down from ambuscade, in cold blood, as a rule no efforts have been made on the part of the State officers to arrest the murderers; but in cases where the officers of the United States have been engaged in enforcement of the laws, and have unfortunately come in conflict with the violators of the law, and homicides have occurred, active steps have been at once taken for the arrest of such officers, and nothing would be left undone by the State authorities to bring them to trial and punishment."

There is no question but that this statement of the Commissioner was a fair presentation of facts; but when he went on to expose the root of the evil, the underlying sentiment that made, and still makes, illicit distilling popular among our mountaineers, I think that he was singularly at fault. This was his explanation—the only one that I have found in all the reports of the Department from 1870 to 1904:

" Much of the opposition to the enforcement of the internal revenue laws [he does not say *all,* but offers no other theory] is properly attributable to a latent feeling of hostility to the government and laws of the United States still prevailing in the breasts of a portion of the people of these districts, and in consequence of this condition of things the officers of the United States have often been treated very much as though they were emissaries from some foreign country quartered upon the people for the collection ot tribute."

This shows an out-and-out misunderstanding of the character of the mountain people, their history, their proclivities, and the circumstances of their lives. The southern mountaineers, as a class, have been remarkably loyal to the Union ever since it was formed. Far more of them fought for the Union than for the Confederacy in our Civil War. And, anyway, politics has never had anything to do with the moonshining question. The reason for illicit distilling is

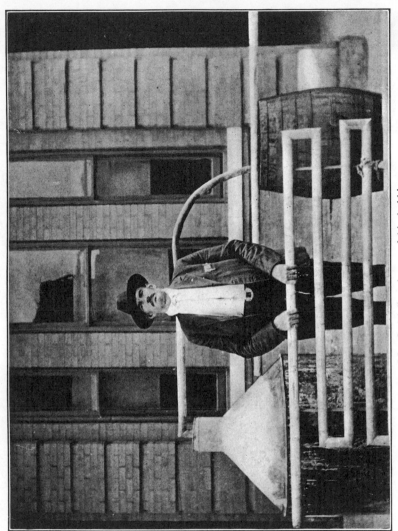

"Mr. Quick," and one of his hobbies.

purely an economic one, as I have shown. If
officers of the Federal Government have been
treated as foreigners, they have met the same
reception that *all* outsiders meet from the mountaineers. A native of the Carolina tidewater is
a " furriner " in the Carolina mountains, and so
is a native of the " bluegrass " when he enters
the eastern hills of his own State. The highlander's word " furriner " means to him what
βάρβαρος did to an ancient Greek. Ordinarily he
is courteous to the unfortunate alien, though
never deferential; in his heart of hearts he regards the queer fellow with lofty superiority.
This trait is characteristic of all primitive peoples, of all isolated peoples. It is provincialism,
pure and simple—a provincialism more crudely
expressed in Appalachia than in Gotham or
The Hub, but no cruder in essence for all that.

The vigorous campaign of 1877 bore such
fruit that, in the following year, the Commissioner was able to report: " We virtually have
peaceable possession of the districts of 4th and
5th North Carolina, Georgia, West Tennessee,
Kentucky, Alabama, and Arkansas, in many of
which formidable resistance to the enforcement
of the law has prevailed. . . . In the western
portion of the 5th Virginia district, in part of
West Virginia, in the 6th North Carolina dis-

trict, in part of South Carolina, and in the 2d and 5th districts of Tennessee, I apprehend further serious difficulties. . . . It is very desirable, in order to prevent bloodshed, that the internal revenue forces sent into these infected regions to make seizures and arrests shall be so strong as to deter armed resistance."

In January, 1880, a combined movement by armed bodies of internal revenue officers was made from West Virginia southwestward through the mountains and foothills infested with illicit distillers. "The effect of this movement was to convince violators of the law that it was the determination of the Government to put an end to frauds and resistance of authority, and since that time it has been manifest to all well-meaning men in those regions of the country that the day of the illicit distiller is past." In his report for 1881-82 the Commissioner declared that "The supremacy of the laws . . . has been established in all parts of the country."

As a matter of fact, the number of arrests per annum, which hitherto had ranged from 1,000 to 3,000, now dropped off considerably, and the casualties in the service became few and far between. But, in 1894, Congress increased the tax on spirits from the old 90 cents figure to $1.10 a gallon. The effect was almost instantaneous.

We have no means of learning how many new moonshine stills were set up, but we do know that the number of seizures doubled and trebled, and that bloodshed proportionally increased.

Then a new factor entered the moonshining problem, and profoundly altered it: the South went "dry."

One might have expected that prohibition would be bitterly opposed in Appalachia, in view of the fact that here the old-fashioned idea still prevailed, in practice, that moderate drinking was neither a sin nor a disgrace, and that a man had the same right to make his own whiskey as his own soup, if he chose to do so. At this period those who fought the liquor traffic on purely moral grounds were a small minority, in the mountains. But they were supported by the blockaders themselves, who were glad to get rid of the competition of registered distilleries and saloons or dispensaries, and the drinking public preferred the native product because it was cheap. Such a combination was irresistible.

Then came the World War. Nearly all of the able-bodied young men went away into military service. A great number of the boys and middle-aged men also left home and went into the shipyards or munition plants. The folks left at home became more abstemious than ever, partly from necessity, partly from loyal eagerness to "do their bit." And there was everywhere a spiritual uplift, due to the universal anxiety and the solemnity of war. The churches gained a remarkable ascendancy that they were quick to utilize as a political power. The Eighteenth Amendment was passed, and the Volstead Act.

The immediate effect of prohibition was to put an enormous premium on illicit distilling. Formerly the profit on moonshine whiskey had been only seventy-five cents to a dollar a gallon, at the still-house; to-day it is three to six dollars. A man working with a still so small that he can pick it up bodily and run away with it, at the first alarm, can make a thousand dollars profit with it in a few weeks. The still itself is the only part of a backwoods distillery that cannot be made right out in the hills from materials found on the spot. The whole outfit can be dismantled in a few minutes, and the metal parts can be hidden in a hole in the ground no bigger than a common trunk.

Human nature proved to be the same old human nature that it had always been. Farmers and others, who never before had been able to make more than the barest subsistence, now saw a chance to get rich in a few months. Thus among a poverty-stricken class of mountaineers the temptation to run secret stills inflamed and spread.

When one man suddenly rises from destitution to affluence, his neighbors are moved to follow his example. Some of the bolder spirits among them will do so, and take chances with the law. The others will become jealous, will play the informer, and neighborhood feuds result. The informers are as secret and underhanded as the law-breakers. Both sides became mean, treacherous, dishonorable; and so the moral fiber of the whole community is impaired.

The greater the reward in sight, the greater risks will be run for it. The blockaders are getting ugly. Arrests have rapidly increased, since prohibition, and so have mortal combats between officers and outlaws. Spies are everywhere, and a hated gendarmerie patrols the country. The war between enforcement agents and blockaders is more widespread and deadly than ever before in our history. We who live in the mountains are fairly within gun-crack of it.

I wish I could share the optimism of those comfortable people who believe that all this will blow over in a few years; but to me the outlook is more serious. I used to think that good roads would help to check moonshining, by making it easier for mountain farmers to market their corn in bulk at a fair profit. Such would probably have been the effect under the old régime. But I never dreamed, in those days, that distilled corn juice would soon be retailing at ten to twenty dollars a gallon. As things are, our new highways will make the distant marketing of blockade liquor a veritable line of trade. "Mountain dew" will be collected by fly-by-night cars and carried to a far extended market.

Observe, please, that this is no argument for or against prohibition. That is not my business. As a descriptive writer it is my duty to collect facts, whether pleasant or unpleasant, regardless of my own or any one else's bias, and present them in orderly sequence. It is for the reader to draw his own conclusions.

CHAPTER IX

THE SNAKE-STICK MAN

I LEFT Hazel Creek in the summer of 1907. After various wanderings, chiefly in the mountains, I came finally to live in Bryson City, the county seat of the same county in which I had first appeared as a resident of the mountains.

It was along in May, I believe, of 1919, that a sturdy, dark-eyed stranger came to the old hotel where I live, and was introduced to the landlord by the Indian Agent from Lufty, who had brought him over in his car.

"Uncle Bill, this is a gentleman from the West who is taking a vacation and wishes to ramble about over the mountains. He would like to stay with you a few weeks."

Mr. Quick, as I shall call the stranger, had the air of a prosperous ranchman of rather retired habit. He engaged one of the best rooms and was given a seat at table alongside of me. We exchanged the usual inanities at supper, but neither of us made advances toward sociability.

Our visitor wore a conspicuous emblem of a fraternal order in which, by the token, he had attained high degree. He went out and made friends at once with brethren of the lodge, but was a bit distant with other people.

There came a fine day when I was cocked up in a chair reading in front of the hotel. Mr. Quick seated himself beside me and became absorbed at once in a yellow-covered book. When the dinner-bell rang we went in, leaving our reading matter on a card table in the office.

It chanced that I was the first one out from dinner. In picking up my magazine I noticed that the stranger's book was entitled *La Guardia Blanca,* which I instantly recognized as a Spanish translation of one of Conan Doyle's novels: a tale of free adventurers of the Middle Ages fighting for fun and booty.

I stood and stared at it like one possessed.

No ordinary American would be reading an English romance in a Spanish version. And here, of all places under the sun!

Thirteen years, off and on, had I dwelt in this remote region of the Great Smoky Mountains, and in all that time I had not till now met man or woman here who knew any foreign tongue, save three or four college men, a casual Jew

Buck's Exit.

peddler or two, and one stray Italian who had been jailed on a charge of assassination.

When the new boarder returned to his tilted chair there was a topic of mutual interest at last. "I see that you read Spanish," I remarked.

"O yes," he replied, brightening, "I speak it, too."

We dropped our books and began a lively conversation. The man's reticence fled. He was interested in the Indians; had been among them for many years, in the West, in Florida. He spoke Creek (or was it Choctaw?) and Navaho and Seminole. Navaho he had found one of the most difficult tongues in the world, the grammar intricate, the pronunciation hard for our ears to catch and our mouths to utter.

He knew the western Cherokees, but not their language. What a romantic history was theirs! How strange that this Eastern Band of ours were still occupying a bit of their ancient stronghold in the Carolina Smokies! It would be amusing for him to pick up a little of the Cherokee language while here on vacation; and Indian relics—he had a collection from other tribes at home in Oklahoma.

One of my own hobbies. Of course I would assist him.

We swapped experiences of western life, and a few confidences. For my part, I was a writer, of a sort; field sports and out-of-the-way places my specialty. Just now I was embarrassed by lack of a camera to illustrate some of my stuff.

Ah! he had a good camera. He would be delighted to accompany me into the hills and make any pictures I wished. Then, very modestly, he admitted that he tried a little writing now and then himself: adventure stories—that sort of thing. Might he see some of my work?

Might a visitor see Mamma's baby? I took him to my office and turned him loose. He devoured books and scrap books, and pored over magazine files, making intelligent comments on what he read.

And so I, too, was a "gun crank." He had been one all his life. What did I think of the Luger? What of the Army automatic pistol? How about the old Frontier model Colt forty-five? He had all three with him; also two self-loading rifles. Might we not go out for a little practice together?

We could, and we did. Mr. Quick gets this *nom de guerre* in the present narrative from the "lightning draw" that he demonstrated with pistols, and his rapid, accurate work with the rifles.

His way of carrying a Luger interested me. It was neither on the hip nor under the left armpit, but in what is called a suspender holster, worn inside the band of the trousers and attached to the right suspender. The holster was made of soft leather with rubber interlining on the back. The top of the holster, running up behind the pistol butt in an inverted V shape, had a slit at the apex in which the suspender cast-off was snapped, the suspender tab that engages the trousers buttons having been removed. The sides of the holster back had buttonholes for the trousers buttons, which latter were sewed to the inside of the trousers band. Thus the holster served to hold up the trousers, as a part of the suspenders, and it could neither sag down much from the pistol's weight nor pull up and interfere when the gun was drawn.

This is about the only way that a rather large pistol can be carried concealed when one is not wearing a coat, and yet be handy for instant drawing. Mr. Quick always wore a waistcoat, generally with only one or two buttons fastened.

The pistol butt was where he could grasp it instantly from any position, standing, sitting, or otherwise. The gun would not fall out if he was scuffling on the ground. A revolver in such position would bulge the vest, but an automatic pistol is so flat that it is not noticeable, except to men who are "wise" to that sort of thing.

One day Mr. Quick was out with a man who was something of a pistol shot himself, and they were practicing together, the other man having a single action Colt revolver in a hip-pocket holster. After Quick had shown some of his "whirling stunts" he changed to the "quick draw." He was using two Lugers.

"Jim," said he. "I can pull both my guns and shoot twice before you can pull your gun and shoot once."

They tried it, and Quick won.

"Now," said Quick, "I believe I can let you take hold of the stock of your pistol, put your thumb on the hammer and your finger on the trigger, and I will stand with my hands at my belt buckle. You count to three, and at the word *three* I'll draw and fire both my guns before you can draw and fire yours."

They tried it, and Quick won.

My new acquaintance and I found that we had many interests in common. We roamed the hills, talking natural history, field sports, comparative scenery, natives and their ways, ever so many things. We went among the

Cherokees and among the white "branch-water
people." Quick was a good photographer, and
he made several pictures to illustrate articles of
mine in *Outing* and *All Outdoors*.

What I most liked about the man was that he
was genuine. Never for a moment did he assume interest for mere politeness sake; nor did
I. I don't believe we ever bored each other in
two months of almost daily association. How
many men or women can say that of each other?

Blessed is the comradeship of hobby-riders,
so long as their extravagances are mutual. One
hobby may do; but Quick and I had a dozen to
share—a whole paddockful, one might say, in
sporting terms.

One day my new companion wanted a straight
stick for a cane. I introduce him to sourwood
shoots, which seem made by nature for that purpose. They grow exceptionally straight and
slender. They season without cracking or
checking, even when peeled green, and turn
lightweight but pretty strong and hard. The
peeled wood is white.

He passed by those that were of proper size
for walking-sticks and selected one thick enough
for a handspike. I marveled, but said nothing.

Next day I observed that he was carving a
big spiral on that sourwood club and shaving

the rest down to cane diameter. Little by little the spiral, that stood in relief, assumed the form of a rattlesnake. Deftly and neatly he carved the snake's scales, the rattle, the wicked flat head and forked tongue. He worked by eye alone, sitting easily in his chair, and used no tool but a pocketknife.

In three days he had a rattlesnake wound round that stick, complete, and painted to the life in watercolors. It was fit to give anyone a jolt, and make him gasp, when the stick was thrust toward him with a twisting motion.

Hitherto Mr. Quick had not made many acquaintances in town or country. But now, as he sauntered down the street flourishing his stick, he set the girls everywhere screaming and giggling, and the gamins crazy with delight. People crowded about and followed him. In a day or so he was on familiar terms with everybody, from the prim school teacher to the lowest-lived bootlegger within five miles.

They called him "the Snake-Stick Man." Nobody now cared what his real name might be; for had he not been christened and adopted by the community for itself? Ah me!

Mr. Quick was affable and full of fun, now that the crowd was with him. He made several snake-sticks, each an improvement on the ear-

lier ones.   On one he had a monkey chasing a
lizard up the snake's tail and stabbing at it with
a devil's trident.   Tourists passing on trains
offered him five to ten dollars for a snake-stick,
but he would not sell.   He gave one to me, and
others to members of his lodge.

But by and by something began to go wrong
with the Snake-Stick Man.   He neglected his
meals, or toyed futilely with them.   He remained much in his room, or took sudden long
walks by himself, and came back with a worried
air as though harassed by some evil spirit.   At
times he sank into deep despondency.   Yet he
complained little, and explained never a word.

I was concerned for his health, but delicate
about intruding into what was his own affair.
Finally, though, I could bear it no longer, and
so I asked him what was the matter, and if I
could do anything for him.

He answered, with obvious reluctance, that
he was cursed with such spells at times.   It was
nervous dyspepsia.   He had tried the stock
remedies.   Nothing would do him any good but
a little whiskey.

Corpo di Baccho!   So that was it.   Well, he
might be a neurasthenic, though he didn't look
it.   Anyhow—

Yes, I did.

But the availabilities, so far as I could reach out, were few and small. Then came other new acquaintances to Mr. Quick's relief. There is a fellow-feeling in this world for nervous dyspeptics—or there was then, in the natal year of nation-wide prohibition, when we did not yet know whether to consider the new crusade as a godsend, a calamity or a joke.

Of course this was moonshine liquor; for it had been a long time since there had been any other kind in our little part of the South. And more of it came to a certain room upstairs in the old Cooper House than could fairly be accounted for in the treatment of one man's gastric neuroses.

Mr. Quick did not know it, but a suspicion was growing, about this time, in the bosom of one H. Kephart, that he, our Snake-Stick Man, was "fixing for a good long drunk," as our mountaineers delicately phrase it.

As it turned out, I was dead wrong. A tablespoonful, in company, was his limit. Stomach so weak it could not stand more at a time. Just "a little dib," you know, now and then, to tone it up. And I know, now, that he never touched a drop unless someone was around.

Neither the Muse of History nor the Goddess of Justice would thank me for saying any more about Mr. Quick's liquor supply. Rather it is up to me to bring this narrative swiftly to its climax.

In July came our summer term of Superior Court. Came, too, on the opening day, several woebegone citizens to a little red brick building that adjoins the court-house and is adorned with iron bars at the windows.

Like lightning from a fair sky there crashed upon us the report, certified and all too true, that our Snake-Stick Man was a secret agent of the Indian Bureau who had been picked for the job of finding out who was making or vending liquor on the Indian Reservation, and to make their paths straight to the chain-gang. Outside of the Reservation he had not meddled.

In our sparsely settled region everybody knows nearly everybody else. It logically follows that when I looked up at those faces behind the bars some of them had a familiar look. It follows that they had seen me running around with the Snake-Stick Man for two months or more. I could put that in my pipe and smoke it.

After the volcano in my bosom had subsided enough for a cool survey of the situation I took a new interest in Mr. Quick. You would have cut him dead, of course. But you are not a sporting writer. In a sense, Mr. Quick and I were now to swap places. Turn about is fair play. He had been using me as a subject of investigation; now it was my turn. I purposed seeing what sort of a fellow he would prove to be when all masks were dropped.

When he returned to the hotel that evening I went straight to him and we had a man-to-man talk.

"So far as my official business here is concerned," said he, "I make no apology. I have been in the Federal service for twenty years. I am, you might say, a soldier; for it amounts to the same thing. I obey orders. My loyalty to my Government is superior to any other consideration."

"But, Kephart," he continued, "I tried my darndest not to deceive you in anything else. If I made any slip in that, I sincerely beg your pardon."

"You didn't," I answered. "You were the real thing. If you had been a poseur, pretending an interest in nature, in literature, and so on, that you did not honestly feel, you could not have put it over, with me, for ten minutes."

There followed a long talk that touched the depths of human nature, but with which neither the Muse of History nor the Goddess of Justice has any business.

I have a pent-up thought or two that I will get off my system. For the average run of detectives and their business, I have little respect. There may be a larger proportion of decent fellows among them than I know of; but I have met some sorry specimens.

I cordially detest the public policy that has quartered an army of Federal spies upon the American people and that was at this time authorizing them to invade homes and to search individuals on mere suspicion. I believe such a policy to be wholly and thoroughly bad.

But here was a different case, and a different sort of man. No common spy, no bluffing rough-neck, no graduate of the penitentiary turned renegade to his own people, could have done what he did. No plausible rogue playing the part of a gentleman could have done it, either.

There have been gentlemen detectives in fiction: Monsieur Dupin and Sherlock Holmes, for example. Never before had I met one in real life. But here he stood.

Think back a bit. He had been posted about me, as one who had written a good deal about the mountain moonshiners and who evidently knew what he was talking about. He wanted to make my acquaintance at the start and yet circumstances did not permit him to tell me frankly who and what he was. How did he go about it?

He made no advances. He was a book-lover himself, and also a frequenter of far places. So he knew from his own experience how it is to be isolated from literary centers. He knew I must be bored with the commonplace. So he simply brought that exotic book within my range of vision, with never a look nor a word, and the trick was turned.

And those snake-sticks for the multitude. Here again was applied psychology. What other trick could have won him the instant attention and good-will of every class of people, in a country town, without his having to say a word for himself?

Here was a detective who actually used brains in his business. Here was a detective who had the instincts of a gentleman, instead of those of a sneak.

Mr. Quick stayed on at our hotel for another month, taking part sometimes in little forays at night that were pulled off by local officers, or by himself with their assistance. His days of usefulness as a detective in western North Carolina were over.   Henceforth he was a straight-out raider with no disguise.

I had long walks and long talks with him again, just as before, and regardless of public comment.   I found him even more interesting in his true character than he had been in the assumed one.   Mystery adds a glamour to commonplace personalities, and they fade out when it is dissolved; but Mr. Quick rather gained when he stepped out into the light.

One day, after telling me of an adventure he had met in our own "big sticks," as we call the forest wilderness that surrounds us, Quick remarked: "Man-hunting is the finest sport in the world."

I kindled at that; for I had heard the same sentiment before, expressed in the very same words, by other man-hunters who were as different from Quick as men can well be.   I kindled because I had often wondered, sportsman that I am, whether I should find it so if the test happened to come my way.   I doubted, but was ready to be convinced.

So when Mr. Quick told me, early one morning, that he was going on a man-hunt across the Smokies into Tennessee, in a region that neither he nor I had ever visited, and he invited me to go along, I equipped myself hastily and stepped into the car that was to take him on the first leg of the journey.

CHAPTER X

A RAID INTO THE SUGARLANDS

SO we were outward bound on a man-hunt, across the Great Smoky Mountains, into the Sugarland country of Tennessee. Whom we might be after, or what for, was little concern of mine. This was supposed to be a sporting proposition, and the arrangements were in the hands of Mr. Quick.

It was a bright morning in mid-August, with a portent of sultriness here in the river valley, but of cool airs and clear prospects on the high ranges that we were heading for.

We sped along the new highway, crossed the Tuckaseegee near Governor's Island, and soon turned northward along a charming tributary, the Okona Lufty. This stream, which is called Lufty for short, has its sources among the precipitous peaks and ridges between Clingman Dome and Mount Guyot—one of the roughest and most heavily timbered regions in eastern America.

There had been no time for proper preparation. We did not even provide ourselves with hob-nailed shoes. I assured Quick that this would give us trouble, but that if he could stand it, I could.

At Birdtown, the site of an ancient Cherokee village, we took on a short, dark, pleasant faced fellow, who was to serve as guide. His Indian name, as nearly as one can spell it, was Dee-yah-katch-*tee* (*a* as in *father*). Out of mercy to the printer let us call him Katch.

We passed the campus of the Indian school at Cherokee and turned up the left fork of Lufty. Now the flivver chugged hard, and squirmed and bumpety-bumped over a road that grew worse and worse. It was ten in the morning when we arrived at Smokemont, a new sawmill village, head of navigation for Ford cars. Ahead of us was a hard day's travel afoot.

At a little wayside store we filled our pockets with such luncheon stuff as the place afforded: some crackers, some "meat by-products with ham flavor," detestable, but standard at nearly every jumping-off place in the United States. This was not my way of starting on a sporting venture; but if Quick could stand that, so could I.

Then we swung into a long, steady climbing stride.

"Court Week" at Bryson City, N. C.

Hitherto there had been little said; but as our legs limbered to their work, so were our tongues loosened. By listening to Quick and Katch it was easy for me to unravel the plot of our adventure.

There was a bad old citizen, a moonshiner, white, with perhaps a streak of red for good measure, and he had two sons who were true to type. Call them Old Man Ruff, and Buck and Jake.

I don't know that I ever saw the senior Ruff, but I remembered the two offsprings well.

Buck cut such a dash when they arrested him, one time, in our town, that they penned him alone in the inner cage of the jail. At night he wrenched off a steel brace from his cot, with which he pried off a hinge and so joined the other prisoners. With their help, using the brace for a tool, he dug a hole through the brick wall. Then it was easy to let himself down with knotted blankets. Exit Buck.

Jake came to town, some months later, and proceeded to make merry after the fashion that our lumberjacks call "hellin' around." When an officer went to run him in, Jake pulled a long-barreled Colt (the only Bisley model I ever saw in the mountains); but he was too fuddled to get the drop. After a season in jail, he was let out on bond. Presto! he jumped it.

The point of it all, for us, was that Katch was Jake's bondsman. Katch now had but a short time to produce the aforesaid Jake, or he must kiss good-bye to five hundred dollars. Nor was that the worst of it: he would lose his wife, too, without even a bye-bye kiss; for Katch solemnly assured us she would "tear up the patch" and forsake him, if he had to part with those five hundred dollars.

"O no, Katch," we soothed him. "She's a well-meaning woman, isn't she?"

"Yes, meanest as hell."

The truth was that Katch had been implicated with the Ruffs in the liquor business, and the bonding had been virtually forced on him, much to his wife's disgust.

Katch recently had been "tipped off" that the three Ruffs had fled together across the state line and that they were hiding out in the Sugarlands. So he brought his troubles to the detective. That gentleman already had federal warrants for the fugitives, but, to provide further against contingencies, he had our sheriff swear him in as a local deputy and give him state warrants as well. He also bore papers for one or two other fugitive citizens of North Carolina who were supposed to be enjoying the innocent hospitality of Tennessee.

My own status in the affair was not yet defined. I had not been sworn in as an officer. Yet Mr. Quick had provided me with a .45 Colt automatic and a pair of handcuffs. I did not assume that he meant me to eat soup with them. Probably the swearing business could be attended to at his convenience. Anyway, I was with the bunch; and bunch it I surely would. This was a sporting proposition.

It is a little over nine miles uphill from Smokemont to a crossing of the divide that we Carolinians call Collins Gap, marked Indian Gap on the government map. This is the only pass but one that is practicable in more than thirty miles of the Smoky range. Leading to it, on the Carolina side, there is a wagon road of fairly easy grade. Beyond the top, on the Tennessee side—but we will come to that.

A logging railroad was being pushed up through the wilderness, along this route. At the second construction camp we found a gang of Indians working on the grade. All of them knew Katch and his troubles, some of them knew me, and we could tell from their sly glances and grins that they identified Quick as the Snake-

Stick Man, and that they felt something was in the wind.

A red athlete on my right sang out to us *"Bon jour."*

It was startling to hear French from a full-blood Cherokee; but I remembered that he and others of his tribe had seen hot service, and acquitted themselves well, "over there."

We stopped for luncheon at a mossy springside in the Beech Flat. It was a cold bite, and a bad one, but we were ravenous, and down it went.

Soon we entered the balsam zone. It was an abrupt change from the world we had emerged from; real mountains now, and a forest reminiscent of the far North.

At a few minutes past 3 p. m. we "topped out" in the Gap. This is probably the deepest sag in twenty miles of divide from Clingman Dome to Mount Guyot. The government map indicates its elevation to be 5,300 feet above sealevel.

If you had before you the Knoxville and Mount Guyot sheets of that map (U. S. Geological Survey) you might get some idea of the kind of country we were in. You would observe from the contour lines that we were surrounded on all sides by high and steep mountains—uninhabited they are, and heavily forest clad—and that we stood upon the state line that marks the end of North Carolina, the beginning of Tennessee.

At this time of year the Gap was a luxurious place on which to lounge and view and dream. We cast ourselves on the grass and took a good smoke as we rested our tired limbs.

Ahead of us was the descent into Tennessee. The road had abruptly ended. Beyond was a steep and rocky trail, going down, down along a brawling torrent into the gloom of narrow gulfs that were choked with laurel and spruce and balsam.

This was the beginning of the Sugarlands, a country of ill fame, hidden deep in remote gorges, difficult of access, tenanted by a sparse population who preferred to be a law unto themselves. For many a year it had been known on our side of the mountains as Blockaders' Glory, which is the same as saying Moonshiners' Paradise, and we all believed it to be fitly named.

Thus doth sinless North Carolina look down upon sinful Tennessee.

Katch was the only one of us who had ever been down that trail. Quick might as well have been on the moon, for all he knew of the land; and it is safe to wager that he would have been equally unconcerned in either situation. His was a temperament that Jules Verne would have loved.

As for me, all I knew of the Sugarlands was what I had glimpsed from afar, standing on some peak of the divide. I had seen the Sugarland Mountain, a long ridge running down from the main divide, but could only guess what lay beyond it from what I saw on the hither side. I recalled now my first impression of that country to the west of it, at the head of the left prong of Little River. It was years ago, of a bitter cold winter evening, that I looked down from the north front of Siler's Bald into a great triangular gulf that is formed by the Miry Ridge and the Sugarland Mountain with the main Smokies as a base.

That was a weird and forbidding land. Vast labyrinths of rhododendron covered those profound and dismal depths, impenetrable, sunless in winter, dead but for the murky evergreen of shrubs and spruces. The place was unearthly in its dreariness and desolation. I turned to my companion mountaineer and asked if it had a name.

"No: not as a whole."

"Let us call it Godforsaken."

"A good name: it is fitten."

But here we were, on the far side of Sugar-land, in summer: a very different prospect. We started down from the Gap at 4 o'clock, passing two recently abandoned browse camps and the ruins of a burned log hut. The trail was what remained of a military road that had been made across the Smokies in the Civil War. What sort of road it must have been, in its prime, may be judged from the fact that cannon had to be dismounted from their carriages and dragged over the bare rocks and clay.

On down we passed through the balsam zone and thence into a forest of great hardwood trees of many species. The trail meandered along the bottom of deep and narrow glens, with great cliffs above, and dense laurel on either side. Seldom could we see out to right or left. There were no side trails.

We slipped and slid. The toes of our street shoes punished us. Rocks of all sizes everywhere. Any boulder less in size than a house we called a "pebble."

Quick asked the Indian: "How do they bury people in this country?"

"Guess they criminate them," answered Katch, meaning cremate, and he misunderstood our laughter.

Down, down, down! And never a sign that

man had ever been here before us, except along the narrow track we followed. The torrent alongside us dashed over ledges and boulders with hiss and roar. The crossings became diffi-cult. There was nowhere a footlog; so we had to jump from one waterworn rock to another, in our smooth-soled shoes. The submerged rocks were slippery as grease. If one of us had fallen, the others might have had to make a litter to bear him out.

Five miles from the Collins Gap, and four-teen from where we had started afoot, we came to the first evidence of settlement. It was a bit of cornfield, perched above the trail at a slope so steep that it must have been dug up with mat-tocks and hoed on hands and knees. A pump-kin broke loose from its vine, as we came along, fell out of the field and burst on the trail like a bomb.

Why would anyone plant corn on such a place? Because the Sugarlanders were a little behind the times: they had not yet learned to make whiskey out of anything more lethal than honest corn.

We passed through a couple of old clearings, very small ones, in each of which stood an aban-doned cabin—just a log pen covered with clap-

"The torrent dashed over ledges and boulders with hiss and roar."

boards, a dirt floor, and a pile of rocks shoulder-high for a chimney.

Then the trail wound tortuously through dense laurel that grew twelve to twenty feet high, gnarled and twisted and with interlocking limbs.

We were following it, Indian file, of course, when Katch, who was in the lead, suddenly stopped as if shot.

"Two or three men have come this way," he whispered, pointing to fresh footprints, "and they dodged aside when they heard us coming toward them."

It was true. The tracks showed that the men were advancing in our direction; that they had heard us at thirty or forty yards and had instantly vanished into the laurel on our left-hand side. No one would do that unless he had reason to dodge all comers.

We parted the laurel carefully and squirmed through it to a little opening diagonally to the rear. There on the ground lay two burlap sacks of rations and clothing, a shotgun, and a small rifle, hastily abandoned by men who had plunged on into the further laurel.

In such a mizmaze of tough and tangled vegetation they would have to crawl. In all probability they were lying flat in it, facing toward us, not twenty yards distant, and with pistols drawn. We, on our side, could not see ten feet into that jungle.

There we stood at gaze, listening, for several minutes. Not a twig cracked. It was certain that the fugitives had not stirred. They were awaiting our move.

It was a rather ticklish situation. If we advanced upon them, we could not help making enough noise for them to locate us. They would see us before we could see them. If they chose to fire, they could do so with certain aim.

And here was the rub: if these fellows were residents of the Sugarlands, instead of the fugitives we were after, and they killed one or more of us, they could readily fix up a story that would clear them in their own court. We were interlopers if we made the least hostile move.

Yet these might be the very men we had come so far to seize. If we let them slip by, they would be gone for good and all.

We consulted in whispers. Then Quick decided to advance. I happened to be on the left, nearest the trail, which was but a few yards away. If the hiding men, instead of resisting, decided to break and run, they would have to get to the trail. So I stepped out to it, to be ready to head them off.

It is lucky I did so, though for a totally unexpected reason.

Quick and Katch started abreast and moved forward into the thicket, stealthily, a foot at a time. It was a tense moment. Then my ear caught a faint sound *from behind*. I wheeled, and there stood a tall youth of nineteen or twenty, in the trail, bending forward on the alert, his shotgun poised, his eyes straining at my comrades. He was pale, but resolute. I well remember the grim set of his jaw.

This fellow had been lagging a little behind his companions, and had come up in our rear, as we were facing back toward the hiding place. He had not seen me at all, as there were some bushes between us. His attention had been riveted on my comrades, who were in his plain view about ten yards away. He could have killed either of them at the first shot, unless I stopped him.

I spoke: "Are those your things in there on the ground?"

He was startled at finding himself suddenly at a disadvantage.

"No," he answered; "they belong to some fellows I'm with."

"Who are you?"

He flushed angrily, as though that were none of my business, but he gave me a name.

My companions heard us, and they came out of the thicket.

"What are you doing here?" demanded the detective sternly.

"Going fishing." The lad's answer was ready and defiant. Of course he was lying, and he knew that we knew it; but every mountaineer is schooled from boyhood to meet such an emergency as this. He knows, as well as any lawyer, upon which side the burden of proof rests.

He was put through a quiz that developed nothing. No doubt he and his party were on the way to some still-house, where they would stay until the "run" was made. But that was no affair of ours.

So we moved on. It looked as though we were to have some queer experiences in the Sugarlands, where the very first person we met drew a gun on us. Very well: this was "a sporting proposition."

Looking backward it seemed a long time since we had breakfasted. Our luncheon up in the Smokies had not counted for much. Canned meat and crackers are poor fuel for mountaineering.

The shades were deepening into twilight in this cleft between the cliffs. So we pressed eagerly on, to find some lodging place for the night, and a hot supper, God willing, to put strength into our weary limbs.

The lad with the shotgun had told us that the first house would be Old Man Warne's.*

We came to it in about half an hour. It was the usual log house of the backwoods, set in a small rocky clearing, against a background of towering wooded mountainside. Here, in the open space, daylight still lingered.

Through a gap opening southeastward we got our first long-range view of a bit of the country through which we had descended. More than three thousand feet above us rose those two sheer pinnacles of rock that they call the Chimneys. They protrude like tusks from the top of a ridge so narrow that a man can sit down astraddle it and toss a pebble a thousand feet down through the air. Yet such is the nature of rock and climate in this region that a cliff, wherever it is not quite vertical, will hold moisture and vegetation. So the Chimneys are

---

* Names here given to natives of the Sugarlands are invented. If I happen to use any that are real in that district, it is accidental. Names of localities are genuine throughout.

not bare, but clothed with little tough
shrubs and bracken, or with balsam and spruce
and rhododendron where the slopes will permit
their roots to grapple. (A photograph of the
summit of one of the Chimneys is shown in this
volume.)

To the northeast of us was a face of Bull-
head Mountain that was vertical, or even over-
hung; and here was naked rock, hundreds of
feet high, in which we could see the mouths of
small caves, like portholes in an old-fashioned
man-o'-war.

From Warne's yard came several hounds and
curs, bristling and bellowing the alarm. Immediately two or three men appeared, among
them a stout old fellow, red-faced, essaying to
smile, but evidently more anxious than pleased
at our sudden advent.

Katch did most of the talking for us. He
told the Warnes what men we were after, and
why, but did not give them our own names nor
credentials. I felt that this was a blunder. In
the mountains it is a stranger's first duty to tell
who he is, where he is from, and whom he
knows that might turn out to be a mutual acquaintance. Whosoever neglects or disdains to
give such information is likely to suffer for it.

Old Man Warne said at once that he had seen no one answering the description of our fugitives from justice. He was plainly nervous. He had instinctive doubts that we were telling him our real business. We had come into his neighborhood suddenly, as it were through the back door. We were armed. Mr. Quick's self-loading Winchester, at least, was conspicuous to everybody. Neither of us, I fancy, was reassuring as to "cut of jib." By this time we were a tough-looking bunch.

When strangers come to a mountain home, and have told who and what they are, then, if the owner likes their appearance, even a little bit, he will politely invite them in to rest. Mr. Warne did not invite us in; nay, he promptly directed us to the next house farther on.

We could fairly feel the flutter of the women and children, who remained indoors peeping out through cracks, and no doubt sighing with relief when we turned and went on down along the Little Pigeon.

Soon we came opposite another cabin, which stood on the far side of the stream from where the trail ran. It was set in a remarkable location.

In front was the wild torrent, now grown in

volume, that boiled and roared between large rocks. Two loose planks, end to end across three of the rocks, served as rude drawbridges spanning the chasm. The rocks were too far apart for a man to leap from one to the other, save at peril of falling stunned or broken into the brawling water, which immediately would sweep him away. With the planks withdrawn, the house would be secure from sudden frontal attack. Behind it rose the steep Sugarland Mountain, across which, as we were to learn on the morrow, there ran but a single difficult trail.

"A natural fortification," remarked Quick to me.

"Yes: let's call it The Castle."

Neither of us three adventurers knew any residents of the Sugarlands. Katch had been advised by someone to seek out a certain Jasper Fenn "who don't fool with liquor, and likely will tell you the truth."

When we came to where the trail broadened into a wagon road, and a footbridge crossed the stream, we knew we were near Fenn's home. Presently it was to be seen: a prosperous looking place, with a fenced front yard in which stood over a hundred bee-gums (hives made of cuts from hollow logs).

Photo by S. H. Essary
One of the Chimney Tops, Great Smoky Mountains.

"Looks more civilized," one of us remarked. "Here, surely, they will invite us in."

The usual challenge came from a dog. The master of the house appeared. Again Katch explained our business, and Quick reinforced him with details.

Mr. Fenn's expression changed from calm to perplexity, and then to embarrassment. He did not invite us in. He protested that he had neither seen nor heard anything of fugitive rogues from North Carolina, and we could plainly see that he did not want to mix in our business. It was also plain that he suspected we might be rogues ourselves, putting up a false story as a blind while nosing into the home affairs of Sugarland.

I happened to stand behind him, as he talked with my companions, and was whittling a groove around my walking-stick to shorten it. The groove completed, I tapped the end of the stick on the ground and snapped it off. Fenn jumped as if a gun had been cocked behind him, and wheeled around. A man so nervous as that may be either cowardly or dangerous. There are mighty few cowards in the mountains, and subsequent events proved that he was not one of them.

Night was fast coming on. We finally asked Fenn outright if he would let us have something to eat. He muttered an excuse, but consulted his wife. She did not welcome the suggestion, but said she could give us "a cold bite." And she did not even warm the coffee.

Now, I have had years of association with mountain people of every degree, and this was the first time I ever was made to feel unwelcome. But it was also the first time I had ever appeared among them as a man-hunter. And I will confess right here that, under the circumstances, I did not blame the Sugarlanders.

When we offered pay for our food the Fenns would not take a cent. They directed us to the next house, but made no suggestion as to where we might find lodging for the night.

We plodded on down the road in gathering darkness.

"Folks around here seem jumpy," I observed.

"Guess we won't get much out of them," said Katch.

"Not much information," answered Quick, "and it looks as if we'd have to bivouac under the clouds."

"It isn't us they're afraid of," I affirmed: "it's each other. When a man fleeing from North Carolina takes refuge in the Sugarlands, it's a cinch that he knows somebody here. He must make a living somehow. The natural occupation for him is blockading or whiskey-running. No doubt the Ruffs would be as welcome at that as anybody. Warne may not know them; Fenn may not know them; but some of their neighbors may be hiding or employing them right now. Hence the theorem: Don't tell anything about anybody, at any time, or you'll get in Dutch with your neighbors."

The next two miles were weary ones, and black night had fallen upon us by the time we came to a place where we thought it might be worth while to apply for shelter.

Dogs rushed at us with fangs glistening and hair on end. When the owner appeared there was the same old round of question and answer. We were not asked to stop for the night. This man, however, did not seem perturbed. He .was smooth and easy in manner; but his eyes betrayed secret amusement at our nightbound plight.

He hinted that a neighbor living back on the mountainside might know something to our advantage, if anybody did. So we stumbled on over the back fields, picking our way with our electric torches, and finally came to a shack not much bigger than a piano-box, or so it seemed in the gloom. Dogs, as usual. We helloed. A lamp was lighted within the house, and a man came out in his bare feet.

No: he knew nothing. But if our scalawags were anywhere in the country they would probably be at one of the lumber camps, several miles on the far side of Sugarland Mountain. A place for us to spend the night? Well, we might try Old Man Tuckett's; he kept visitors sometimes.

SCENE AT OLD MAN TUCKETT'S.

10 P. M.

Two narrow beds: Katch in one of them; a boy of the household in the other.

One wide bed: Quick and Kephart inspecting it. This bed has a trough in the center. Straw mattress underneath, feather mattress on top, quilts over all.

Kephart enters and tries to lie down on the far side. Feather mattress slides with him into trough.

Quick gets in on near side. Mattress slips and piles him on top of Kephart.

Sundry remarks. Each man grabs his edge of bed, wriggles toward it, and holds on.

10:10 P. M.

Slap. Scratch. "This damned hole is alive with fleas!"

4 A. M.

"Say, Quick, are you awake?"

"Haven't slept a wink all night."

"Neither have I; but 'man-hunting is the finest sport in the world.' "

"Shut up! You'll get 'a cold bite' for breakfast pretty soon."

He guessed wrong. We had things served piping hot on the table, soon after daylight: hot corn bread, hot coffee, and hot *groundhog*.

I'll wager my flint and steel and tinder-box that the groundhog's ghost danced a joyful jig around that breakfast table. They're all in cahoot, in Sugarland.

Out again on the road, we turned back along our previous day's line of march, and went to a house set in a field. No one was at home but an old lady. She was a motherly looking soul, neat, handsome, and with gracious manner. But the moment we announced our mission she fell into a fidget of fear. She tried bravely to smile, but her mouth twisted awry. Her clasped hands trembled, and her fingers wove in and out like a bashful schoolgirl's.

I pitied her. She dared not tell anything at all—though evidently knowing nothing useful to us—dared not say more than yes or no, lest she should get in wrong with her neighbors.

Poor soul! she had to live here. I was ashamed of myself for bothering her, and so were the other men. We said little, and passed on.

Then we met a man coming with eager announcement in his eyes. He was one we had noticed the day before. He said that a lumberjack, passing in the night, had told him of a fellow who matched our description of Jake Ruff, and who was dodging. He had been recently seen at Barradale's upper logging camp on Rough Creek.

Yet when our informant was through with this, his manner suddenly changed. He lifted his hand as though taking an oath, his eyes flashed, and he fairly trembled with earnestness as he exclaimed: "Now, men, if you ever breathe who it was told you this, I'll follow you to your graves or I'll kill you!"

I was astounded at the folly of such a threat. Here we stood, three armed men confronting him, and he knew that one of us was a Federal officer, with the whole power of the Government backing him. And yet, if we should tell where we got this information, he swore to our faces that he would follow us up and kill us, though it should take a lifetime for him to do it.

You who read these lines may scoff and say

that the man was bluffing. I who write them know that he meant just what he said. His conduct in other affairs, that have nothing to do with this story, amply proved the man's character and nerve.

Rough Creek is a branch of Little River, west of Sugarland Mountain, and it drains that dismal gulf which, you may remember, I had called Godforsaken. To get there we had to go back upstream along the Little Pigeon to the place we called The Castle, cross over, and follow a trail, a mere footpath, that marks a long diagonal up the side of the steep ridge. For Sugarland Mountain is, in fact, a "razorback" ridge, rising 1,500 feet above its corresponding valley, and running for about eight miles down from the Smoky divide, without a single gap along the crest. It forms a rampart tedious to scale from either side.

The top of the ridge, where we crossed it, is only five feet wide. The descent is as steep on the other side, but, instead of thick woods it is mostly burnt-over ground, grown up in fire-cherry, except where the evergreen laurel had shielded it. We were well winded by the time we reached a cabin at the foot of the trail.

We followed an old logging road about a mile and a half up Rough Creek to Barradale's camp. This camp was a new location, with flume, portable mill and cook-house just finished, and shacks under construction.

I introduced my companions to Barradale, whom I happened to know, and told him what we were after. He said that the description of Jake might fit some one of his hands: we could see when the men came in to dinner.

Soon they began to arrive. Down below us, about a hundred and fifty yards, I espied a fellow from the Carolina side who was also a bond-jumper and for whom Quick had a warrant. We watched him giving a hand at some odd job, but let him alone for the present lest our more important quarry should take alarm. Presently he saw us, straightened up for an instant, and then plunged into the laurel and was gone.

The cookee banged his poker on a piece of iron swung from a string, to call all hands to dinner. The word got about that we were hunting somebody. Several of the men became nervous, having unpleasant pasts of their own, no doubt. Some were mean looking, some sullen, some indifferent, many joyful at the prospect of a row.

We took places with them at the long table. There were grins back and forth, and scowls,

but the crew ate in a silence that fairly gave one
the creeps. It seemed ominous of trouble all
around. And that is what might have happened if an arrest had been tried in their presence. One never can tell, in one of these mountain lumber camps. But it may have been only
a regulation. In some camps all unnecessary
talk at meals is prohibited. I asked a woods-
boss, once upon a time, why the men were
treated so, like convicts. He answered:

"If you had to run a hell-roarin' bunch like
mine, you'd know why. Their idea of conversation is an argument; their idea of argument
is a rumpus. I can't afford that where there's
two hundred dollars' worth of crockery lyin'
handy."

But nothing developed at our dinner. All
the men were in, and not a Ruff among them.
The suspect proved to be another man from
Lufty, also dodging, but not our Jake at all.

We left the camp and started back toward the
Sugarlands, disappointed and silent. It was
hard to have come so far and done all that
work for nothing. Quick asked me: "How
do you like the sport of man-hunting?"

"Bully; for a chap who is bone-weary, flea-
bitten and groundhog-fed."

"Do you always win at any other game?"

234 OUR SOUTHERN HIGHLANDERS

"Who would play if he did?"

At the foot of the mountain, where our trail met the road, there was a shack, and here we made inquiry once more. The man and his wife assured us that two young strangers and an old one had passed them hurriedly on the way to the works on Fish Camp Prong, three miles below.

It was a slender chance; but Quick and Katch decided to follow it, if I would return to the Sugarlands and make arrangements for lodging. And so we parted.

I climbed the mountain and rested a bit on the narrow top. Starting to descend, I stepped far down on a mossy stone that slipped and threw me. In regaining balance I wrenched my right knee. It began to puff up immediately, and I found that I could not walk downhill, but had to hobble sidewise with the help of a staff.

It took me two hours to reach the bottom of the ridge. I stripped partially and bathed my game leg in the cold water of the torrent. Then painfully I made my way to Jasper Fenn's. He saw me at a distance and came to meet me at the gate. I told him of our ill luck, and he invited me to come in and rest on the porch.

We chatted there in the grateful sunlight.

And then something happened that amused me so much that I will tell it here, trusting the reader not to think it is mere vanity that makes me print it.

In order to win Fenn's confidence in my reliability, to the extent of getting lodging for myself and friends, I told him of some of my early adventures in the Hazel Creek country. It so chanced that I mentioned, among my old neighbors, Quill Rose (this is a real name), who had been famous for half a century, in western Carolina, as a blockader and an original genius. To me, Quill was always a humorous character, despite his undoubted handiness as a gun-fighter. And I told a funny story or two about my acquaintance with him.

Fenn exclaimed: "Quill Rose! Why, I saw a picture of him and his wife and two of Jake Rose's daughters, one time, in a book."

"Where did you get the book?"

"Some furrin women came in here and started a settlement-house. They had the book, and they borried it to us to read. It was called *Our Southern Highlanders.*"

"How did you like it?"

"Fine. Did you ever see it?"

"I wrote it."

Fenn's eyes nearly popped out of his head.

For a moment he was dumbfounded. Then he seized me by the arm and half dragged, half carried me, crippled as I was, back to the kitchen, crying to his wife: "Mary—Mary— here's the man who wrote *that book!*" *

From that moment all suspicion was banished. I was welcome: so were my friends. And Mary proved herself a most excellent cook. There was no more "cold bite." The feast that evening will always be a joy to remember.

By an hour after dark I gave up expecting Quick and Katch. They had only one electric torch, and I knew that its battery was about played out. As my leg was quite stiff and painful, I went early to bed. Two or three hours later I was aroused by my comrades' helloes and Fenn's welcome at the door. They had found their way back through the darkness, after all, but were empty-handed, and exhausted by the hard day's tramp.

Next morning I tried to take up the trail on our return journey, but it was too much for the game leg. My companions hired a mule for me to ride, and a boy to bring it back.

It turned out that the three Ruffs had not

* An old edition of the present volume. The native mountaineers often refer to it simply as "that book."

been in the Sugarlands. The tip that Katch had been given was false. But all three of them were captured, not long afterward, on the Carolina side. So Katch did not lose either his five hundred dollars or his better half.

Some time after our little raid, a tragedy occurred at Jasper Fenn's. One of his neighbors came armed to Fenn's home and called him out, accusing Fenn, I am told, of having done something unethical according to blockaders' standard. Fenn shot him dead from the porch. A trial resulted in acquittal, on the ground of self-defence.

CHAPTER XI

THE KILLING OF HOL ROSE

AMONG the boarders at the old Cooper House, in my time, there have been some interesting characters. One of them was a United States deputy marshal, suave, dignified, a keen judge of human nature, who had the knack of arresting men without trouble. There was something in his look and manner that soothed wild fellows instead of infuriating them. He would say:

"Jim, I have a paper to serve on you. I'm sorry; but of course it has to be done. Now if you'll come along quietly, and behave, I'll treat you like a gentleman. I don't want to put handcuffs on such a man as you."

The average hill-billy, when he is at all sober, respects such treatment and will go along without any fuss.

One day this officer, returning from a tour of duty, came to me and said: "Kep, I had to serve a paper on one of your kinsfolk, down on Hanging Dog, last week."

"The deuce you did! I didn't know I had any relatives in North Carolina."

"Well, they spell the name just as you do and pronounce it the same way."

"What kind of people are they?"

He answered mischievously: "Nicest kind of people: they make *good* liquor."

"Well, Charlie, if you find any of my kinsfolk making bad liquor, just hang them, with my compliments; but when they're making pure double-distilled corn, I want you to treat them right."

"I did. I told the old man that I wouldn't arrest him at all if he'd give me his word to appear before the United States Commissioner at two o'clock the next Wednesday; and he said 'All right.' "

"Very considerate. Did he show up?"

"Sure, he showed up, punctual to the minute, and he made bond. Then he invited me to come and stay with him any time I'm down there. We're the best of friends."

This was eight or nine years ago, when moonshining was only an offence against the internal revenue law—a form of tax-dodging—and trading in this contraband liquor was a sort of smuggling. So long as the conspirators were not caught, their conscience was as serene as that of the lady of fashion who smuggles jewels past the customs officers when arriving from Europe. And, in fact, their offence was virtually the same as hers.

Old-time blockaders of this sort were shown a good deal of consideration by the better class of federal officials, who made allowance for environment and tradition. When a man, otherwise of good repute, was haled before a court in spring or summer, for illicit distilling, and it was found that he had no one left at home to look after the farm, it was customary for the judge to parole him until the following winter, so that he could go back and make his crop. This being done, and his family provided for, the man would return without escort, give himself up, and serve his term.

Still, even in the old days, there always were some moonshiners in the mountains who had to be handled with severity, if they were caught at all. They were not amateurs, but professionals. Among them were some desperadoes, men already stained with blood and reckless or ruthless about shedding more.

It was among such a class that Hol Rose spent a part of his young manhood. By nature and by training, Rose was something of a bravo. He had to be such, so long as he mixed

Photo by Kyle Jenkins

A Hunter's Cabin.

with the wild crew who made a lifelong business of blockading. I do not mean that he was particularly quarrelsome or underhanded; but he had the mountaineer's pride of "nerve" developed to the point of arrogance, and that was sure, sooner or later, to strike a spark of fierce resentment in someone of temper similar to his own. In the mountains they do not settle such affairs with fist fights, but with knives or pistols.

Hol told me himself that he had killed two men in Georgia, but I have forgotten how he said the fracas arose. He said he "had it to do."

Later in life, Hol settled down, quit drinking, and made a fair name for himself. He seemed to have an ambition to aid in law enforcement, and was appointed deputy sheriff in our county.

It was at this time that I became acquainted with him. He boarded for a while at the Cooper House, and we saw a good deal of each other. Among his friends he was a jolly fellow, fond of chaffing, and yet with a certain reserve that impressed one as a dead-line.

As soon as he became an officer, Rose displayed more than usual activity in running down offenders. He would take more trouble, and run greater risks, than the average county officer. Man-hunting, for him, was a sport: he thoroughly enjoyed it.

One day he went after a man who, so he told me, had sworn to resist arrest, and who was known to be a powerful fellow with plenty of nerve. Rose testified in court, when the case came up for trial, that when he started to read his warrant the man slapped him in the face and ran away; that he ran in pursuit of the fugitive, fell, and his gun was accidentally discharged. Anyway, the aforesaid runaway is now minus a leg. Rose lost his job as deputy for having displayed excessive zeal.

In various cities that I have lived in it is a common practice for policemen to shoot at men who try to run away from them, and I never knew of one of them being disciplined for having done so. But here, in the mountains, the law and the custom are that an officer must catch his man by running him down, if he can; he must not shoot unless dangerous resistance is offered.

After the passage of the Volstead Act, Rose was appointed deputy prohibition enforcement officer in our county. He at once began to display an ambition to make a record for vigorous enforcement, and he lived up to it. He made many raids, captured many stills, arrested block-

aders and bootleggers and anybody that he
found with even a flask of liquor in his possession. He went beyond the limit of his authority in doing so.

He used to ask me sometimes to help him
with his official reports, as he had no typewriter
and the papers had to be made out in duplicate.
He kept a pocket diary, and from it he filled in
the reports, stating for every day in the month
just where he was, how many miles he traveled,
and what he did in an official way.   From this
I know how active the man was, and to what
pains he went to carry the law unto the lawless.

It is not my intention to praise nor to criti-
cize, but simply to narrate facts.   It is a fact
that Rose's methods in searching and seizing
were, in some cases, considered high-handed by
a large part of the community.   It was common
talk that he searched men or their belongings,
not only without warrant, but with an over-
bearing manner that was bound to excite bitter
feeling and resentment.   It was common to hear
men say to each other: "It wouldn't surprise
me, any day, to hear that Hol Rose had been
killed."

I had been hearing a good deal of gossip
about him and the risks he ran, and, knowing it
to be mainly true, I spoke to him about it one

day when he came in for help with his report.

"Hol," said I, "don't you know that it is illegal for you to make searches and seizures without a warrant?"

"No, it isn't," he replied.

"Did you ever read the Constitution of the United States?"

"No; but I'm ordered to do these things, and I'll obey orders."

"One of these days some fellow is going to plug you for it."

"Well, if he does, it will be from behind or from the bushes."

There was something in the tone of his voice, and his downcast, thoughtful face, that pierced my heart. It was the voice and the manner of one confronting death, and realizing it, but game to die with his boots on, face to the front.

A few weeks later—it was on the 25th of October, 1920—as I was going for the afternoon mail, a neighbor asked me: "Have you heard of the killing?"

"No. Who?"

"Babe Burnett has killed Hol Rose, over on Brush Creek. Charlie Beck, who was with Rose, has 'phoned in to the sheriff. Reed, at Asheville, has been notified, and he has called out all his men in this district. He is coming himself, with Lyerly's bloodhounds."

The first of the federal officers came in on the 7 o'clock train from Dillsboro. I was invited to go out in his car, with three others. It is eighteen miles from our town, Bryson, the county seat, to Burnett's farm on Brush Creek. There is a good road most of the way, though it has several hairpin curves along the edge of precipices. We made fast time for a while.

My thoughts went back to the previous week, when "Babe" Burnett had been in to the county fair and had stayed at the Cooper House. He complained that although he had a good orchard the apples were going to waste because it would not pay to haul them to market.

Burnett was a man of about 60 years, tall, spare-built, dark, wrinkled, with determined expression and quick nervous movements, a vigorous talker, with snapping eyes.

There was record that, about five years before, he had an altercation with a mail-carrier, whom he assaulted and left for dead. He escaped to Canada and thence to the State of Washington, but returned to his old home here about three years later. He told us that he was dissatisfied and wanted to sell his farm and move west again.

I thought of him now: a wild-eyed fugitive among the rocks and thickets, slipping about with gun in hand, prepared to sell his life dearly if his hiding place were found. I thought of his anguished wife, alone in her desolated home, with a murdered man lying in her dooryard, and an armed posse with blood-hounds coming to take her husband dead or alive.

And I thought of Hol Rose: yesterday a mountain cavalier, handsome, well groomed, debonair, proud of his daring, vain of his record as a hunter of men; but to-night lying stark and stained in his own blood, done forever with his gallantries and his ambitions.

The men beside me had their minds on the work ahead. The deputy marshal on my right, leaning forward on his high-power rifle, exclaimed: "I'd rather do this than anything else I ever did in my life."

And the local officer on my left smiled back, with a glint in his eye, as though to say: "You're right, comrade; man-hunting is the finest sport in the world."

I could appreciate their feeling. It was as though one's hunting companion had been killed by a wild beast, and it was up to his partners to stalk and slay it; except that a mur-

derous man is more cunning and more dangerous than any beast, and so the stimulus to battle
is greater.

But my mind went back again to that forlorn
woman on the mountain, and her desperate
broken heart. In the face of such tragedy it
would be sacrilege to speak of sport.

We came finally to a rough and narrow by-
road, up which we had to turn, driving the big
car carefully, feeling our way around the twists
and among the rocks. A couple of miles
further we discovered the cars of the sheriff's
posse, and a rude little sled such as highlanders
use where wheeled vehicles cannot go. Around
the sled was clustered the group of men, con-
versing solemnly in low tones.

Rose's body had just been brought down off
the mountain on this sled, and there it lay, face
up, the hands bound together so they would not
dangle in going over the rocky ground. The
face was calm and unmarred. On Hol's breast
there was a group of shot-holes, centered over
the heart, and tinged with red.

Charlie Beck was there: he who had been
Rose's companion on the raid. Charlie was a
veteran of the Philippines, where he had been
captured by savages and held prisoner for a
month in the wilds of the interior. Of late

years, here at home, he had often been employed as deputy by local or federal authorities when "bad men" were to be taken.

Beck told us that Rose had asked him, this morning, to go along on a raid after blockade stills. He had answered: "Wait a bit; I have only eight cartridges." Rose said that would be plenty, as he did not expect any trouble. Rose himself was in the habit of carrying a shotgun when he thought there was danger of resistance, and Beck, at such time, would take his Winchester rifle; but this time they set forth with nothing but their side arms.

They traveled southward among the Alarka Mountains to the home of Burnett, where Rose suspected there was some distilling going on. Here they found two barrels of apple pomace in a state of fermentation. Burnett said he was intending to make vinegar out of the pomace. Rose told him it was against the law to make vinegar in that way, as there was alcohol in the pomace. Rose and Beck, at Burnett's direction, went over to the orchard and found five other barrels of pomace, and near by found a "still place" with fresh ashes in the furnace, but no still. When they returned to the house, having destroyed the pomace, Burnett had gone away.

The officers then went to other farms in the neighborhood and did some searching without result. In the afternoon they returned to Burnett's home, to arrest him. They found him at his crib unloading corn fodder. When Burnett saw them he started to run away. The officers threw off their coats, drew their pistols, and charged after Burnett, calling on him to halt.

As they ran around the corner of the barn, Rose being in the lead, a shot was fired from a strawstack about twenty paces away. Beck said he could not see the man who fired it, as the fellow was behind the stack, or hugging close to its side, but he saw the straw blown aside by the blast of the gun.

He heard Rose cry out: "Babe, you have killed me!" Then, in a moment: "I believe I'm rallying." A few seconds later Beck, who by this time had advanced a little ahead of Rose, was half deafened by a pistol-shot close to his ear. Turning quickly, he saw Rose sagging down with his pistol pointing upward. Hol evidently had fired wild in his death struggle. He expired in two or three minutes.

Meantime Beck had plenty to occupy him. He expected to be fired at himself, by the man behind the strawstack, or by others, for there might be several of them in ambush. He watched for a head to appear from behind the strawstack.

It developed, however, that Burnett, immediately after firing, had run along a gully straight away from the strawstack, and Beck did not see him until he emerged, about seventy yards away, running through bushes as high as his waist. Beck fired his eight cartridges at the man, but he told us he did not think he hit him, as he had only an army pistol. He told me: "If I had had my rifle, I could have hit him."

He said that Mrs. Burnett protested: "He didn't do it," meaning her husband; and "I didn't see anything." Beck replied: "If you'll come and look at this man lying dead here, you'll see something."

Beck then went about the neighborhood trying to get someone to go to the nearest telephone and call up the sheriff. But no one would stir. Everybody wanted to keep out of the mess—to keep from being a witness in court. So Beck had to go himself, leaving his comrade where he had fallen. The first telephones that he tried were not working, and he had to walk seven miles before he found one that was in order. Then he returned alone to the Burnett house, which was now deserted, and he waited there through the long hours until the sheriff arrived.

Anyone who knows these mountains, and the character of moonshine bands, will understand that there was no sport in that tired man's lonely vigil. It took grit; but the strain must have been anything but pleasant.

That night, in the mountain glen, Rose's body was transferred to a motor truck, and most of us came back with it, arriving in town about midnight. Several officers accompanied Charlie Beck back to the Burnett house and waited there for the reinforcements they knew were on the way.

At 3 o'clock in the morning I was awakened by the deep bellow of bloodhounds. These animals are silent when trailing (unlike foxhounds or deerhounds), but they exercise their throats sometimes when idle or when being transported. Reed's men from Asheville were passing in their car, on the way to Brush Creek, carrying the two dogs with them.

The animals took up the trail at Burnett's and followed it straight to the home of a neighbor, three-quarters of a mile away. The neighbor's wife said that Burnett had come there wounded in the leg by a gunshot. She had dressed the wound with turpentine and bound it up to staunch the blood. It is not unlikely that some of the turpentine found its way to Burnett's feet. That would account for the failure of the dogs to trace the man beyond this house.

(Burnett told me afterwards that when the officers came near his hiding place he slipped out, circled, came in behind them, and followed after them till they gave up the chase. It was the safest place for him to be.)

Rose was buried by his lodge in the little cemetery on a hilltop overlooking our town.

Burnett slipped away to an adjoining county, where he had friends who would succor him and get him in secret communication with attorneys. So he stayed out all winter, and until May of the following year. Then, acting on advice of counsel, he came in to our town and gave himself up to the sheriff. He was put in jail to await trial in July. While he was there, other prisoners on two occasions broke jail and escaped, but he refused to accompany them.

Outsiders may wonder why the mountain moonshiners, as a rule, do not stay away for good and all, once they have escaped from officers; especially those charged with a serious felony, such as murder. Generally they come back sometime and stand trial. One reason is that most of them are freeholders, and they come back to get their property out of the clutches of the law. Another reason is that murder, unless plainly of the first degree, is an offence that is apt to be treated very leniently in mountain courts.

*   *   *   *   *

Meantime, in the old Cooper House, there was developing an extraordinary romance. Two of Burnett's sons came on from Idaho, soon after the old man got into his trouble. One of them, Verlin, stayed on, and appeared to be in communication with his father, who was still hiding out. He boarded off and on, at the Cooper House.

Our cook was Ima Rose, daughter of Hol Rose, well named and blooming. Truth to tell, she was one of the prettiest mountain girls of the buxom type that I ever saw.

Verlin Burnett was a dashing ex-marine.

The whole countryside wondered what would happen when these two young and vital representatives of the hostile clans had to meet daily under the same roof.

What did happen was so unexpected that it made everybody gasp. Verlin and Ima fell in love with each other. Their passion was reckless. They went abroad together.

One of Ima's cousins, a man with "a record," came to town and (so I was credibly informed) bluntly told Verlin that he would kill him if he did not stop going with Ima.

But the young folks merely stopped promenading and took to automobiling. Ima tried to learn how to drive the car. She sped round a corner, knocked two wheels off a car parked opposite our hotel, ricochetted across the street, hit our telephone pole, broke it short off at the butt, and alighted from her battered car smiling and unhurt.

Next day the loving couple eloped. My suitcase disappeared at the same time (I'll be hanged if I ever taught it such tricks). Within a few days we learned that Verlin and Ima were married in another county. Sometime later they were reported to have been seen back in the Alarka Mountains, both of them carrying guns.

Weeks later, when I opened my bedroom door one morning, there stood my runaway suitcase. I picked it up angrily and shook it; but no, it didn't glug.

Imagine my predicament if it had glugged! There was no scrap of paper, no sign whatever, to prove in whose company that vagabond suitcase had been roaming since last I saw it. And suppose I had found inside it, let me say, three half-gallon fruit jars full of white corn liquor. What should I have done?

Under our present law, if I kept that gallon and a half of illicit spirits, I would be guilty of "retailing," even though I did nothing at all with it.

If I carried it out to pour it into the river, and was intercepted, I would be guilty of "transporting."

For either of these crimes I could be sent to the chain-gang.

There was one thing I might lawfully do, in such a case: I might stand there in my tracks and drink every drop of that liquor, and the law could do nothing at all to me. But I am physically restrained from that: my belly is too small and my head too weak.

But I might report the matter to the sheriff. Yes: in my case it would be safe to do so; for I have never made nor sold liquor. Just one little query enters here (bad little query, shameful query, but it will come in), namely: What would become of that liquor if I turned it over to the authorities?

You may try in vain, in our town (where no liquor can be obtained on medical prescription, not even to save a life), you will try in vain to get a few ounces of whiskey for a sick person, from all that is confiscated and stored in jail. What ever does become of the gallons and gallons of that stuff? Nobody seems to know, though everybody thinks he "as good as knows." Should I encourage such practices? O fie, O foh, O fum!

* * * * *

Since Rose was a federal officer, killed in (presumably) the line of duty, a layman might expect that Burnett would be tried for murder in a federal court. But federal courts have no jurisdiction in murder cases, since the United States, in their national capacity, have no common law. Consequently Burnett had to be tried in a state court.

On the morning of July 28th, 1921, in our court house, was opened the case of State of North Carolina *vs.* J. E. ("Babe") Burnett, charged with the murder of James Holland Rose, F. P. A.

The Grand Jury twice refused to send in a true bill; but, under pressure from the Court, finally returned one. A jury was secured next day, and the case proceeded to trial.

Charlie Beck was the only eye-witness for the State. His testimony was substantially what he

Splitting Clapboards.

told us on the night after the killing, with certain additions brought out by examination.
Being asked if Rose carried a warrant for the
arrest of Burnett, he replied: "If he did, I
didn't know it."

"Did you have a warrant yourself?"

"No."

"When you were shooting at Burnett, after
Rose was killed, did you try to kill him?"

"Yes, I tried to kill him."

"Why did you try to kill Burnett when you
had no warrant for him?"

"Because he had killed my friend."

Counsel for the defence tried repeatedly to
inject into the evidence the question of the right
of the officers to search the premises of Burnett, and to arrest him, without a proper warrant. The State attempted to show that Rose
did have a warrant, but this effort completely
broke down.

Burnett took the stand in his own defence.
He admitted that he had intended to make
brandy of his surplus apples, but said that someone stole his still. Then, to keep his fruit from
going to waste, he had prepared to use the pomace of crushed apples for making vinegar, not
knowing that he was violating any law in doing
this.

He said that he found the officers at his house in the morning when he was returning from work in the field; that Rose said: "I am a revenue officer and am hunting your whiskey"; that neither of the officers showed any warrant; that he voluntarily assisted them in searching the premises, and even directed them to some barrels of apple pomace in the orchard that were near an old still furnace that he had repaired. The officers found the still place but did not thereupon arrest him, but went away.

Burnett swore that when the officers went out into the orchard he went to drive his cattle up on the mountain to keep them off his crops, which were not under fence, as was his custom, and that he did not leave with any purpose of flight. When he returned, Rose and Beck had gone somewhere, and he ate his dinner and then went to hauling up his corn fodder.

He testified that he was at the crib unloading the fodder when Rose and his assistant came the second time; that they charged him with pistols drawn; that he ran toward and around the barn, the officers pursuing him; that Rose fired one shot at him, hitting him in the leg; that he fell over the bars at the end of the barn near the strawstack, where he had left his shotgun in the morning when he had returned from a squirrel

hunt; that Rose was still pointing his pistol at
him, and that Beck also had a pistol drawn; and
that he then seized his gun and fired at Rose,
as the only thing he could do to save himself.

He swore that he at no time saw any warrant
or heard any claim of one; that he heard no call
to halt, and did not hear either of the men speak
during the occurrence; that after he fired, he
continued his flight, and that he was shot at
several times by Beck until he passed out of
view.

Mrs. Burnett testified that one of the men
fired at her husband as he went toward the barn
from the crib; that she did not hear them make
any call to her husband, but that they were advancing toward him with their pistols out.

These were the high spots of the trial. The
rest was mostly the usual drone of court proce-
dure.

The State in its arguments insisted that Burnett was guilty of murder in the first degree, the
fact that he had his gun at the strawstack, and
that he ran toward it at the approach of the
officers, and killed Rose as soon as he had secured the gun, showing premeditation; that in
the act of secreting the gun and shooting from
behind the stack, Burnett was making a secret

assault upon the officers, and that therefore he could not claim self-defence; that the officers were using no more force than was necessary in making the arrest; that, at the time of the killing, the Lever Act was in force (a war-time anti-profiteering and food-conservation statute) which made it a felony to ferment fruits or grains; and that the officers found evidence that such a felony had been committed, and that therefore they had a right to arrest without warrant.

The defence claimed that the officers had no warrant for the arrest of Burnett; that the Lever Act was discredited by having been subsequently declared unconstitutional; that Rose had the reputation of being a violent and dangerous man; that the officers were engaged in an unlawful assault upon Burnett, and that he, fearing for his life, had a right to shoot.

The Judge, in his charge to the jury, instructed them that the Lever Act was in effect at the time of the killing, and that under its provisions the officers did have a right to arrest Burnett without a warrant.

The jury at first stood for acquittal, by a large majority; but on the third day of the trial it returned a verdict of murder in the second degree. The Judge sentenced Burnett to serve twelve years in the state prison at hard labor.

An appeal was taken. The Supreme Court of North Carolina, at the fall term of 1921, ruled that Rose was not charged with the duty of enforcing the Lever Act, nor clothed with the power incident to such enforcement; but that he was a prohibition officer charged only with the duties of enforcing the National Prohibition Act and the Harrison Narcotic Act, under which the unlawful distillation of spirits for the first offence is only a misdemeanor, and that Rose had no power of arrest without warrant unless he found the person or persons charged "in the act of operating an illicit distillery"; further, that from all the testimony in this case it appeared that the prisoner, at the time of the attempted arrest, was not engaged in operating an illicit distillery, but was at his corn crib, on his own premises, unloading fodder, and consequently was not liable to arrest without a warrant. On these facts the Supreme Court remanded the case for a new trial.

At his second trial in our Superior Court, Burnett was acquitted. He was immediately re-arrested by federal officers, and, at the time of this writing, is under bond for appearance at

the next Federal Court for trial on the charge
of assaulting a government officer: the same offence under a different name.

There is a principle involved in this case that
is of more importance than the guilt or inno-
cence of the man accused. It is the principle
that officers, and courts as well, should themselves respect the supreme law of the land.

Hol Rose lost his life in trying to make an
illegal arrest. He did not know that it was illegal—he was no lawyer, only an enforcement
agent who depended upon his superiors to de-
fine his duties and powers. Once when he had
been warned, in a friendly way, that he had no
right to search, seize, or make an arrest, without
a warrant, except where a particular felony was
being committed, he had answered in all seriousness: "I am ordered to do it, and I will obey
orders." In that case, he was the victim, not
merely of his own impulsiveness, but of unlawful instructions issued to him by someone higher
up.

The United States Supreme Court has repeatedly ruled that no federal officer has a right
to make searches and seizures without due process of law, as defined in the 4th amendment to
the Constitution. It has been obliged to do this
more than once because inferior courts have

shown a tendency to ignore the fundamental rights of citizens in this respect. So, in one of its recent decisions (Gouled *vs.* U. S., Feb. 28, 1921) the Supreme Court has felt it necessary to restate the law in stern and unmistakable terms.—

"It would not be possible to add to the emphasis with which the framers of our Constitution and this Court [cases cited] have declared the importance to political liberty and to the welfare of our country of the due observance of the rights guaranteed under the Constitution by these two amendments [4th and 5th]. The effect of the decisions cited is:

"That such rights are declared to be indispensable to the 'full enjoyment of personal security, personal liberty and private property;' that they are to be regarded as of the very essence of constitutional liberty; and that the guaranty of them is as important and as imperative as are the guaranties of the other fundamental rights of the individual citizen—the right to trial by jury, to the writ of habeas corpus, and to due process of law.

"It has been repeatedly decided that these amendments should receive a liberal construction, *so as to prevent stealthy encroachment upon or 'gradual depreciation' of the rights secured by them, by imperceptible practice of courts, or by well-intentioned but mistakenly over-zealous executive officers.*"

There is a lesson here for our citizenry at large. Zealots injure their own cause by their own excesses. In numerous cases the provisions of the 18th amendment to the Constitution have

264 OUR SOUTHERN HIGHLANDERS

been enforced by systematically violating other, and more fundamental, parts of the same Constitution. That is a dangerous thing to do; for nothing is so provocative of lawlessness as the policy of an administration or a ruling class to "do evil, that good may come."

CHAPTER XII

THE OUTLANDER AND THE NATIVE

AMONG the many letters that come to me from men who think of touring or camping in Highland Dixie there are few but ask, " How are strangers treated? "

This question, natural and prudent though it be, never fails to make me smile, for I know so well the thoughts that lie back of it: " Suppose one should blunder innocently upon a moonshine still—what would happen? If a feud were raging in the land, how would a stranger fare? If one goes alone into the mountains, does he run any risk of being robbed? "

Before I left the tame West and came into this wild East, I would have asked a few questions myself, if I had known anyone to answer them. As it was, I turned up rather abruptly in a backwoods settlement where the " furriner " was more than a nine-days wonder. I bore no credentials; and it was quite as well. If I had presented a letter from some clergyman or from the President of the United States it would have been—just what I was myself—a curiosity: as when the puppy discovers some weird and marvelous new bug.

Everyone greeted me politely but with unfeigned interest. I was welcome to sup and bed wherever I went. Moonshiners and man-slayers were as affable as common folks. I dwelt alone for a long time, first in open camp, afterwards in a secluded hut. Then I boarded with a native family. Often I left my belongings to look out for themselves whilst I went away on expeditions of days or weeks at a time. And nobody ever stole from me so much as a fish-hook or a brass cartridge. So, in the retrospect, I smile.

Does this mean, then, that Poe's characterization of the mountaineers is out of date? Not at all. They are the same " fierce and uncouth race of men " to-day that they were in his time. Homicide is so prevalent in the districts that I personally am acquainted with that nearly every adult citizen has been directly interested in some murder case, either as principal, officer, witness, kinsman, or friend.

This grewsome subject I shall treat elsewhere, in detail. It is introduced here only to emphasize a fact pertinent to the present topic, namely: that the private wars of the highlanders are limited to their own people.

And here is another significant fact: as regards personal property I do not know any race in the world that is more honest than our backwoodsmen of the southern mountains. As soon as you leave the railroad you enter a land where sneak-thieves are rare and burglars almost unheard of. In my own country and all those adjoining it there has been only one case of highway robbery and only one of murder for money, so far as I can learn, in the past *forty* years.

The mountain code of conduct is a curious mixture of savagery and civility. One man will kill another over a pig or a panel of fence (not for the property's sake, but because of hot words ensuing) and he will "come clear" in court because every fellow on the jury feels he would have done the same thing himself under similar provocation; yet these very men, vengeful and cruel though they are, regard hospitality as a sacred duty toward wayfarers of any degree, and the bare idea of stealing from a stranger would excite their instant loathing or white-hot scorn.

There are some "dark corners" of the mountains, mostly on or near state boundary lines, where there are bands of desperadoes who defy the law. But elsewhere anyone of tact and common sense can go as he pleases through Appalachia without being molested. Tact, however, implies the will and the insight to put yourself truly in the other man's place. Imagine yourself born, bred, circumstanced like him. It implies, also, the courtesy of doing as you would be done by if you were in that fellow's shoes. No arrogance, no condescension, but man to man on a footing of equal manliness.

And there are "manners" in the rudest community: customs and rules of conduct that it is well to learn before one goes far afield. For example, when you stop at a mountain cabin, if no dogs sound an alarm, do not walk up to the door and knock. You are expected to call out *Hello!* until someone comes to inspect you. None but the most intimate neighbors neglect this usage, and there is mighty good reason back of it in a land where the path to one's door may be a warpath.

If you are armed, as a hunter, do not fail to remove the cartridges from the gun, in your host's presence, before you set foot on his porch. Then give him the weapon or stand it in a corner or hang it up in plain view. Even our sheriff, when he stopped with us, would lay his revolver on the mantel-shelf and leave it there until he went his way. If you think a moment you can see the courtesy of such an act. It proves that the guest puts implicit trust in the honor of his host and in his ability to protect all within his house. There never has been a case in which such trust was violated.

I knew a traveler who, spending the night in a one-room cabin, was fool enough (I can use no milder term) to thrust a loaded revolver under his pillow when he went to bed. In the morning his weapon was still there, but empty, and its cartridges lay conspicuously on a table across the room. Nobody said a word about the incident: the hint was left to soak in.

The only real danger that one may encounter from the native people, so long as he behaves himself, is when he comes upon a man who is wild with liquor and cannot sidestep him. In such case, give him the glad word and move on at once. I have had a drunken "ball-hooter" (log-roller) from the lumber camps fire five shots around my head as a *feu-de-joie*, and then stand tantalizingly, with hammer cocked over the sixth cartridge, to see what I would do about it. As it chanced, I did not mind his fireworks, for my head was a-swim with the rising fever of erysipelas and I had come dragging my heels many an irk mile down from the mountains to find a doctor. So I merely smiled at the fellow and asked if he was having a good time. He grinned sheepishly and let me pass unharmed.

The chief drawback to travel in this region, aside from the roads, is not the character of the people, but the quality of bed and board. Of course there are good hotels at most of the summer resorts, but these are few and scattering, at present, for a territory so immense. In mos' regions where there is noble scenery, unspoiled forest, and good fishing, the accommodations are extremely rude. Many of the village inns are dirty, and their tables a shock and a despair to the hungry pilgrim. There are blessed exceptions, to be sure, but on the other hand the traveler sometimes will encounter a cuisine that is neither edible nor speakable, and will be shown to a bed wherein it needs no Sherlock Holmes to detect that the previous biped retired with his boots on, or at least with much realty attached to his person. Such places often are like that unpronounceable town in Russia of which Paragot said: "The bugs are the most companionable creatures in it, and they are the cleanest."

If one be of the same mind as the plain-spoken Dr. Samuel Johnson, that "the finest landscape in the world is not worth a damn without a cozy inn in the foreground," he should keep to the stock show-places of our highlands or seek other playgrounds.

By far the most comfortable way to stay in the back country at present is in a camp of one's own where he can keep things tidy and have food to suit him. If you be, though, of stout stomach and wishful to get true insight into mountain ways and character you can find some sort of boarding-place almost anywhere. In such case go first to the sheriff of the county (in person, not by letter). This officer is a walking bureau of information and dispenses it freely to any stranger. He knows almost every man in the county, his character and his circumstances. He may be depended upon to direct you to the best stopping-places, will tell you how to get hunting and fishing privileges, and will recommend a good packer or teamster if such help is wanted.

Along the railways and main county roads the farmers show a well-justified mistrust about admitting company for the night. But in the back districts the latch-string generally is out to all comers. "If you-uns can stand what we-uns has ter, w'y come right in and set you a cheer."

If the man of the house has misgivings as to the state of the larder, he will say: "I'll ax

272 OUR SOUTHERN HIGHLANDERS

the woman gin she can git ye a bite." Seldom
does the wife demur, though sometimes her pa-
tience is sorely tried.

A stranger whose calked boots betrayed his
calling stopped at Uncle Mark's to inquire,
"Can I git to stay all night?" Aunt Nance,
peeping through a crack, warned her man in a
whisper: "Them loggers jest louzes up folkses
houses." Whereat Mark answered the lumberjack: "We don't ginerally foller takin' in
strangers."

Jack glanced significantly at the lowering
clouds, and grunted: "Uh—looks like I could
stand hitched all night!"

This was too much for Mark. "Well!" he
exclaimed, "mebbe we-uns can find ye a pallet
—I'll try to enjoy ye somehow." Which, being
interpreted, means, "I'll entertain you as best I
can."

The hospitality of the backwoods knows no
bounds short of sickness in the family or downright destitution. Travelers often innocently
impose on poor people, and even criticise the
scanty fare, when they may be getting a lion's
share of the last loaf in the house. And few
of them realize the actual cost of entertaining
company in a home that is long mountain miles
from any market. Fancy yourself making a

A Natural "Bald," (Part of the Summit of Thunderhead Mountain.)

Photo by S. H. Essary

twenty-mile round trip over awful roads to carry back a sack of flour on your shoulder and a can of oil in your hand; then figure what the transportation is worth.

Once when I was trying a short-cut through the forest by following vague directions I swerved to the wrong trail. Sunset found me on the summit of an unfamiliar mountain, with cold rain setting in, and below me lay the impenetrable laurel of Huggins's Hell. I turned back to the head of the nearest water course, not knowing whither it led, fought my way through thicket and darkness to the nearest house, and asked for lodging. The man was just coming in from work. He betrayed some anxiety but admitted me with grave politeness. Then he departed on an errand, leaving his wife to hear the story of my wanderings.

I was eager for supper; but madame made no move toward the kitchen. An hour passed. A little child whimpered with hunger. The mother, flushing, soothed it on her breast.

It was well on in the night when her husband returned, bearing a little "poke" of cornmeal. Then the woman flew to her post. Soon we had hot bread, three or four slices of pork, and black coffee unsweetened — all there was in the house.

It developed that when I arrived there was

barely enough meal for the family's supper and breakfast. My host had to shell some corn, go in almost pitch darkness, without a lantern, to a tub-mill far down the branch, wait while it ground out a few spoonfuls to the minute and bring the meal back.

Next morning, when I offered pay for my entertainment, he waved it aside. "I ain't never tuk money from company," he said, " and this ain't no time to begin."

Laughing, I slipped some silver into the hand of the eldest child. "This is not pay; it's a present." The girl was awed into speechlessness at sight of money of her own, and the parents did not know how to thank me for her, but bade me "Stay on, stranger; pore folks has a pore way, but you're welcome to what we got."

This incident is a little out of the common, nowadays; but it is typical of what was customary until lumbering and other industrial works began to invade the solitudes. To-day it is the rule to charge twenty-five cents a meal and the same for lodging, regardless of what the fare and the bed may be. When you think of it, this is right, for "the porer folks is the harder it is to *git* things."

The mountaineers always are eager for news.

In the drab monotony of their shut-in lives the
coming of an unknown traveler is an event that
will set the whole neighborhood gossiping.
Every word and action of his will be discussed
for weeks after he has gone his way. This, of
course, is a trait of rural people everywhere;
but imagine, if you can, how it may be intensified where there are no newspapers, few visitors, and where the average man gets maybe
two or three letters a year !

Riding up a branch road, you come upon a
white-bearded patriarch who halts you with a
wave of the hand.

"Stranger—meanin' no harm—*whar* are you
gwine ?"

You tell him.

"What did you say your name was ?"

You had not mentioned it; but you do so
now.

"What mought you-uns foller for a living ?"

It is wise to humor the old man, and tell him
frankly what is your business "up this 'way-off
branch."

Half a mile farther you espy a girl coming
toward you. She stops like a startled fawn,
wide-eyed with amazement. Then, at a bound,
she dodges into a thicket, doubles on her course
and runs back as fast as her nimble bare legs

can carry her to report that "Some-*body* 's comin' !"

At the next house, stopping for a drink of water, you chat a few moments. High up the opposite hill is a half-hidden cabin from which keen eyes scrutinize your every move, and a woman cries to her boy: "Run, Kit, down to Mederses, and ax who *is* he !"

As you approach a cross-roads store every idler pricks up to instant attention. Your presence is detected from every neighboring cabin and cornfield. Long John quits his plowing, Red John drops his axe, Sick John ("who 's allers ailin', to hear *him* tell") pops out of bed, and Lyin' John (whose "mouth ain't no praar-book, if it *does* open and shet") grabs his hat, with "I jes' got ter know who that feller is !" Then all Johns descend their several paths, to congregate at the store and estimate the stranger as though he were so many board-feet of lumber in the tree or so many pounds of beef on the hoof.

In every settlement there is somebody who makes a pleasure of gathering and spreading news. Such a one we had—a happy-go-lucky fellow from whom, they said, "you can hear the news jinglin' afore he comes within gun-shot." It amused me to record the many ways he had of announcing his mission by indirection. Here is the list :

"I'm jes' broguin' about."

"Yes, I'm jest cooterin' around."

"I'm santerin' about."

"Oh, I'm jes' prodjectin' around."

"Jist traffickin' about."

"No, I ain't workin' none—jest spuddin' around."

"Me? I'm jes' shacklin' around."

"Yea, la ! I'm jist loaferin' about."

And yet one hears that our mountaineers have a limited vocabulary !

Although this is no place to discuss the mountain dialect, I must explain that to "brogue" means to go about in brogues (brogans nowadays). A "cooter" is a box-tortoise, and the noun is turned into a verb with an ease characteristic of the mountaineers. "Spuddin' around" means toddling or jolting along. To "shummick" (also "shammick") is to shuffle about, idly nosing into things, as a bear does when there is nothing serious in view. And "shacklin' around" pictures a shackly, loose-jointed way of walking, expressive of the idle vagabond.

A stranger takes the mountaineers for simple characters that can be gauged at a glance. This illusion—for it is an illusion—comes from the childlike directness with which they ask him the most intimate questions about himself, from the genuine good-will with which they admit him to their homes, and from the stark open-ness of their domestic affairs in houses where no privacy can possibly exist.

In so far as simplicity means only a shrewd regard for essentials, a rigid exclusion of what-ever can be done without, perhaps no white race is nearer a state of nature than these highlanders of ours. Yet this relates only to the externals of life. Diogenes sat in a tub, but his thoughts were deep as the sea. And whoever estimates our mountaineers as a shallow-minded or open-minded people has much to learn.

When Long John asks, "What you aimin' to do up hyur? How much money do you make? Whar's your old woman?" he does not really expect sincere answers. Certainly he will take them with more than a grain of salt. Conver-sation, with him, is a game. In quizzing you, the interests that he is actually curious about lie hidden in the back of his head, and he will pro-ceed toward them by cunning circumventions, seeking to entrap you into telling the truth by accident. Being himself born to intrigue and skilled in dodging the leading question, he as-sumes that you have had equal advantages.

When you discuss with him any business of serious concern, if you should go straight to the point, and open your mind frankly, he would be nonplussed.

The fact is that our highlanders are a sly, suspicious, and secretive folk. That, too, is a state of nature. Primitive society is by no means a Utopia or a Garden of Eden. In wilderness life the feral arts of concealment, spying, false "leads," and doubling on trails are the arts self-preservative. The native backwoodsman practices them as instinctively and with as little compunction upon his own species as upon the deer and the wolf from whom he learned them.

As a friend, no one will spring quicker to your aid, reckless of consequences, and fight with you to the last ditch; but fear of betrayal lies at the very bottom of his nature. His sleepless suspicion of ulterior motives is no more, no less, than a feral trait, inherited from a long line of forebears whose isolated lives were preserved only by incessant vigilance against enemies that stalked by night and struck without warning.

Casual visitors learn nothing about the true character of the mountaineers. I am not speaking of personal but of race character—type. No outsider can discern and measure those powerful but obscure motives, those rooted prejudices, that constitute their real difference from other men, until he has lived with the people a long time on terms of intimacy.   Nor can anyone be trusted to portray them if he holds a brief either for or against this people.   The fluttering tourist marks only the oddities he sees, without knowing the reason for them.   On the other hand, a misguided champion flies to arms at first mention of an unpleasant fact, and either denies it, clamoring for legal proof, or tries to befog the whole subject and run it on the rocks of altercation.

The mountaineers are high-strung and sensitive to criticism.   No one has less use for "that worst scourge of avenging heaven, the candid friend."   Of late years they are growing conscious of their own belatedness, and that touches a tender spot.   "Hit don't take a big seed to hurt a sore tooth."   Since they do not see how anyone can find beauty or historic interest in ways of life that the rest of the world has cast aside, so they resent every exposure of their peculiarities as if that were holding them up to ridicule or blame.

Strange to say, it provokes them to be called mountaineers, that being a "furrin word" which they take as a term of reproach.   They

call themselves mountain people, or citizens;
sometimes humorously "mountain boomers,"
the word boomer being their name for the common red squirrel which is found here only in
the upper zones of the mountains. Backwoodsman is another term that they deem opprobrious. Among themselves the backwoods are
called "the sticks." Hillsman and highlander
are strange words to them—and anything that
is strange is suspicious. Hence it is next to impossible for anyone to write much about these
people without offending them or else falling
into singsong repetition of the same old terms.

I have found it beyond me to convince anyone
here that my studies of the mountain dialect are
made from any better motive than vulgar curiosity. It has been my habit to jot down, on the
spot, every dialectical word or variant or idiom
that I hear, along with the phrase or sentence
in which it occurred; for I never trust memory
in such matters. And although I tell frankly
what I am about, and why, yet all that the folks
can or will see is that—

> A chiel 's amang ye, takin' notes
> And, faith, he'll prent 'em.

Nothing worse than dour looks has yet befallen me, but other scribes have not got off so

easy. On more than one occasion newspaper men who went into eastern Kentucky to report feuds were escorted forcibly to the railroad and warned never to return. The feudists are scarce to blame, for the average news story of their wars is neither sacred nor profane history. It is bad enough to be shown up as an assassin; but when one is posed as "cocking the *trigger*' of a gun, or shooting a "forty-four" bullet from a thirty-caliber "automatic *revolver*," who in Kentucky could be expected to stand it?

The novelists have their troubles, too. President Frost relates that when John Fox gave a reading from his Cumberland tales at Berea College "the mountain boys were ready to mob him. They had no comprehension of the nature of fiction. Mr. Fox's stories were either true or false. If they were true, then he was 'no gentleman' for telling all the family affairs of people who had entertained him with their best. If they were not true, then, of course, they were libellous upon the mountain people. Such an attitude may remind us of the general condemnation of fiction by the 'unco gude' a generation ago.'

As for settlement workers, let them teach more by example than by precept. Bishop Wilson has given them some advice that cannot be bettered : "It must be said with emphasis that our problem is an exceedingly delicate one. The highlanders are Scotch-Irish in their high-spiritedness and proud independence. Those who would help them must do so in a perfectly frank and kindly way, showing always genuine interest in them but never a trace of patronizing condescension. As quick as a flash the mountaineer will recognize and resent the intrusion of any such spirit, and will refuse even what he sorely needs if he detects in the accents or the demeanor of the giver any indication of an air of superiority."

"The worker among the mountaineers," he continues, "must 'meet with them on the level and part on the square' and conquer their oftentimes unreasonable suspicion by genuine brotherly friendship. The less he has to say about the superiority of other sections or of the deficiencies of the mountains, the better for his cause. The fact is that comparatively few workers are at first able to pass muster in this regard under the searching and silent scrutiny of the mountain people."

Allow me to add that this is no place for the "unco gude" to exercise their talents, but rather for those whose studies and travels have taught them both tolerance and hopefulness.

Some well-meaning missionaries are shocked and scandalized at what seems to them incurable perversity and race degeneration. It is nothing of the sort. There are reasons, good reasons, for the worst that we find in any Hellfer-Sartin or Loafer's Glory. All that is the inevitable result of isolation and lack of opportunity. It is no more hopeless than the same features of life were in the Scotch highlands two centuries ago.

But it must be known that the future of this really fine race is, at bottom, an economic problem, which must be studied hand-in-hand with the educational one. Civilization only repels the mountaineer until you show him something to gain by it—he knows by instinct what he is bound to lose. There is no use in teaching cleanliness and thrift to serfs or outcasts. The *independence* of the mountain farm must be preserved, or the fine spirit of the race will vanish and all that is manly in the highlander will wither to the core.

It is far from my own purpose to preach or advise. "Portray the struggle, and you need write no tract." Still farther is it from my thought to let characterization degenerate into caricature. Wherever I tell anything that is unusual or below the average of backwoods life,

I give fair warning that it is admitted only for spice or contrast, and let it go at that. But even in writing with severe restraint it will be necessary at times to show conditions so rude and antiquated that professional apologists will growl, and many others may find my statements hard to credit as typical of anything at all in our modern America.

So, let me remind the reader again that full three-fourths of our mountaineers still live in the eighteenth century, and that in their far-flung wilderness, away from large rivers and railways, the habits, customs, morals of the people have changed but little from those of our old colonial frontier; in essentials they are closely analogous to what we read of lower-class English and Scottish life in Covenanter and Jacobite times.

CHAPTER XIII

THE PEOPLE OF THE HILLS

IN delineating a strange race we are prone to disregard what is common in our own experience and observe sharply what is odd. The oddities we sketch and remember and tell about. But there is little danger of misrepresenting the physical features and mental traits of the hill people, because among them there is one definite type that greatly predominates. This is not to be wondered at when we remember that fully three-fourths of our highlanders are practically of the same descent, have lived the same kind of life for generations, and have intermarried to a degree unknown in other parts of America.

Our average mountaineer is lean, inquisitive, shrewd. If that be what constitutes a Yankee, as is popularly supposed outside of New England, then this Yankee of the South is as true to type as the conventional Uncle Sam himself

A fat mountaineer is a curiosity. The hill folk even seem to affect a slender type of comeliness. In Alice MacGowan's *Judith of the Cumberlands*, old Jepthah Turrentine says of one of his sons : "I named that boy after the finest man that ever walked God's green earth —and then the fool had to go and git fat on me! Think of me with a *fat* son! I allers did hold that a fat woman was bad enough, but a fat man ort p'intedly to be led out and killed !"

Spartan diet does not put on flesh. Still, it should be noted that long legs, baggy clothing, and scantiness or lack of underwear make people seem thinner than they really are. Our highlanders are conspicuously a tall race. Out of seventy-six men that I have listed just as they occurred to me, but four are below average American height and only two are fat. About two-thirds of them are brawny or sinewy fellows of great endurance. The others generally are slab-sided, stoop-shouldered, but withey. The townsfolk and the valley farmers, being better nourished and more observant of the prime laws of wholesome living, are noticeably superior in appearance but not in stamina.

Nearly all males of the back country have a grave and deliberate bearing. They travel with the long, sure-footed stride of the born woodsman, not graceful and lithe like a moccasined Indian (their coarse brogans forbid it), but shambling as if every joint had too much play. There is nothing about them to suggest the Swiss or Tyrolean mountaineers; rather they resemble the gillies of the Scotch Highlands. Generally they are lean-faced, sallow, level-browed, with rather high cheek-bones. Gray eyes predominate, sometimes vacuous, but oftener hard, searching, crafty—the feral eye of primitive man.

From infancy these people have been schooled to dissimulate and hide emotion, and ordinarily their faces are as opaque as those of veteran poker players. Many wear habitually a sullen scowl, hateful and suspicious, which in men of combative age, and often in the old women, is sinister and vindictive. The smile of comfortable assurance, the frank eye of good-fellowship, are rare indeed. Nearly all of the young people and many of the adults plant themselves before a stranger and regard him with a fixed stare, peculiarly annoying until one realizes that they have no thought of impertinence.

Many of the women are pretty in youth; but hard toil in house and field, early marriage, frequent child-bearing with shockingly poor attention, and ignorance or defiance of the plainest necessities of hygiene, soon warp and

"She knows no other lot."

age them. At thirty or thirty-five a mountain woman is apt to have a worn and faded look, with form prematurely bent—and what wonder? Always bending over the hoe in the cornfield, or bending over the hearth as she cooks by an open fire, or bending over her baby, or bending to pick up, for the thousandth time, the wet duds that her lord flings on the floor as he enters from the woods—what wonder that she soon grows short-waisted and round-shouldered?

The voices of the highland women, low toned by habit, often are singularly sweet, being pitched in a sad, musical, minor key. With strangers, the women are wont to be shy, but speculative rather than timid, as they glance betimes with "a slow, long look of mild inquiry, or of general listlessness, or of unconscious and unaccountable melancholy." Many, however, scrutinize a visitor calmly for minutes at a time or frankly measure him with the gipsy eye of Carmen.

Outsiders, judging from the fruits of labor in more favored lands, have charged the mountaineers with indolence. It is the wrong word. Shiftless many of them are—afflicted with that malady which Barrie calls "acute disinclination to work"—but that is not so much in their physical nature as in their economic outlook.

Rarely do we find mountaineers who loaf all day on the floor or the doorstep like so many of the poor whites of the lowlands. If not laboring, they at least must be doing something, be it no more than walking ten miles to shoot a squirrel or visit a crony.

As a class, they have great and restless physical energy. Considering the quantity and quality of what they eat there is no people who can beat them in endurance of strain and privation. They are great walkers and carriers of burdens. Before there was a tub-mill in our settlement one of my neighbors used to go, every other week, thirteen miles to mill, carrying a two-bushel sack of corn (112 pounds) and returning with his meal on the following day. This was done without any pack-strap but simply shifting the load from one shoulder to the other, betimes.

One of our women, known as "Long Goody" (I measured her; six feet three inches she stood) walked eighteen miles across the Smokies into Tennessee, crossing at an elevation of 5,000 feet, merely to shop more advantageously than she could at home. The next day she shouldered fifty pounds of flour and some other groceries, and bore them home before nightfall. Uncle Jimmy Crawford, in his seventy-second year, came to join a party of us on a bear hunt. He walked twelve miles across the mountain, carrying his equipment and four days' rations for himself *and dogs*. Finding that we had gone on ahead of him he followed to our camp on Siler's Bald, twelve more miles, climbing another 3,000 feet, much of it by bad trail, finished the twenty-four-mile trip in seven hours—and then wanted to turn in and help cut the nightwood. Young mountaineers afoot easily outstrip a horse on a day's journey by road and trail.

In a climate where it showers about two days out of three through spring and summer the women go about, like the men, unshielded from the wet. If you expostulate, one will laugh and reply: "I ain't sugar, nor salt, nor nobody's honey." Slickers are worn only on horseback—and two-thirds of our people had no horses. A man who was so eccentric as to carry an umbrella is known to this day as "Umbrell'" John Walker.

In winter, one sometimes may see adults and children going barefoot in snow that is ankle deep. It used to be customary in our settlement to do the morning chores barefooted in the snow. "Then," said one, "our feet 'd tingle and burn, so 't they wouldn't git a bit cold all day when we put our shoes on." I knew a family whose children had no shoes all one winter, and occasionally we had zero weather.

It seems to have been common, in earlier times, to go barefooted all the year. Frederick Law Olmsted, a noted writer of the Civil War period, was told by a squire of the Tennessee hills that "a majority of the folks went barefoot all winter, though they had snow much of the time four or five inches deep; and the man said he didn't think most of the men about here had more than one coat, and they never wore one in winter except on holidays. 'That was the healthiest way,' he reckoned, 'just to toughen yourself and not wear no coat.' No matter how cold it was, he 'didn't wear no coat.'" One of my own neighbors in the Smokies never owned a coat until after his marriage, when a friend of mine gave him one.

It is the usual thing for men and boys to wade cold trout streams all day, come in at sunset, disrobe to shirt and trousers, and then sit in the piercing drafts of an open cabin drying out before the fire, though the night be so cool that a stranger beside them shivers in his dry flannels. After supper, the women, if they have been wearing shoes, will remove them to ease their feet, no matter if it be freezing cold—and the cracks in the floor may be an inch wide.

In bear hunting, our parties usually camped at about 5,000 feet above sea level. At this elevation, in the long nights before Christmas, the cold often was bitter and the wind might blow a gale. Sometimes the native hunters would lie out in the open all night without a sign of a blanket or an axe. They would say: "La! many's the night I've been out when the frost was spewed up so high [measuring three or four inches with the hand], and that right around the fire, too." Cattle hunters in the mountains never carry a blanket or a shelter-cloth, and they sleep out wherever night finds them, often in pouring rain or flying snow. On their arduous trips they find it burden enough to carry the salt for their cattle, with a frying-pan, cup, corn pone, coffee, and "sow-belly," all in a grain sack strapped to the man's back.

Such nurture, from childhood, makes white men as indifferent to the elements as Fuegians. And it makes them anything but comfortable companions for one who has been differently reared. During "court week" when the hotels at the county-seat are overcrowded with countrymen, the luckless drummers who happen to be there have continuous exercise in closing doors. No mountaineer closes a door behind

him. Winter or summer, doors are to be shut
only when folks go to bed. That is what they
are for. After close study of mountain speech
I have failed to discern that the word draft is
understood, except in parts of the Virginia and
Kentucky mountains, where it means a brook.
One is reminded of the colonial, who, visiting
England, remarked of the British people: "It
is a survival of the fittest—the fittest to exist in
fog." Here, it is the fittest to survive cold, and
wet, and drafts.

Running barefooted in the snow is exceptional nowadays; but it is by no means the limit
of hardiness or callosity that some of these people display. It is not so long ago that I passed
an open lean-to of chestnut bark far back in the
wilderness, wherein a family of Tennesseans
was spending the year. There were three children, the eldest a lad of twelve. The entire
worldly possessions of this family could easily
be packed around on their backs. Poverty,
however, does not account for such manner of
living. There is none so poor in the mountains
that he need rear his children in a bark shed.
It is all a matter of taste.

There is a wealthy man known to everyone
around Waynesville, who, being asked where
he resided, as a witness in court, answered:

"Three, four miles up and down Jonathan Creek." The judge was about to fine him for contempt, when it developed that the witness spoke literal truth. He lives neither in house nor camp, but perambulates his large estate and when night comes lies down wherever he may happen to be. In winter he has been known to go where some of his pigs bedded in the woods, usurp the middle for himself, and borrow comfort from their bodily heat.

This man is worth over a hundred thousand dollars. He visited the world's fairs at Chicago and St. Louis, wearing the old long coat that serves him also as blanket, and carrying his rations in a sack. Far from being demented, he is notoriously so shrewd on the stand and so learned in the law that he is formidable to every attorney who cross-questions him.

I cite these last two instances not merely as eccentricities of character, but as really typical of the bodily stamina that most of the mountaineers can display if they want to. Their smiling endurance of cold and wet and privation would have endeared them to the first Napoleon, who declared that those soldiers were the best who bivouacked shelterless throughout the year.

In spite of such apparent "toughness," the

mountaineers are not a notably healthy people. The man who exposes himself wantonly year after year must pay the piper. Sooner or later he "adopts a rheumatiz," and the adoption lasts till he dies. So also in dietary matters. The backwoodsmen through ruthless weeding-out of the normally sensitive have acquired a wonderful tolerance of swimming grease, doughy bread and half-fried cabbage; but, even so, they are gnawed by dyspepsia. This accounts in great measure for the "glunch o' sour disdain" that mars so many countenances. A neighbor said to me of another: "He has a gredge agin all creation, and glories in human misery." So would anyone else who ate at the same table. Many a homicide in the mountains can be traced directly to bad food and the raw whiskey taken to appease a soured stomach.

Every stranger in Appalachia is quick to note the high percentage of defectives among the people. However, we should bear in mind that in the mountains proper there are few, if any, public refuges for this class, and that home ties are so powerful that mountaineers never send their "fitified folks" or "half-wits," or other unfortunates, to any institution in the lowlands, so long as it is bearable to have them around. Such poor creatures as would be segregated in

more advanced communities, far from the public eye, here go at large and reproduce their
kind.

Extremely early marriages are tolerated, as
among all primitive people. I knew a hobbledehoy of sixteen who married a frail, tubercu-
lous girl of twelve, and in the same small settlement another lad of sixteen who wedded a girl of
thirteen. In both cases the result was wretched
beyond description.

The evil consequences of inbreeding of persons closely akin are well known to the mountaineers; but here knowledge is no deterrent,
since whole districts are interrelated to start
with. Owing to the isolation of the clans, and
their extremely limited travels, there are abundant cases like those caustically mentioned in
King Spruce: "All Skeets and Bushees, and
married back and forth and crossways and up-
side down till ev'ry man is his own grand-
mother, if he only knew enough to figger
relationship."

The mountaineers are touchy on these topics
and it is but natural that they should be so.
Nevertheless it is the plain duty of society to
study such conditions and apply the remedy.
There was a time when the Scotch people (to
cite only one instance out of many) were in

still worse case, threatened with race degeneration; but improved economic conditions, followed by education, made them over into one of the most vigorous of modern peoples.

When I lived up in the Smokies there was no doctor within sixteen miles (and then, none who ever had attended a medical school). It was inevitable that my first-aid kit and limited knowledge of medicine should be requisitioned until I became a sort of "doctor to the settlement."* My services, being free, at once became popular, and there was no escape; for, if I treated the Smiths, let us say, and ignored a call from the Robinsons, the slight would be resented by all Robinson connections throughout the land. So my normal occupations often were interrupted by such calls as these:

"John's Lize Ann she ain't much; cain't you-uns give her some easin'-powder for that hurtin' in her chist?"

"Old Uncle Bobby Tuttle's got a pone come up on his side; looks like he mought drap off, him bein' weak and right narvish and sick with a head-swimmin'."

---

* In mountain dialect such words as settlement, government, studyment (reverie) are accented on the last syllable, or drawled with equal stress throughout.

"Ike Morgan Pringle's a-been horse-throwed down the clift, and he's in a manner stone dead."

"Right sensibly atween the shoulders I've got a pain; somethin' 's gone wrong with my stummick; I don't 'pear to have no stren'th left; and sometimes I'm nigh sifflicated. Whut you reckon ails me?"

"Come right over to Mis' Fullwiler's, quick; she's fell down and busted a rib inside o' her!"

On these errands of mercy I soon picked up some rules of practice that are not laid down in the books. I learned to carry not only my own bandages but my own towels and utensils for washing and sterilizing. I kept my mouth shut about germ theories of disease, having no troops to enforce orders and finding that mere advice incited downright perversity. I administered potent drugs in person and left nothing to be taken according to direction except placebos.

Once, in forgetfulness, I left a tablet of corrosive sublimate on the mantel after dressing a wound, and the man of the house told me next day that he had " 'lowed to swaller it and see if it wouldn't ease his headache!" A geologist and I, exploring the hills with a mountaineer, fell into discussion of filth diseases and germs, not realizing that we were overheard. Hap-

pening to pass an ant-hill, Frank remarked to
me that formic acid was supposed to be antagonistic to the germ of laziness. Instantly we
heard a growl from our woodsman: "By God,
I was *expectin'* to hear the like o' that!"

Ordinarily wounds are stanched with dusty
cobwebs and bound up in any old rag. If in-
fection ensues, Providence has to take the
blame. A woman gashed her foot badly with
an axe; I asked her what she did for it; dis-
dainfully she answered, "Tied it up in sut and
a rag, and went to hoein' corn."

An injured person gets scant sympathy, if
any. So far as outward demeanor goes, and
public comment, the witnesses are utterly callous. The same indifference is shown in the
face of impending death. People crowd
around with no other motive, seemingly, than
morbid curiosity to see a person die. I asked
our local preacher what the folks would do
if a man broke his thigh so that the bone pro-
truded. He merely elevated his eyebrows and
replied: "We'd set around and sing until he
died."

The mountaineers' fortitude under severe
pain is heroic, though often needless. For all
minor operations and frequently for major ones
they obstinately refuse to take an anesthetic,

being perversely suspicious of everything that they do not understand. Their own minor surgery and obstetric practice is barbarous. A large proportion of the mountain doctors know less about human anatomy than a butcher does about a pig's. Sometimes this ignorance passes below ordinary common sense. There is a "doctor" still practicing who, after a case of confinement, sits beside the patient and presses hard upon the hips for half an hour, explaining that it is to "push the bones back into place; don't you know they allers comes uncoupled in the socket?" This, I suppose, is the limit; but there are very many practicing physicians in the back country who could not name or locate the arteries of either foot or hand to save their lives.

It was here I first heard of "tooth-jumping." Let one of my old neighbors tell it in his own way:

"You take a cut nail (not one o' those round wire nails) and place its squar p'int agin the ridge of the tooth, jest under the edge of the gum. Then jump the tooth out with a hammer. A man who knows how can jump a tooth without it hurtin' half as bad as pullin'. But old Uncle Neddy Cyarter went to jump one of his own teeth out, one time, and missed the nail and mashed his nose with the hammer. He had the weak trembles."

"I have heard of tooth-jumping," said I, "and reported it to dentists back home, but they laughed at me."

"Well, they needn't laugh; for it's so. Some men git to be as experienced at it as tooth-dentists are at pullin'. They cut around the gum, and then put the nail at jest sich an angle, slantin' downward for an upper tooth, or upwards for a lower one, and hit one lick."

"Will the tooth come at the first lick?"

"Ginerally. If it didn t, you might as well stick your head in a swarm o' bees and ferget who you are."

"Are back teeth extracted in that way?"

"Yes, sir; any kind of a tooth. I've burnt my holler teeth out with a red-hot wire."

"Good God!"

"Hit's so. The wire'd sizzle like fryin'."

"Kill the nerve?"

"No; but it'd sear the mar so it wouldn't be so sensitive."

"Didn't hurt, eh?"

"Hurt like hell for a moment. I held the wire one time for Jim Bob Jimwright, who couldn't reach the spot for hisself. I *told* him to hold his tongue back; but when I touched the holler he jumped and wropped his tongue agin the wire. The words that man used ain't fitty to tell."

Some of the ailments common in the mountains were new to me. For instance, "dew pizen," presumably the poison of some weed, which, dissolved in dew, enters the blood through a scratch or abrasion. As a woman described it, "Dew pizen comes like a risin', and laws-a-marcy how it does hurt! I stove a brier in my heel wunst, and then had to hunt cows every morning in the dew. My leg swelled up black to clar above the knee, and Dr. Stinchcomb lanced the place seven times. I lay on a pallet on the floor for over a month. My leg like to killed me. I've seed persons jest a lot o' sores all over, as big as my hand, from dew pizen."

A more mysterious disease is "milk-sick," which prevails in certain restricted districts, chiefly where the cattle graze in rich and deeply shaded coves. If not properly treated it is fatal both to the cow and to any human being who drinks her fresh milk or eats her butter. It is not transmitted by sour milk or by buttermilk. There is a characteristic fetor of the breath. It is said that milk from an infected cow will not foam and that silver is turned black by it.

Mountaineers are divided in opinion as to whether this disease is of vegetable or of mineral origin; some think it is an efflorescence from gas that settles on plants. This much is certain: that it disappears from "milk-sick coves" when they are cleared of timber and the sunlight let in. The prevalent treatment is an emetic, followed by large doses of apple brandy and honey; then oil to open the bowels. Perhaps the extraordinary distaste for fresh milk and butter, or the universal suspicion of these foods that mountaineers evince in so many localities, may have sprung up from experience with "milk-sick" cows. I have not found this malady mentioned in any treatise on medicine; yet it has been known from our earliest frontier times. Abraham Lincoln's mother died of it.

That the hill folk remain a rugged and hardy people in spite of unsanitary conditions so gross that I can barely hint at them, is due chiefly to their love of pure air and pure water. No mountain cabin needs a window to ventilate it: there are cracks and cat-holes everywhere, and, as I have said, the doors are always open except at night. "Tight houses," sheathed or plastered, are universally despised, partly from inherited shiftlessness, partly for less obvious reasons.

A Mountain Home

One of Miss MacGowan's characters fairly insulted the neighborhood by building a modern house. "Why lordy ! Lookee hyer, Creed," remonstrated Doss Provine over a question of matching boards and battening joints, "ef you git yo' pen so almighty tight as that you won't git no fresh air. Man's bound to have ventilation. Course you can leave the do' open all the time like we-all do; but when you're a-holdin' co't and sech-like maybe you'll want to shet the do' sometimes—and then whar'll ye git breath to breathe ? . . . All these here glass winders is blame foolishness to *me*. Ef ye need light, open the do'. Ef somebody comes that ye don't want in, you can shet it and put up a bar. But saw the walls full o' holes an' set in glass winders, an' any feller that's got a mind to can pick ye off with a rifle ball as easy as not whilst ye set by the fire of an evenin'."

When mountain people move to the lowlands and go to living in tight-framed houses, they soon deteriorate like Indians. It is of no use to teach them to ventilate by lowering windows from the top. That is some more "blame foolishness"—their adherence to old ways is stubborn, sullen, and perverse to a degree that others cannot comprehend. Then, too, in the lowlands, they simply cannot stand the water.

As Emma Miles says: "No other advantages will ever make up for the lack of good water. There is a strong prejudice against pumps; if a well must be dug, it is usually left open to the air, and the water is reached by means of a hooked pole which requires some skillful manipulation to prevent losing the bucket. Cisterns are considered filthy; water that has stood overnight is 'dead water,' hardly fit to wash one's face in. The mountaineer takes the same pride in his water supply as the rich man in his wine cellar, and is in this respect a connoisseur. None but the purest and coldest of freestone will satisfy him."

Once when I was staying in a lumber camp on the Tennessee side, near the top of Smoky, my friend Bob and I tramped down to the nearest town, ten miles, for supplies. We did not start until after dinner and intended to spend the night at a hotel. It was a sultry day and we arrived very thirsty. Bob took some ice-water into his mouth, and instantly spat it out, exclaiming: "Be damned if I'll stay here; that ain't fit to drink; I'm goin' back." And back he would have gone, ten miles up a hard grade, at night, if someone had not shown us a spring.

A little colony of our Hazel Creek people took a notion to try the Georgia cotton mills.

They nearly died there from homesickness, tight houses, and "bad water." All but one family returned as soon as they possibly could. While trying to save enough money to get away one old man said: "I lied to my God when I left the mountains and kem to these devilish cotton mills. Ef only He'd turn me into a varmint I'd run back to-night! Boys, I dream I'm in torment; an' when I wake up, I lay thar an' think o' the spring branch runnin' over the root o' that thar poplar; an' I say, could I git me one drink o' that water I'd be content to lay me down and die!"

Poor old John! In his country there are a hundred spring branches running over poplar roots; but *"that thar* poplar": we knew the very one he meant. It was by the roadside. The brooklet came from a disused still-house hidden in laurel and hemlock so dense that direct sunlight never penetrated the glen. Cold and sparkling and crystal clear, the gushing water enticed every wayfarer to bend and drink, whether he was thirsty or no. John is back in his own land now, and doubtless often goes to drink of that veritable fountain of youth.

CHAPTER XIV

THE LAND OF DO WITHOUT

HOMESPUN jeans and linsey used to be
the universal garb of the mountain people. Nowadays you will seldom find
them, except in far-back places. Shoddy "store
clothes" are cheaper and easier to get. And
this is a sorry change, for the old-time material
was sound and enduring, the direct product of
hard personal toil, and so it was prized and
taken care of; whereas such stuff as a backwoodsman can buy in his crossroads store is
flimsy, soon loses shape and breaks down his
own pride of personal appearance. Our average
hillsman now goes about in a dirty blue shirt,
wapsy and ragged trousers toggled up with a
nail or two, thick socks sagging untidily over
rusty brogans, and a huge, black, floppy hat
that desecrates the landscape. Presently his
hatband disappears, to be replaced with a
groundhog thong, woven in and out of knife
slits, like a shoestring.

When he comes home he "hangs his hat on

the floor" until his wife picks it up. He never brushes it. In time that battered old headpiece becomes as pliant to its owner's whim, as expressive of his mood, as a clown's cap in the circus. Commonly it is a symbol of shiftlessness and unconcern. A touch, and it becomes a banner of defiance to law and order. To meet on some lonesome road at night a horseman enveloped to the heels in a black slicker and topped with one of those prodigious funnels that conceals his features like a cowl, is to face the Ku Klux or the Spanish Inquisition.

When your young mountaineer is properly filled up on corn liquor and feels like challenging the world, the flesh, and the devil, he pins up the front of his hat with a thorn, sticks a sprig of balsam or cedar in the thong for an aigrette, and then gallops forth with bottle and pistol to tilt against whatsoever may dare oppose him. And on the gray dawn of the morning after you may find *that hat* lying wilted in a corner, as crumpled, spiritless and forlorn as —its owner, upon whom we charitably drop the curtain.

I doubt, though, if anywhere in this wide world mere personal appearance is more deceitful than among our mountaineers. The slovenly lout whom you shrink from approaching against the wind is one of the most independent and self-satisfied fellows on earth, as quick to resent alms as to return a blow. And it is wonderful what soap and clean clothes will do! About the worst specimen of tatterdemalion that I ever saw outside of trampdom used to come into town every week, always with a loaded Winchester on his shoulder. He may have washed his face now and then, but there was no sign that he ever combed his mane. I took him for one of those defectives alluded to in a previous chapter; but no, I was told he was "nobody's fool." The rifle, it was explained, never left his hand when he was abroad: they said that a feud was brewing "over on 'Larky,'" and that this man was "in the bilin'." Well, it boiled over, and the person in question killed two men in front of his own door.

When the prisoner was brought into court I could not recognize him. A bath, the barber, and a new store suit had transformed him into a right good-looking fellow—anything but a tramp, anything but a desperado. He bore himself throughout that grilling ordeal like the downright man he was, made out a clear case of self-defense, was set at liberty and—promptly reverted to a condition in which he is recognizable once more.

The women of the back country usually go bareheaded around home and often barefooted, too, as did the daughters of Highland chiefs a century or two ago, and for the same reason: simply that they feel better so. When "visitin'" or expecting visitors their extremities are clad. They make their own dresses and the style seems never to change. When traveling horseback they use a man's saddle and ride astride in their ordinary skirts with an ingenuity of "tucking up" that is beyond my understanding (as no doubt it should be). Often one sees a man and a woman riding a-pillion, in which case the lady perches sidewise, of course.

If I were disposed to startle the reader, after the manner of impressionistic writers who strive after effect at any cost, I could fill a book with oddities observed in the mountains, and that without exaggeration by commission or omission. Let one or two anecdotes suffice; and then we will get back to our averages again. I took down the following incident verbatim (save for proper names) from lips that I know to be truthful. It is introduced here as a specimen of vivid offhand description in few words:

"There was a fam'ly on Pick-Yer-Flint that was named Higgins, and another named the McBees. They married through and through

till the whole gineration nigh run out; though
what helped was that they'd fly mad sometimes
and kill one another like fools. They had great
big heads and mottly faces—ears as big as
sheepskins. Well, when they dressed up to
come to church the men—grown men—'d have
shirts made of this common domestic, with the
letters *AAA* on their backs; and them barefooted, and some without hats, but with three
yards of red ribbon around their necks. The
sleeves of their shirts looked like a whole web of
cloth jest sewed up together; and them sleeves'd
git full o' wind, and that red ribbon aflyin'—
O my la !

"There was lots o' leetle boys of 'em that
kem only in their shirt-tails. There was cracks
between the logs that a dog could jump through,
and them leetle fellers 'd git 'em a crack and
grin in at us all through the sarmon. 'T ain't
no manner o' use to ax me what the tex' was
that day ! "

I may explain that it still is common in many
districts of the mountain country for small boys
to go about through the summer in a single
abbreviated garment and that they are called
"shirt-tail boys."

Some of the expedients that mountain girls in-
vent to make themselves attractive are bizarre

in the extreme. Without invading the sanctities of toilet, I will cite one instance that is interesting from a scientific viewpoint. They told me that a certain blue-eyed girl thought that black eyes were "purtier" and that she actually changed her eyes to jet black whenever she went to "meetin' " or other public gathering. While I could see how the trick might be worked, it seemed utterly absurd that an unschooled maid of the wilderness could acquire either the knowledge or the means to accomplish such change. Well, one day I was called to treat a sick baby. While waiting for the medicine to react I chanced to mention this tale as it had been told me. The father, who had blue eyes, solemnly assured me that there was "no lie about it," and said he would convince me in a few minutes.

He stepped to the garden and plucked a leaf of jimson weed. His wife crushed the leaf and instilled a drop of its juice into one of his eyes. I took out my watch. One side of the eyeball reddened slightly. The man said "hit smarts a leetle—not much." Within fifteen minutes the pupil had expanded like a cat's eye in the dark, leaving a rim of blue iris so thin as to be quite unnoticeable without close inspection. The eye consequently was jet black and its expression utterly changed. My host said it did not affect his vision materially, save that "things glimmer a bit." I met him again the next day and he still was an odd-looking creature indeed, with one eye a light blue and the other an absolute black. The thing puzzled me until I recalled that the Latin name of jimson weed is *Datura stramonium;* then, in a flash, it came to me that stramonium is a powerful mydriatic.

If our man-killer, hitherto mentioned, had had blue or gray eyes and had not chosen to stand trial, then, with a cake of soap and a new suit and a jimson leaf he might have made himself over so that his own mother would not have known him. These simple facts are offered gratis to writers of detective tales, whose stock of disguises nowadays is so threadbare and (pardon me) so absurd.

The mountain home of to-day is the log cabin of the American pioneer—not such a lodge as well-to-do people affect in Adirondack "camps" (which cost more than framed structures of similar size), but a pen that can be erected by four "corner men" in one day and is finished by the owner at his leisure. The commonest type is a single large room, with maybe a narrow porch in front and a plank door, a big stone chimney at one end, a single sash for a window at the other, and a seven or eight-foot lean-to at the rear for kitchen.

Some of the early settlers, who had first choice of land, took pains in building their houses, squaring the logs like bridge timbers, joining them closely, smoothing their puncheons with an adze almost as truly as if they were planed, and using mortar instead of clay in laying chimney and hearth. But such houses nowadays are rare. If a man can afford so much effort as all that he will build a framed dwelling. If not, he will content himself with such a cabin as I have described. If he prospers he may add a duplicate of it alongside and cover the whole with one roof, leaving a ten or twelve-foot entry between.

In Carolina they seldom build a house of round logs, but rather hew the inner and outer faces flat, out of a curious notion that this adds an appearance of finish to the structure. If only they would turn the logs over, so that the flat faces joined, leaving at least the outside in the natural round, the house would need hardly any chinking and the effect would be far more pleasing to good taste. As it is they merely notch the logs at the corners, leaving wide spaces to be filled up with splits, rocks, mud–

anything to keep out the weather. As a matter of fact, few houses ever are thoroughly chinked and he who would take pains to make a workmanlike job of chinking would be ridiculed as "fussin' around like an old granny-woman." Nobody but a tenderfoot feels drafts, you know.

It is hard to keep such a dwelling clean, even if the family be small. The whole structure being built of green timber throughout, soon shrinks, checks, warps and sags, so that there cannot be a square joint, a neat fit, a perpendicular face, or a level place anywhere about it. The roof droops in a season or two, the shingles curl and leaky places open. Flooring shrinks apart, leaving wide and irregular cracks through which the winter winds are sucked upward as through so many flues (no mountain home has a cellar under it). Everywhere there are crannies and rough surfaces to hold dust and soot, there being probably not a single planed board in the whole house.

But, for all that, there is something very attractive and picturesque about the little old log cabin. In its setting of ancient forests and mighty hills it fits, it harmonizes, where the prim and precise product of modern carpentry would shock an artistic eye. The very roughness of the honest logs and the home-made furniture gives texture to the picture. Having no mathematically straight lines nor uniform curves, the cabin's outlines conform to its surroundings. Without artificial stain, or varnish, or veneer, it *is* what it seems, a genuine thing, a jewel in the rough. And it is a home. When wind whistles through the cracks and snow sifts into the corners of the room, one draws his stumpy little split-bottomed chair close to the wide hearth and really knows the comfort of fire leaping and sap singing from big birch logs.

Every room except the kitchen (if there be a kitchen) has a couple of beds in it: enough all told for the family and, generally, one spare bed. If much company comes, some pallets are made on the floor for the women and children of the household. In a single-room cabin there usually is a cockloft, reached by a ladder, for storage, and maybe a bunk or two. Closets and pantries there are none, for they would only furnish good harborage for woods-rats and other vermin.

Everything must be in sight and accessible to the housewife's little sedge broom. Linen and small articles of apparel are stored in a chest or a cheap little tin trunk or two. Most of the family wardrobe hangs from pegs in the walls

318 OUR SOUTHERN HIGHLANDERS

or nails in the loft beams, along with strings of dried apples, peppers, bunches of herbs, twists of tobacco, gourds full of seeds, the hunter's pouch, and other odd bric-a-brac interesting to "furrin" eyes. The narrow mantel-shelf holds pipes and snuff and various other articles of frequent use, among them a twig or two of sweet birch that has been chewed to shreds at one end and is queerly discolored with something brown (this is what the mountain woman calls her "tooth brush" — a snuff stick, understand).

For wall decorations there may be a few gaudy advertisements lithographed in colors, perhaps some halftones from magazines that travelers have left (a magazine is always called a "book" in this region, as, I think, throughout the South). Of late years the agents for photo-enlarging companies have invaded the mountains and have reaped a harvest; for if there be one curse of civilization that our hillsman craves, it is a huge *tinted* "family group" in an abominable rococo frame.

There is an almanac in the cabin, but no clock. "What does man need of a clock when he has a good-crowin' rooster?" Strange as it may seem, in this roughest of backwoods countries I have never seen candles, unless they were brought in by outsiders like myself. Beef, you must remember, is exported, not eaten, by our farmers, and hence there is no tallow to make candles with. Instead of these, every home is provided with a kerosene lamp of narrow wick, and seldom do you find a chimney for it. This is partly because lamp chimneys are hard to carry safely over the mountain roads and partly because "man can do without sich like, anyhow." But kerosene, also, is hard to transport, and so one sometimes will find pine knots used for illumination; but oftener the woman will pour hog's grease into a tin or saucer, twist up a bit of rag for the wick and so make a "slut" that, believe me, deserves the name. In fact, the supply of pine knots within convenient distance of home is soon exhausted, and anyway, as the mountaineer disdains to be forehanded, he would burn up the knots for kindling rather than save any for illumination.

Very few cabins have carpet on the floor. It would hold too much mud from the feet of the men who would not use a scraper if there was one. Beds generally are bought, nowadays, at the stores, but some are home-made, with bedcords of bast rope. Tables and chairs mostly are made on the spot or obtained by barter from some handy neighbor. In many homes you will still find the ancient spinning-wheel, with a hand-loom on the porch and in the loft there will be a set of quilting frames for making "kivers."

Out in the yard you see an ash hopper for running the lye to make soap, maybe a few bee gums sawed from hollow logs, and a crude but effective cider press. At the spring there is a box for cold storage in summer. Near by stands the great iron kettle for boiling clothes, making soap, scalding pigs, and a variety of other uses. Alongside of it is the "battlin' block" on which the family wash is hammered with a beetle ("battlin' stick") if the woman has no washboard, which very often is the case.

Naturally there can be no privacy and hence no delicacy, in such a home. I never will forget my embarrassment about getting to bed the first night I ever spent in a one-room cabin where there was a good-sized family. I did not know what was expected of me. When everybody looked sleepy I went outdoors and strolled around in the moonlight until the women had time to retire. On returning to the house I found them still bolt upright around the hearth. Then the hostess pointed to the bed I was to occupy and said it was ready whenever I was. Well, I "shucked off my clothes," tumbled in, turned my face to the wall, and imme-

"Be it ever so humble——"

diately everybody else did the same. That is the way to do : just *go* to bed ! I lay there awake for a long time. Finally I had to roll over. A ruddy glow from the embers showed the family in all postures of deep, healthy slumber. It also showed something glittering on the nipple of the long, muzzle-loading rifle that hung over the father's bed. It was a bright, new percussion cap, where a greased rag had been when I went out for my moonlight stroll. There was no need of a curtain in that house. They could do without.

I have been describing an average mountain home. In valleys and coves there are better ones, of course. Along the railroads, and on fertile plateaus between the Blue Ridge and the Unakas, are hundreds of fine farms, cultivated by machinery, and here dwell a class of farmers that are scarcely to be distinguished from people of similar station in the West. But a prosperous and educated few are not the people. When speaking of southern mountaineers I mean the mass, or the average, and the pictures here given are typical of that mass. It is not the well-to-do valley people, but the real mountaineers, who are especially interesting to the reading public; and they are interesting *chiefly* because they preserve traits and manners that have been transmitted almost unchanged from ancient times—because, as John Fox puts it, they are "a distinct remnant of an Anglo-Saxon past."

Almost everywhere in the backwoods of Appalachia we have with us to-day, in flesh and blood, the Indian-fighter of our colonial border—aye, back of him, the half-wild clansman of elder Britain—adapted to other conditions, but still virtually the same in character, in ideas, in attitude toward the outer world. Here, in great part, is spoken to-day the language of Piers the Ploughman, a speech long dead elsewhere, save as fragments survive in some dialects of rural England.

No picture of mountain life would be complete or just if it omitted a class lower than the average hillsman I have been describing. As this is not a pleasant topic, I shall be terse. Hundreds of backwoods families, large ones at that, exist in "blind" cabins that remind one somewhat of Irish hovels, Norwegian saeters, the "black houses" of the Hebrides, the windowless rock piles inhabited by Corsican shepherds and by Basques of the Pyrenees. Such a cabin has but one room for all purposes. In rainy or gusty weather, when the two doors must be closed, no light enters the room save through

cracks in the wall and down the chimney.   In
the damp climate of western Carolina such an
interior is fusty, or even wet.   In many cases
the chimney is no more than a semi-circular pile
of rough rocks and rises no higher than a man's
shoulder, hence the common saying, "You can
set by the fire and spit out through the chimbly."
When the wind blows "contrary" one's lungs
choke and his eyes stream from the smoke.

In some of these places you will find a "pet
pig" harbored in the house.   I know of two
cases where the pig was kept in a box directly
under the table, so that scraps could be chucked
to him without rising from dinner.

Hastening from this extreme, we still shall
find dire poverty the rule rather than the exception among the multitude of "branch-water
people."   One house will have only an earthen
floor; another will be so small that "you cain't
cuss a cat in it 'thout gittin' ha'r in yer teeth."
Utensils are limited to a frying-pan, an iron pot,
a coffee-pot, a bucket, and some gourds.   There
is not enough tableware to go around, and children eat out of their parents' plates, or all
"soup-in together" around one bowl of stew or
porridge.

Even to families that are fairly well-to-do
there will come periods of famine, such as Lin-

324 OUR SOUTHERN HIGHLANDERS

coln, speaking of his boyhood, called "pretty
pinching times." Hickory ashes then are used
as a substitute for soda in biscuits, and the empty
salt-gourd will be soaked for brine to cook with.
Once, when I was boarding with a good family,
our stores ran out of everything, and none of
our neighbors had the least to spare. We had
no meat of any kind for two weeks (the game
had migrated) and no lard or other grease for
nearly a week. Then the meal and salt played
out. One day we were reduced to potatoes
"straight," which were parboiled in fresh
water, and then burnt a little on the surface as
substitute for salt. Another day we had not a
bite but string beans boiled in unsalted water.

It is not uncommon in the far backwoods for
a traveler, asking for a match, to be told there
is none in the house, nor even the pioneers' flint
and steel. Should the embers on the hearth go
out, someone must tramp to a neighbor's and
fetch fire on a torch. Hence the saying : "Have
you come to borry fire, that you're in sich a
hurry you can't chat?"

The shifts and expedients to which some of
the mountain women are put, from lack of utensils and vessels, are simply pathetic. John Fox
tells of a young preacher who stopped at a cabin
in Georgia to pass the night. "His hostess, as

a mark of unusual distinction, killed a chicken, and dressed it in a pan. She rinsed the pan and made up her dough in it. She rinsed it again and went out and used it for a milk-pail. She came in, rinsed it again, and went to the spring and brought it back full of water. She filled up the glasses on the table, and gave him the pan with the rest of the water in which to wash his hands. The woman was not a slattern; it was the only utensil she had."

Such poverty is exceptional; yet it is an all but universal rule that anything that cannot be cooked in a pot or fried in a pan must go begging in the mountains. Once I helped my hostess to make kraut. We chopped up a hundred pounds of cabbage with no cutter but a tin coffee-can, holding this in the two hands and chopping downward with the edge. Many times I stopped to hammer the edge smooth on a round stick. Verily this is the land of make-it-yourself-or-do-without!

Yet, however destitute the mountain people may be, they are never abject. The mordant misery of hunger is borne with a sardonic grin. After a course of such diet as described above, a woman laughingly said to me, "I'm gittin' the dropsy—the meat is all droppin' off my bones." During the campaign of 1904 a brother

Democrat confided to me that "The people around hyur is so pore that if free silver war shipped in by the carload, we-uns couldn't pay the freight." So, when a settlement is dubbed Poverty, it is with no suggestion of whining lament, but with the stoical good-humor that shows in Needmore, Poor Fork, Long Hungry, No Pone, and No Fat—all of them real names.

Occasionally, as at "hog-killin' time," the poorest live in abundance; occasionally, as at Christmas, they will go on sprees. But, taking them the year through, the highlanders are a notably abstemious race. When a family is reduced to dry corn bread and black coffee unsweetened—so much and no more—it will joke about the lack of meat and vegetables. And, when there is meat, two mountaineers engaged in hard outdoor work will consume less of it than a northern office-man would eat. Indeed, the heartiness with which "furriners" stuff themselves is a wonder and a merriment to the people of the hills. When a friend came to visit me, the landlady giggled an aside to her husband: "Git the almanick and see when that feller 'll full!" (as though she were bidding him look to see when the moon would be full).

In truth, it is not so bad to be poor where everyone else is in the same fix. One does not lose caste nor self-respect. He is not tempted by a display of good things all around him, nor is he embittered by the haughtiness and extravagance of the rich. And, socially, the mountaineer is a democrat by nature: equal to any man, as all men are equal before him. Even though hunger be eating like a slow acid into his vitals, he still will preserve a high spirit, a proud independence, that accepts no favor unless it be offered in a neighborly way, as man to man. I have never seen a mountain beggar; never heard of one.

Charity, or anything that smells to him like charity, is declined with patrician dignity or open scorn. In the last house up Hazel Creek dwelt "old man" Stiles. He had a large family, and was on the verge of destitution. His eldest son, a veteran from the Philippines, had been invalided home, and died there. Jack Coburn, in the kindness of his heart, sent away and got a blank form of application to the Government for funeral expenses, to which the family was entitled by law. He filled it out, all but the signature, and rode away up to Stiles's to have the old man sign it. But Stiles peremptorily refused to accept from the nation what was due his dead son. "I ain't that hard pushed yit," was his first and last word on the subject. This might seem to be the very perversity of ignorance; but it was, in fact, renunciation on a point of honor, and native pride refused to see the matter in any other light.

The mountaineer, born and bred to Spartan self-denial, has a scorn of luxury, regarding its effeminacies with the same contempt as does the nomadic Arab. And any assumption of superiority he will resent with blow or sarcasm. A ragged hobbledehoy stood on the Vanderbilt grounds at Biltmore, mouth open but silent, watching a gardener at work. The latter, annoyed by the boy's vacuous stare, spoke up sharply: "What do you want?" Like a flash the lad retorted: "Oh, dad sent me down hyur to look at the place—said if I liked it, he mought buy it for me."

Once, as an experiment, I took a backwoodsman from the Smokies to Knoxville, and put him up at a good hotel. Was he self-conscious, bashful? Not a bit of it. When the waiter brought him a juicy tenderloin, he snapped: "I don't eat my meat raw!" It was hard to find anything on the long menu that he would eat. On the street he held his head proudly erect, and regarded the crowd with an expression of "Tetch me gin ye dar!" Although the surroundings were as strange to him as a city of

Mars would be to us, he showed neither concern nor approval, but rather a fine disdain, like that of Diogenes at the country fair: "Lord, how many things there be in this world of which Diogenes hath no need!"

The poverty of the mountain people is naked, but high-minded and unashamed. To comment on it, as I have done, is taken as an impertinence. This is a fine trait, in its way, though rather hard on a descriptive writer whose motives are ascribed to mere vulgarity and a taste for scandal-mongering. The people, of course, have no ghost of an idea that poverty may be more picturesque than luxury; and they are quite as far from conceiving that a plain and friendly statement of their actual condition, published to the world, is the surest way to awaken the nation to consciousness of its duties toward a region that it has so long and so singularly neglected.

The worst enemies of the mountain people are those public men who, knowing the true state of things, yet conceal or deny the facts in order to salve a sore local pride, encourage the supine fatalism of "what must be will be," and so drug the highlanders back into their Rip Van Winkle sleep.

CHAPTER XV

HOME FOLKS AND NEIGHBOR PEOPLE

DESPITE the low standard of living that prevails in the backwoods, the average mountain home is a happy one, as homes go. There is little worry and less fret. Nobody's nerves are on edge. Our highlander views all exigencies of life with the calm fortitude and tolerant good-humor of Bret Harte's southwesterner, "to whom cyclones, famine, drought, floods, pestilence and savages were things to be accepted, and whom disaster, if it did not stimulate, certainly did not appall."

It is a patriarchal existence. The man of the house is lord. He takes no orders from anybody at home or abroad. Whether he shall work or visit or roam the woods with dog and gun is nobody's affair but his own. About family matters he consults with his wife, but in the end his word is law. If Madame be a bit shrewish he is likely to tolerate it as natural to the weaker vessel; but if she should go too far he checks her with a curt " Shet up! " and the incident is closed.

" The woman," as every wife is called, has her kingdom within the house, and her man seldom meddles with its administration. Now and then he may grumble " A woman 's allers findin' somethin' to do that a man can't see no sense in;" but, then, the Lord made women fussy over trifles—His ways are inscrutable—so why bother about it?

The mountain farmer's wife is not only a household drudge, but a field-hand as well. She helps to plant, hoes corn, gathers fodder, sometimes even plows or splits rails. It is the commonest of sights for a woman to be awkwardly hacking up firewood with a dull axe. When her man leaves home on a journey he is not likely to have laid in wood for the stove or hearth: so she and the children must drag from the hillsides whatever dead timber they can find.

Outside the towns no hat is lifted to maid or wife. A swain would consider it belittled his dignity. At table, if women be seated at all, the dishes are passed first to the men; but generally the wife stands by and serves. There is no conscious discourtesy in such customs; but they betoken an indifference to woman's weakness, a disregard for her finer nature, a denial of her proper rank, that are real and deep-seated in the mountaineer. To him she is little more than a sort of superior domestic animal. The chivalric regard for women that characterized our pioneers of the Far West is altogether lacking in the habits of the backwoodsman of Appalachia.

And yet it is seldom that a highland woman complains of her lot. She knows no other. From aboriginal times the men of her race have been warriors, hunters, herdsmen, clearers of forests, and their women have toiled in the fields. Indeed she would scarce respect her husband if he did not lord it over her and cast upon her the menial tasks. It is "manners" for a woman to drudge and obey. All respectable wives do that. And they stay at home where they belong, never visiting or going anywhere without first asking their husband's consent.

I am satisfied that there is less bickering in mountain households than in the most advanced society of Christendom. Certainly there are fewer divorces in proportion to the marriages. This is not by grace of any uncommon regard for the seventh commandment, but rather from a more tolerant attitude of mind.

Mountain women marry early, many of them at fourteen or fifteen, and nearly all before they are twenty. Large families are the rule, seven to ten children being considered normal, and fifteen is not an uncommon number; but the infant mortality is high.

The children have few toys other than rag dolls, broken bits of crockery for " play-purties," and such " ridey-hosses " and so forth as they make for themselves. They play few games, but rather frisk about like young colts without aim or method. Every mountain child has at least one dog for a playfellow, and sometimes a pet pig is equally familiar. In many districts there is not enough level land for a ballground. A prime amusement of the small boys is " rocking " (throwing stones at marks or at each other), in which rather doubtful pastime they become singularly expert.

To encourage a child to do chores about the house and stable, he may be promised a pig of his own the next time a sow litters. To know when to look for the pigs an expedient is practiced that I never heard of elsewhere: the child bores a small hole at the base of his thumbnail. I was assured by a mountain preacher that the hole " will grow out to the edge of the nail in three months and twenty-four days "—the period, he said, of a sow's gestation (in reality the average term is about three months).

Most mountaineers are indulgent, super-indulgent parents. The oft-heard threat " I'll w'ar ye out with a hick'ry!" is seldom carried out. The boys, especially, grow up with little restraint beyond their own natural sense of filial duty. Little children are allowed to eat and drink anything they want—green fruit, adulterated candy, fresh cider, no matter what—to the limit of repletion; and fatal consequences are not rare. I have observed the very perversity of license allowed children, similar to what Julian Ralph tells of a man on Bullskin Creek, who, explaining why his child died, said that " No one couldn't make her take no medicine; she just wouldn't take it; she was a Baker through and through, and you never could make a Baker do nothin' he didn't want to!"

The saddest spectacle in the mountains is the tiny burial-ground, without a headstone or headboard in it, all overgrown with weeds, and perhaps unfenced, with cattle grazing over the low mounds or sunken graves. The spot seems never to be visited between interments. I have remarked elsewhere that most mountaineers are singularly callous in the presence of serious injury or death. They show a no less remarkable lack of reverence for the dead. Nothing on earth can be more poignantly lonesome than one of these mountain burial-places, nothing so mutely evident of neglect.

Funeral services are extremely simple. In the backwoods, where lumber is scarce, a coffin will be knocked together from rough planks taken from someone's loft, or out of puncheons hewn from the green trees. It is slung on poles and carried like a litter. The only exercises at the grave are singing and praying; and sometimes even those are omitted, as in case no preacher can be summoned in time.

In all back settlements that I have visited, from Kentucky southward, there is a strange custom as to the funeral sermon, that seems to have no analogue elsewhere. It is not preached until long after the interment, maybe a year or several years. In some districts the practice is to hold joint services, at the same time and place, for all in the neighborhood who died within the year. The time chosen will be after the crops are gathered, so that everybody can attend. In other places a husband's funeral sermon is postponed until his wife dies, or *vice versa,* though the interval may be many years. These collective funeral services last two or three days, and are attended by hundreds of people, like a camp-meeting.

Strange scenes sometimes are witnessed at the

graveside, prompted perhaps by weird superstitions. At one of our burials, which was attended by more than the usual retinue of kinsfolk, there were present two mothers who bore
each other the deadliest hate that women know.
Each had a child at her breast. When the clods
fell, they silently exchanged babies long enough
for each to suckle her rival's child. Was it a
reconciliation cemented by the very life of their
blood? Or was it a charm to keep off evil
spirits? No one could (or would) explain it to
me.

Weddings never are celebrated in church, but
at the home of the bride, and are jolly occasions,
of course. Often the young men, stimulated
with more or less "moonshine," add the literally stunning compliment of a shivaree.

The mountaineers have a native fondness for
music and dancing, which, with the shouting-
spells of their revivals, are the only outlets for
those powerful emotions which otherwise they
studiously conceal. The harmony of " part
singing " is unknown in the back districts, where
men and women both sing in a jerky treble.
Most of their music is in the weird, plaintive
minor key that seems spontaneous with primitive
people throughout the world. Not only the tone,
but the sentiment of their hymns and ballads is

Photo by J. O. Morrell

"Come in and Rest."

usually of a melancholy nature, expressing the wrath of God and the doom of sinners, or the luckless adventures of wild blades and of maidens all forlorn. A highlander might well say, with the clown in *A Winter's Tale,* "I love a ballad but even too well; if it be doleful matter, merrily set down, or a very pleasant thing indeed, and sung lamentably."

But where banjo and fiddle enter, the vapors vanish. Up strike The Fox Chase, Shady Grove, Gamblin' man, Sourwood Mountain, and knees are limbered, and merry voices rise.—

> Call up your dog, O call up your dog!
> Call up your dog!
> Call up your dog!
> Let 's a-go huntin' to ketch a groundhog.
> Rang tang a-whaddle linky day!

Wherever the church has not put its ban on "twistifications" the country dance is the chief amusement of young and old. I have never succeeded in memorizing the queer "calls" at these dances, in proper order, and so take the liberty of quoting from Mr. Haney's *Mountain People of Kentucky.*—

"Eight hands up and go to the left; half and back; corners turn; partners sash-i-ate. First four, forwards and back; forward again and cross over; forward and back and home you go. Gents stand and ladies swing in the center; own partners and half sash-i-ate.

"Eight hands and gone again; half and back; partners by the right and opposite by the left—sash-i-ate. Right hands across and howdy do? Left and back and how are you? Opposite partners, half sash-i-ate and go to the next (and so on for each couple).

"All hands up and go to the left. Hit the floor. Corners turn and sash-i-ate. First couple cage the bird with three arms around. Bird hop out and hoot-owl in; three arms around and hootin' agin. Swing and circle four, ladies change and gents the same; right and left; the shoo-fly swing (and so on for each couple)."

In homes where dancing is not permitted, and often in others, "play-parties" are held, at which social games are practiced with childlike abandon: Roll the Platter, Weavilly Wheat, Needle's Eye, We Fish Who Bite, Grin an' Go 'Foot, Swing the Cymblin, Skip t' m' Lou (pronounced "Skip-tum a-loo") and many others of a rollicking, half-dancing nature.

Round the house; skip t' m' Lou, my darlin'.
Steal my partner and I'll steal again; skip (etc.).
Take her and go with her—I don't care; skip (etc.).
I can get another as pretty as you; skip (etc.),
Pretty as a red-bird, and prettier too; skip (etc.).

A substitute for the church fair is the "poke-supper," at which dainty pokes (bags) of cake and other home-made delicacies are auctioned off to the highest bidder. Whoever bids-in a poke is entitled to eat with the girl who prepared it, and escort her home. The rivalry excited among the mountain swains by such artful lures may be judged from the fact that, in a neighborhood where a man's work brings only a dollar a day, a pretty girl's poke may be bid up to ten, twenty, or even fifty dollars.

As a rule, the only holidays observed in the mountains, outside the towns, are Christmas and New Year's. Christmas is celebrated after the southern fashion, which seems bizarre indeed to one witnessing it for the first time. The boys and men, having no firecrackers (which they would disdain, anyway), go about shooting revolvers and drinking to the limit of capacity or supply. Blank cartridges are never used in this uproarious jollification, and the courses of the bullets are left to chance, so that discreet people keep their noses indoors. Christmas is a day of license, of general indulgence, it being tacitly assumed that punishment is remitted for any ordinary sins of the flesh that may be committed on that day. There is no church festivity, nor are Christmas trees ever set up. Few mountain children hang up their stockings, and many have never heard of Santa Claus.

New Year's Day is celebrated with whatever effervescence remains from Christmas, and in the same manner; but generally it is a feeble reminder, as the liquid stimulus has run short and there are many sore heads in the neighborhood.

Most of the mountain preachers nowadays denounce dances and " play-parties " as sinful diversions, though their real objection seems to be that such gatherings are counter-attractions that thin out the religious ones. Be that as it may, they certainly have put a damper on frolics, so that in very many mountain settlements " goin' to meetin' " is recognized primarily as a social function and affords almost the only chance for recreation in which family can join family without restraint.

Meetings are held in the log schoolhouse. The congregation ranges itself, men on one side, women on the other, on rude benches that sometimes have no backs. Everybody goes. If one judged from attendance he would rate our highlanders as the most religious people in America. This impression is strengthened, in a stranger, by the grave and astoundingly patient attention that is given an illiterate or nearly illiterate minister while he holds forth for two or three mortal hours on the beauties of predestination, free-will, foreordination, immersion, foot-washing, or on the delinquencies of "them acorn-fed critters that has gone New Light over in Cope's Cove."

After an *al fresco* lunch, everybody doggedly returns to hear another circuit-rider expound and denounce at the top of his voice until late afternoon—as long as "the spirit lasts" and he has "good wind." When he warms up, he throws in a gasping *ah* or *uh* at short intervals, which constitutes the "holy tone." Doctor MacClintock gives this example: "Oh, brethren, repent ye, and repent ye of your sins, ah; fer if ye don't, ah, the Lord, ah, he will grab yer by the seat of yer pants, ah, and hold yer over hell fire till ye holler like a coon!"

During these services there is a good deal of running in and out by the men and boys, most of whom gradually congregate on the outside to whittle, gossip, drive bargains, and debate among themselves some point of dogma that is too good to keep still about.

Nearly all of our highlanders, from youth upward, show an amazing fondness for theological dispute. This consists mainly in capping texts, instead of reasoning, with the single-minded purpose of confusing or downing an opponent. Into this battle of memories rather than of wits the most worthless scapegrace will enter with keen gusto and perfect seriousness. I have known two or three hundred mountain lumber-jacks, hard-swearing and hard-drinking tough-as-they-make-'ems, to be whetted to a fighting edge over the rocky problem " Was Saul damned? " (Can a suicide enter the kingdom of heaven?)

The mountaineers are intensely, universally Protestant. You will seldom find a backwoodsman who knows what a Roman Catholic is. As John Fox says, " He is the only man in the world whom the Catholic Church has made little or no effort to proselyte. Dislike of Episcopalianism is still strong among people who do not know, or pretend not to know, what the word means. ' Any Episcopalians around here?' asked a clergyman at a mountain cabin. ' I don't know,' said the old woman. ' Jim's got the skins of a lot o' varmints up in the loft. Mebbe you can find one up thar.' "

The first settlers of Appalachia mainly were Presbyterians, as became Scotch-Irishmen, but they fell away from that faith, partly because the wilderness was too poor to support a regular ministry, and partly because it was too democratic for Calvinism with its supreme authority of the clergy. This much of seventeenth century Calvinism the mountaineer retains: a passion for hair-splitting argument over points of doctrine, and the cocksure intolerance of John Knox; but the ancestral creed itself has been forgotten.

The circuit-rider, whether Methodist or Baptist, found here a field ripe for his harvest. Being himself self-supporting and unassuming, he easily won the confidence of the people. He preached a highly emotional religion that worked his audience into the ecstasy that all primitive people love. And he introduced a mighty agent of evangelization among outdoor folk when he started the camp-meeting.

The season for camp-meetings is from mid-August to October. The festival may last a week in one place. It is a jubilee-week to the work-worn and home-chained women, their only diversion from a year of unspeakably monotonous toil. And for the young folks, it is their theater, their circus, their county fair. (I say this with no disrespect: " big-meetin' time " is a gala week, if there be any such thing at all in the mountains—its attractiveness is full as much secular as spiritual to the great body of the people.)

It is a camp by day only, or up to closing time. No mountaineer owns a tent. Preachers and exhorters are housed nearby, and visitors from all the country scatter about with their friends, or sleep in the open, cooking their meals by the wayside.

In these backwoods revival meetings we can witness to-day the weird phenomena of ungovernable shouting, ecstasy, bodily contortions, trance, catalepsy, and other results of hypnotic suggestion and the contagious one-mindedness of an overwrought crowd. This is called " taking a big through," and is regarded as the madness of supernatural joy. It is a mild form of that extraordinary frenzy which swept the Kentucky settlements in 1800, when thousands of men and women at the camp-meetings fell victims to " the jerks," " barking exercises," erotic vagaries, physical wreckage, or insanity, to which the frenzy led.

Many mountaineers are easily carried away by new doctrines extravagantly presented. Religious mania is taken for inspiration by the superstitious who are looking for " signs and wonders." At one time Mormon prophets lured women from the backwoods of western Carolina and eastern Tennessee. Later there was a similar exodus of people to the Castellites, a sect of whom it was commonly remarked that " everybody who joins the Castellites goes crazy." In our day the same may be said of the Holy Rollers and Holiness People.

In a feud town of eastern Kentucky, not long ago, I saw two Holiness exhorters prancing before a solemnly attentive crowd in the court-house square, one of them shouting and exhibiting the " holy laugh," while the other pointed to the Cumberland River and cried, "I don't say *if* I had the faith, I say I *have* the faith, to walk over that river dry-shod!" I scanned the crowd, and saw nothing but belief, or willingness to believe, on any countenance. Of course, most mountaineers are more intelligent than that; but few of them are free from superstitions of one kind or other. There are to-day many believers in witchcraft among them (though none own it to any but their intimates) and nearly everybody in the hills has faith in portents.

The mountain clergy, as a general rule, are hostile to "book larnin'," for "there ain't no Holy Ghost in it." One of them who had spent three months at a theological school told President Frost, "Yes, the seminary is a good place ter go and git rested up, but 'tain't worth while fer me ter go thar no more 's long as I've got good wind."

It used to amuse me to explain how I knew

that the earth was a sphere; but one day, when I was busy, a tiresome old preacher put the everlasting question to me: "Do you believe the yearth is round?" An impish perversity seized me and I answered, "No—all blamed humbug!" "Amen!" cried my delighted catechist, "I knowed in reason you had more sense."

In general the religion of the mountaineers has little influence on every-day behavior, little to do with the moral law. Salvation is by faith alone, and not by works. Sometimes a man is "churched" for breaking the Sabbath, "cussin'," "tale-bearin'"; but sins of the flesh are rarely punished, being regarded as amiable frailties of mankind. It should be understood that the mountaineer's morals are "all tail-first," like those of Alan Breck in Stevenson's *Kidnapped*.

One of our old-timers nonchalantly admitted in court that he and a preacher had marked a false corner-tree which figured in an important land suit. On cross-examination he was asked:

"You admit that you and Preacher X—— forged that corner-tree? Didn't you give Preacher X—— a good character, in your testimony? Do you consider it consistent with his profession as a minister of the Gospel to forge corner-trees?"

"Aw," replied the witness, "religion ain't got nothin' to do with corner-trees!"

John Fox relates that, "A feud leader who had about exterminated the opposing faction, and had made a good fortune for a mountaineer while doing it, for he kept his men busy getting out timber when they weren't fighting, said to me in all seriousness:

"'I have triumphed agin my enemies time and time agin. The Lord's on my side, and I gits a better and better Christian ever' year.'

"A preacher, riding down a ravine, came upon an old mountaineer hiding in the bushes with his rifle.

"'What are you doing there, my friend?'

"'Ride on, stranger,' was the easy answer. 'I'm a-waitin' fer Jim Johnson, and with the help of the Lawd I'm goin' to blow his damn head off.'"

But let us never lose sight of the fact that these people, intellectually, are not living in our age. To judge them fairly we must go back and get a medieval point of view, which, by the way, persisted in Europe and America until well into the Georgian period. If history be too dry, read Stevenson's *Kidnapped,* and especially its sequel *David Balfour,* to learn what that viewpoint was. The parallel is so close—

eighteenth century Britain and twentieth century Appalachia—that here we walk the same
paths with Alan and David, the Edinboro' law-
sharks, Katriona and Lady Allardyce. The
only difference of moment is that we have no
aristocracy.

As for the morals of our highlanders, they are
precisely what any well-read person would expect after taking their belatedness into consideration. In speech and conduct, when at ease
among themselves, they are frank, old-fashioned
Englishmen and Scots, such as Fielding and
Smollet and Pepys and Burns have shown us
to the life. Their manners are boorish, of
course, judged by a feminized modern standard,
and their home conversation is as coarse as the
mixed-company speeches in Shakespeare's com-
edies or the offhand pleasantries of Good Queen
Bess.

But what is refinement? What is morality?

" I don't mind," said the Belovéd Vagabond,
" I don't mind the frank dungheap outside a
German peasant's kitchen window; but what I
loathe and abominate is the dungheap hidden
beneath Hedwige's draper papa's parlor floor."
And we do well to consider that fine remark
by Sir Oliver Lodge: " Vice is reversion to a
lower type *after perception of a higher.*"

I have seen the worst as well as the best of Appalachia. There *are* " places on Sand Mountain " — scores of them — where unspeakable orgies prevail at times. But I know that between these two extremes the great mass of the mountain people are very like persons of similar station elsewhere, just human, with human frailties, only a little more honest, I think, in owning them. And even in the tenebra of far-back coves, where conditions exist as gross as anything to be found in the wynds and closes of our great cities, there is this blessed difference: that these half-wild creatures have not been hoplessly submerged, have not been driven into desperate war against society. The worst of them still have good traits, strong characters, something responsive to decent treatment. They are kind-hearted, loyal to their friends, quick to help anyone in distress. They know nothing of civilization. They are simply *the unstarted* — and their thews are sound.

CHAPTER XVI

THE MOUNTAIN DIALECT

ONE day I handed a volume of John Fox's stories to a neighbor and asked him to read it, being curious to learn how those vivid pictures of mountain life would impress one who was born and bred in the same atmosphere. He scanned a few lines of the dialogue, then suddenly stared at me in amazement.

"What's the matter with it?" I asked, wondering what he could have found to startie him at the very beginning of a story.

"Why, that feller *don't know how to spell!*"

Gravely I explained that dialect must be spelled as it is pronounced, so far as possible, or the life and savor of it would be lost. But it was of no use. My friend was outraged. "That tale-teller then is jest makin' fun of the mountain people by misspellin' our talk. You educated folks don't spell your own words the way you say them."

A most palpable hit; and it gave me a new point of view.

To the mountaineers themselves their speech is natural and proper, of course, and when they see it bared to the spotlight, all eyes drawn toward it by an orthography that is as odd to them as it is to us, they are stirred to wrath, just as we would be if our conversation were reported by some Josh Billings or Artemas Ward.

The curse of dialect writing is elision. Still, no one can write it without using the apostrophe more than he likes to; for our highland speech is excessively clipped. " I'm comin' d'reck'ly " has a quaintness that should not be lost. We cannot visualize the shambling but eager mountaineer with a sample of ore in his hand unless the writer reports him faithfully: " Wisht you'd 'zamine this rock fer me—I heern tell you was one o' them 'sperts."

Although the hillsmen save some breath in this way, they waste a good deal by inserting sounds where they do not belong. Sometimes it is only an added consonant: gyarden, acrost, corkus (caucus) ; sometimes a syllable: loaferer, musicianer, suddenty. Occasionally a word is both added to and clipped from, as cyarn (carrion). They are fond of grace syllables: " I gotta me a deck o' cyards." " There ain't nary bitty sense in it."

More interesting are substitutions of one sound for another. In mountain dialect all vowels may be interchanged with others. Various sounds of *a* are confused with *e*, as hed (had), kem (came), keerful; or with *i*, grit (grate), rifle (raffle); with *o*, pomper, toper (taper), wrop; or with *u*, fur, ruther. So any other vowel may serve in place of *e*: sarve, chist. upsot, turrible. Any other may displace *i*: arn (iron), eetch, hender, whope or whup. The *o* sounds are more stable, but we have crap (crop), yan, clus, and many similar variants. Any other vowel may do for *u*: braysh or bresh (brush), shet, sich, shore (sure).

Mountaineers have peculiar difficulty with diphthongs: haar (hair), cheer (chair), brile, and a host of others. The word coil is variously pronounced quile, querl or quorl.

Substitution of consonants is not so common as of vowels, but most hillsmen say nabel (navel), ballet (ballad), Babtis', rench or rinch, brickle (brittle), and many say atter or arter, jue (due), tejus, vascinator (fascinator— a woman's scarf). They never drop *h*, nor substitute anything for it.

The word woman has suffered some strange sea-changes. Most mountaineers pronounce it correctly, but some drop the *w* ('oman), others

Photo by Paul Fink

The Alum Cave, Great Smoky Mountains.

add an *r* (womern and wimmern), while in Michell County, North Carolina, we hear the extraordinary forms ummern and dummern ("La, look at all the dummerunses a-comin'!")

On the other hand, some words that most Americans mispronounce are always sounded correctly in the southern highlands, as dew and new (never doo, noo). Creek is always given its true *ee* sound, never crick. Nare (as we spell it in dialect stories) is simply the right pronunciation of ne'er, and nary is ne'er a, with the *a* turned into a short *i* sound.

It should be understood that the dialect varies a good deal from place to place, and, even in the same neighborhood, we rarely hear all families speaking it alike. Outlanders who essay to write it are prone to err by making their characters speak it too consistently. It is only in the backwoods, or among old people and the penned-at-home women, that the dialect is used with any integrity. In railroad towns we hear little of it, and farmers who trade in those towns adapt their speech somewhat to the company they may be in. The same man, at different times, may say can't and cain't, set and sot, jest and jes' and jist, atter and arter or after, seed and seen, here and hyur and hyar, heerd and heern or heard, sich and sech, took and tuk—there is no uniformity about it. An unconscious sense of euphony seems to govern the choice of hit or it, there or thar.

Since the Appalachian people have a marked Scotch-Irish strain, we would expect their speech to show a strong Scotch influence. So far as vocabulary is concerned, there is really little of it. A few words, caigy (cadgy), coggled, fer nent, gin for if, needcessity, trollop, almost exhaust the list of distinct Scotticisms. The Scotch-Irish, as we call them, were mainly Ulstermen, and the Ulster dialect of to-day bears little analogy to that of Appalachia.

Scotch influence does appear, however, in one vital characteristic of the pronunciation: with few exceptions our highlanders sound *r* distinctly wherever it occurs, though they never trill it. In the British Isles this constant sounding of *r* in all positions is peculiar, I think, to Scotland, Ireland, and a few small districts in the northern border counties of England. With us it is general practice outside of New England and those parts of the southern lowlands that had no flood of Celtic immigration in the eighteenth century. I have never heard a Carolina mountaineer say niggah or No'th Ca'lina, though in the last word the syllable *ro* is often elided.

In some mountain districts we hear do' (door), flo', mo', yo', co'te, sca'ce (long *a*), pusson; but such skipping of the *r* is common only where lowland influence has crept in. Much oftener the *r* is dropped from dare, first, girl, horse, nurse, parcel, worth (dast, fust, gal, hoss, nuss, passel, wuth). By way of compensation the hillsmen sometimes insert a euphonic *r* where it has no business; just as many New Englanders say, "The idear of it!"

Throughout Appalachia such words as last, past, advantage, are pronounced with the same vowel sound as is heard in man. This helps to delimit the people, classifying them with Pennsylvanians and Westerners: a linguistic grouping that will prove significant when we come to study the origin and history of this isolated race.

An editor who had made one or two short trips into the mountains once wrote me that he thought the average mountaineer's vocabulary did not exceed three hundred words. This may be a natural inference if one spends but a few weeks among these people and sees them only under the prosaic conditions of workaday life. But gain their intimacy and you shall find that even the illiterates among them have a range of expression that is truly remarkable. I have myself taken down from the lips of Carolina mountaineers some eight hundred dialectical or obsolete words, to say nothing of the much greater number of standard English terms that they command.

Seldom is a " hill-billy " at a loss for a word. Lacking other means of expression, there will come "spang " from his mouth a coinage of his own. Instantly he will create (always from English roots, of course) new words by combination, or by turning nouns into verbs or otherwise interchanging the parts of speech.

Crudity or deficiency of the verb characterizes the speech of all primitive peoples. In mountain vernacular many words that serve as verbs are only nouns of action, or adjectives, or even adverbs. " That bear 'll meat me a month." " They churched Pitt for tale-bearin'." " Granny kept faultin' us all day." " Are ye fixin' to go squirrelin'? " " Sis blouses her waist a-purpose to carry a pistol." " My boy Jesse book-kept for the camp." " I disgust bad liquor." " This poke salat eats good." " I ain't goin' to bed it no longer " (lie abed). " We can muscle this log up." " I wouldn't pleasure them enough to say it." " Josh ain't much on sweet-heartin'." " I don't confidence them dogs much." " The creek away up thar turkey-tails out into numerous leetle forks."

A verb will be coined from an adverb: "We better git some wood, bettern we?" Or from an adjective: "Much that dog and see won't he come along" (pet him, make much of him). "I didn't do nary thing to contrary her." "Baby, that onion 'll strong ye!" "Little Jimmy fell down and benastied himself to beat the devil."

Conversely, nouns are created from verbs. "Hit don't make no differ." "I didn't hear no give-out at meetin'" (announcement). "You can git ye one more gittin' o' wood up thar." "That Nantahala is a master shut-in, jest a plumb gorge." Or from an adjective: "Them bugs—the little old hatefuls!" "If anybody wanted a history of this county for fifty years he'd git a lavish of it by reading that mine-suit testimony." Or from an adverb: "Nance tuk the biggest through at meetin'!" (shouting spell). An old lady quoted to me in a plaintive quaver:

"It matters not, so I've been told,
Where the body goes when the heart grows cold;

"But," she added, "a person has a rather about where he'd be put."

In mountain vernacular the Old English strong past tense still lives in begun, drunk, holped, rung, shrunk, sprung, stunk, sung, sunk, swum. Holp is used both as preterite and as infinitive: the *o* is long, and the *l* distinctly sounded by most of the people, but elided by such as drop it from almost, already, self (the *l* is elided from help by many who use that form of the verb).

Examples of a strong preterite with dialectical change of the vowel are bruk, brung, drap or drapped, drug, friz, roke or ruck (raked), saunt (sent), shet, shuck (shook), whoped (long *o*). The variant whupped is a Scotticism. Whope is sometimes used in the present tense, but whup is more common. By some the vowel of whup is sounded like *oo* in book (Mr. Fox writes "whoop," which, I presume, he intends for that sound).

In many cases a weak preterite supplants the proper strong one: div, driv, fit, gi'n or give, rid, riv, riz, writ, done, run, seen or seed, blowed, crowed, drawed, growed, knowed, throwed.

There are many corrupt forms of the verb, such as gwine for gone or going, mought (mowt) for might, clim, het, ort or orter, wed (weeded), war (was or were—the *a* as in far), shun (shone), cotch (in all tenses) or cotched, fotch or fotched, borned, hurted, dremp.

Peculiar adjectives are formed from verbs.
" Chair-bottoming is easy settin'-down work."
" When my youngest was a leetle set-along
child " (interpreted as " settin' along the
floor "). " That Thunderhead is the torn-
downdest place!" " Them's the travellinest
hosses ever I seed." " She's the workinest
woman!" " Jim is the disablest one o' the
fam'ly." " Damn this fotch-on kraut that
comes in tin cans!"

A verb may serve as an adverb: " If I'd a-
been thoughted enough." An adverb may be
used as an adjective: " I hope the folks with
you is gaily " (well). An adjective can serve
as an adverb: " He laughed master." Sometimes a conjunction is employed as a preposi-
tion: " We have oblige to take care on him."

These are not mere blunders of individual
illiterates, but usages common throughout the
mountains, and hence real dialect.

The ancient syllabic plural is preserved in
beasties (horses), nesties, posties, trousies (these
are not diminutives), and in that strange word
dummerunses that I cited before.

Pleonasms are abundant. " I done done it "
(have done it or did do it). " Durin' the
while." " In this day and time." " I thought
it would surely, undoubtedly turn cold." " A

small, little bitty hole." "Jane's a tol'able big, large, fleshy woman." "I ginerally, usually take a dram mornin's." "These ridges is might' nigh straight up and down, and, as the feller said, perpendic'lar."

Everywhere in the mountains we hear of biscuit-bread, ham-meat, rifle-gun, rock-clift, ridin'-critter, cow-brute, man-person, women-folks, preacher-man, granny-woman and neighbor-people. In this category belong the famous double-barreled pronouns: we-all and you-all in Kentucky, we-uns and you-uns in Carolina and Tennessee. (I have even heard such locution as this: "Let's we-uns all go over to youerunses house.") Such usages are regarded generally as mere barbarisms, and so they are in English, but Miss Murfree cites correlatives in the Romance languages: French *nous autres,* Italian *noi altri,* Spanish *nosotros.*

The mountaineers have some queer ways of intensifying expression. "I'd *tell* a man," with the stress as here indicated, is simply a strong affirmative. "We had one more *time*" means a rousing good time. "P'int-blank" is a superlative or an epithet: "We jist p'int-blank got it to do." "Well, p'int-blank, if they ever come back again, I'll move!"

A double negative is so common that it may

be crowded into a single word: "I did it the unthoughtless of anything I ever done in my life." Triple negatives are easy: "I ain't got nary none." A mountaineer can accomplish the quadruple: "That boy ain't never done nothin' nohow." Yea, even the quintuple: "I ain't never seen no men-folks of no kind do no washin'."

On the other hand, the veriest illiterates often startle a stranger by glib use of some word that most of us picked up in school or seldom use informally. "I can make a hunderd pound o' pork outen that hog—tutor it jist right." "Them clouds denote rain." "She's so dilitary!" "They stood thar and caviled about it." "That exceeds the measure." "Old Tom is blind, but he can discern when the sun is shinin'." "Jerry proffered to fix the gun for me." I had supposed that the words cuckold and moon-calf had none but literary usage in America, but we often hear them in the mountains, cuckold being employed both as verb and as noun, and moon-calf in its baldly literal sense that would make Prospero's taunt to Caliban a superlative insult.

Our highlander often speaks in Elizabethan or Chaucerian or even pre-Chaucerian terms. His pronoun hit antedates English itself, being the Anglo-Saxon neuter of he. Ey God, a favorite expletive, is the original of egad, and goes back of Chaucer. Ax for ask and kag for keg were the primitive and legitimate forms, which we trace as far as the time of Layamon. When the mountain boy challenges his mate: " I dar ye—I ain't afeared!" his verb and participle are of the same ancient and sterling rank. Afore, atwixt, awar, heap o' folks, peart, up and done it, usen for used, all these everyday expressions of the backwoods were contemporary with the *Canterbury Tales*.

A man said to me of three of our acquaintances: " There's been a fray on the river—I don't know how the fraction begun, but Os feathered into Dan and Phil, feedin' them lead." He meant fray in its original sense of deadly combat, as was fitting where two men were killed. Fraction for rupture is an archaic word, rare in literature, though we find it in *Troilus and Cressida.* " Feathered into them!" Where else can we hear to-day a phrase that passed out of standard English when " villainous saltpetre " supplanted the long-bow? It means to bury an arrow up to the feather, as when the old chronicler Harrison says, " An other arrow should haue beene fethered in his bowels."

Our schoolmaster, composing a form of oath

for the new mail-carrier, remarked: " Let me study this thing over; then I can edzact it "—a verb so rare and obsolete that we find it in no American dictionary, but only in Murray.

A remarkable word, common in the Smokies, is dauncy, defined for me as " mincy about eating," which is to say fastidious, over-nice. Dauncy probably is a variant of daunch, of which the Oxford *New English Dictionary* cites but one example, from the *Townley Mysteries* of *circa* 1460.

A queer term used by Carolina mountaineers, without the faintest notion of its origin, is doney (long *o*) or doney-gal, meaning a sweetheart. Its history is unique. British sailors of the olden time brought it to England from Spanish or Italian ports. Doney is simply *doña* or *donna* a trifle anglicized in pronunciation. Odd, though, that it should be preserved in America by none but backwoodsmen whose ancestors for two centuries never saw the tides!

In the vocabulary of the mountaineers I have detected only three words of directly foreign origin. Doney is one. Another is kraut, which is the sole contribution to highland speech of those numerous Germans (mostly Pennsylvania Dutch) who joined the first settlers in this region, and whose descendants, under wondrously anglicized names, form to-day a considerable element of the highland population. The third is sashiate (French *chassé*), used in calling figures at the country dances.

There is something intrinsically, stubbornly English in the nature of the mountaineer: he will assimilate nothing foreign. In the Smokies the Eastern Band of Cherokees still holds its ancient capital on the Okona Lufty River, and the whites mingle freely with these redskins, bearing them no such despite as they do negroes, but eating at the same table and admitting Indians to the white compartment of a Jim Crow car. Yet the mountain dialect contains not one word of Cherokee origin, albeit many of the whites can speak a little Cherokee.

In our county some Indians always appear at each term of court, and an interpreter must be engaged. He never goes by that name, but by the obsolete title linkister or link'ster, by some lin-gis-ter.

Many other old-fashioned terms are preserved in Appalachia that sound delightfully quaint to strangers who never met them outside of books. A married woman is not addressed as Missis by the mountaineers, but as Mistress when they speak formally, and as Mis' or Miz' for a contraction. We will hear an aged man referred to as "old Grandsir'" So-and-So. "Back this letter for me" is a phrase unchanged from the days before envelopes, when an address had to be written on the back of the letter itself. "Can I borry a race of ginger?" means the unground root—you will find the word in *A Winter's Tale*. "Them sorry fellers" denotes scabby knaves, good-for-nothings. Sorry has no etymological connection with sorrow, but literally means sore-y, covered with sores, and the highlander sticks to its original import.

We have in the mountains many home-born words to fit the circumstances of backwoods life. When maize has passed from the soft and milky stage of roasting-ears, but is not yet hard enough for grinding, the ears are grated into a soft meal and baked into delectable pones called gritted-bread.

In some places to-day we still find the ancient quern or hand-mill, jocularly called an armstrong-machine. Someone who irked from turning it invented the extraordinary improvement that goes by the name of pounding-mill. This consists of a pole pivoted horizontally on top of a post and free to move up and down like the walking-beam of an old-fashioned engine. To one end of this pole is attached a heavy pestle that works in a mortar underneath. At the other end is a box into which water flows from an elevated spout. When the box fills it will go down, lifting the pestle; then the water spills out and the pestle's weight lifts the box back again.

Who knows what a toddick or taddle is? I did not until my friend Dargan reported it from the Nantahala. " Ben didn't git a full turn o' meal, but jest a toddick." When a farmer goes to one of our little tub-mills, mentioned in previous chapters, he leaves a portion of the meal as toll. This he measures out in a toll-dish or toddick or taddle (the name varies with the locality) which the mill-owner left for that purpose. Toddick, then, is a small measure. A turn of meal is so called because " each man's corn is ground in turn—he waits his turn."

When one dines in a cabin back in the hills he will taste some strange dishes that go by still stranger names. Beans dried in the pod, then boiled "hull and all," are called leather-breeches (this is not slang, but the regular name). Green beans in the pod are called snaps; when shelled they are shuck-beans. The old Germans taught their Scotch and English neighbors the merits of scrapple, but here it is known as poor-do.

Lath-open bread is made from biscuit dough, with soda and buttermilk, in the usual way, except that the shortening is worked in last. It is then baked in flat cakes, and has the peculiar property of parting readily into thin flakes when broken edgewise. I suppose that poor-do was originally poor-doin's, and lath-open bread denotes that it opens into lath-like strips. But etymology cannot be pushed recklessly in the mountains, and I offer these clews as a mere surmise.

Your hostess, proffering apple sauce, will ask, " Do you love sass? " I had to kick my chum Andy's shin the first time he faced this question. It is well for a traveler to be forewarned that the word love is commonly used here in the sense of like or relish.

If one is especially fond of a certain dish he declares that he is a fool about it. " I'm a plumb fool about pickle-beans." Conversely, " I ain't much of a fool about liver " is rather more than a hint of distaste. " I et me a bait " literally means a mere snack, but jocosely it may admit a hearty meal. If the provender be scant the hostess may say, " That's right at a smidgen," meaning little more than a mite; but if plenteous, then there are rimptions.

To " grabble 'taters " is to pick from a hill

368 OUR SOUTHERN HIGHLANDERS

of new potatoes a few of the best, then smooth back the soil without disturbing the immature ones.

If the house be in disorder it is said to be all gormed or gaumed up, or things are just in a mommick.

When a man is tired he likely will call it worried; if in a hurry, he is in a swivvet; if nervous, he has the all-overs; if declining in health, he is on the down-go. If he and his neighbor dislike each other, there is a hardness between them; if they quarrel, it is a ruction, a rippit, a jower, or an upscuddle—so be it there are no fatalities which would amount to a real fray.

A choleric or fretful person is tetchious. Survigrous (ser-*vi*-grus) is a superlative of vigorous (here pronounced *vi*-grus, with long *i*) : as "a survigrous baby," "a most survigrous cusser." Bodaciously means bodily or entirely: "I'm bodaciously ruint" (seriously injured). "Sim greened him out bodaciously" (to green out or sap is to outwit in trade). To disfurnish or discon*fit* means to incommode: "I hope it has not disconfit you very bad."

To shamp means to shingle or trim one's hair. A bastard is a woods-colt or an outsider. Slaunchways denotes slanting, and si-godlin or

"Making 'Lasses."

si-antigodlin is out of plumb or out of square
(factitious words, of course—mere nonsense
terms, like catawampus).

Critter and beast are usually restricted to
horse and mule, and brute to a bovine. A bull
or boar is not to be mentioned as such in mixed
company, but male-brute and male-hog are used
as euphemisms.*

A female shoat is called a gilt. A spotted
animal is said to be pieded (pied), and a
striped one is listed. In the Smokies a toad is
called a frog or a toad-frog, and a toadstool is
a frog-stool. The woodpecker is turned around
into a peckerwood, except that the giant woodpecker (here still a common bird) is known as
a woodcock or woodhen.

What the mountaineers call hemlock is the
shrub leucothoe. The hemlock tree is named
spruce-pine, while spruce is he-balsam, balsam
itself is she-balsam, laurel is ivy, and rhododendron is laurel. In some places pine needles are
called twinkles, and the locust insect is known
as a ferro (Pharaoh?). A treetop left on the

---

* So also in the lowland South. An extraordinary affec-
tation of propriety appeared in a dispatch to the *Atlanta
Constitution* of October 29, 1912, which reported that an
exhibitor of cattle at the State fair had been seriously
horned by a *male cow.*

ground after logging is called the lap. Sobby wood means soggy or sodden, and the verb is to sob.

Evening, in the mountains, begins at noon instead of at sunset. Spell is used in the sense of while ("a good spell atterward") and soon for early ("a soon start in the morning"). The hillsmen say "a year come June," "Thursday 'twas a week ago," and "the year nineteen and eight."

Many common English words are used in peculiar senses by the mountain folk, as call for name or mention or occasion, clever for obliging, mimic or mock for resemble, a power or a sight for much, risin' for exceeding (also for inflammation), ruin for injure, scout for elude, stove for jabbed, surround for go around, word for phrase, take off for help yourself. Tale always means an idle or malicious report.

Some highland usages that sound odd to us are really no more than the original and literal meanings, as budget for bag or parcel, hampered for shackled or jailed. When a mountain swain "carries his gal to meetin'" he is not performing so great an athletic feat as was reported by Benjamin Franklin, who said, "My father carried his wife with three children to New England" (from Pennsylvania).

A mountaineer does not throw a stone; he
" flings a rock." He sharpens tools on a grind-
in'-rock or whet-rock. Tomato, cabbage, molasses and baking powder are always used as
plural nouns. " Pass me them molasses."
" I'll have a few more of them cabbage."
" How many bakin'-powders has you got? "

Many other peculiar words and phrases are
explained in their proper place elsewhere in
this volume.

The speech of the southern highlanders is
alive with quaint idioms. " I swapped hosses,
and I'll tell you fer why." " Your name ain't
much common." " Who got to beat? " " You
think me of it in the mornin'." " I 'low to go
to town to-morrow." " The woman's aimin' to
go to meetin'." " I had in head to plow to-day,
but hit's come on to rain." " I've laid off and
laid off to fix that fence." " Reckon Pete was
knowin' to the sarcumstance? " " I'll name it
to Newt, if so be he's thar." " I knowed in
reason she'd have the mullygrubs over them
doin's." " You cain't handily blame her."

" Air ye plumb bereft? " " How come it was
this: he done me dirt." " I ain't carin' which
nor whether about it." " Sam went to Andrews
or to Murphy, one." " I tuk my fut in my hand
and lit out." " He lit a rag fer home." " Don't

much believe the wagon 'll come to-day."
" 'Tain't powerful long to dinner, I don't
reckon." " Phil's Ann give it out to each and
every that Walt and Layunie 'd orter wed."
" Howdy, Tom: light and hitch."
" Reckon I'd better git on."
" Come in and set."
" Cain't stop long."
" Oh, set down and eat you some supper!"
" I've been."
" Won't ye stay the night? Looks like to me
we'll have a rainin', windin' spell."
" No: I'll haffter go down."
" Well, come agin, and fix to stay a week.
" You-uns come down with me."
" Won't go now, I guess, Tom."
" Giddep! I'll be back by in the mornin'."
" Farwell!"
Rather laconic. Yet, on occasion, when the
mountaineer is drawn out of his natural reserve
and allows his emotions free rein, there are few
educated people who can match his picturesque
and pungent diction. His trick of apt phrasing
is intuitive. Like an artist striking off a portrait or a caricature with a few swift strokes
his characterization is quick and vivid.
Whether he use quaint obsolete English or
equally delightful perversions, what he says

will go straight to the mark with epigrammatic force.

I cannot quit this topic without reference to the bizarre and original place-names that sprinkle the map of Appalachia.

Many readers of John Fox's novels take for granted that the author coined such piquant titles as Lonesome, Troublesome, Hell fer Sartin, and Kingdom Come. But all of these are real names in the Kentucky mountains. They denote rough country, and the country *is* rough, so that to a traveler it is plain enough why travel and travail were used interchangeably in old editions of Shakespeare. There is nothing like first-hand knowledge of mountain roads to revive sixteenth-century habits of thought and speech. The most scrupulous visitor will fain admit the aptness of mountain nomenclature.

Kentucky has no monopoly of grotesque and whimsical local names. The whole Appalachian region, from the Virginias to Alabama, is peppered with them. Whatever else the southern mountaineer may be, he is original. Elsewhere throughout America we have place-names imported from the Old World as thick as weeds; but the pioneers of the southern hills either forgot that there was an Old World or they disdained to borrow from it.

374 OUR SOUTHERN HIGHLANDERS

Personal names applied to localities are common enough, but they are those of actual settlers, not of notables honored from afar (Mitchell, LeConte, Guyot, were not the highlanders' names for those peaks). Often a surname is put to such use, as Jake's Creek, Old Nell Knob, and Big Jonathan Run. We even have Granny's Branch, and Daddy and Mammy creeks.

In the main it is characteristic of our Appalachian place-names that they are descriptive or commemorate some incident. The Shut-in is a gorge; the Suck is a whirlpool; Pinch-gut is a narrow passage between the cliffs. Calfkiller Run is "whar a meat-eatin' bear was usin'," and Barren She Mountain was the deathground of a she-bear that had no cubs. Kemmer's Old Stand was a certain hunter's favorite ambush on a runway. Meat-scaffold Branch is where venison was hung up for "jerking." Graining-block Creek was a trappers' rendezvous, and Honey Camp Run is where the bee hunters stayed. Lick-log denotes a notched log used for salting cattle. Still-house Branch was a moonshiners' retreat. Skin-linn Fork is where the bast was peeled from young lindens. Big Butt is what Westerners call a butte. Ball-play Bottom was a lacrosse field of the Indians.

Pizen Gulch was infested with poison ivy or sumach. Keerless Knob is " a joyful place for wild salat" (*amaranthus*). A " hell " or " slick " or " woolly-head " or "yaller patch " is a thicket of laurel or rhododendron, impassable save where the bears have bored out trails.

The qualities of the raw backwoodsmen are printed from untouched negatives in the names he has left upon the map. His literalness shows in Black Rock, Standing Stone, Sharp Top, Twenty Mile, Naked Place, The Pocket, Tumbling Creek, and in the endless designations taken from trees, plants, minerals, or animals noted on the spot. Incidents of his lonely life are signalized in Dusk Camp Run, Mad Sheep Mountain, Dog Slaughter Creek, Drowning Creek, Burnt Cabin Branch, Broken Leg, Raw Dough, Burnt Pone, Sandy Mush, and a hundred others. His contentious spirit blazes forth in Fighting Creek, Shooting Creek, Gouge-eye, Vengeance, Four Killer, and Disputanta.

Sometimes even his superstitions are commemorated. In Owesley County, Kentucky, is a range of hills bearing the singular name of Whoop fer Larrie. A party of hunters, so the legend goes, had encamped for the night in the shelter of a bluff. They were startled from

376 OUR SOUTHERN HIGHLANDERS

sleep by a loud rumble, as of some wagon hurrying along the pathless ridge, and they heard a voice shouting " Whoop fer Larrie! Whoop fer Larrie!" The hills would return no echo, for the cry came from a riotous " ha'nt."

A sardonic humor, sometimes smudged with " that touch of grossness in our English race," characterizes many of the backwoods placenames. In the mountains of Old Virginia we have Dry Tripe settlement and Jerk 'em Tight. In West Virginia are Take In Creek, Get In Run, Seldom Seen Hollow, Odd, Buster Knob, Shabby Room, and Stretch Yer Neck. North Carolina has its Shoo Bird Mountain, Big Bugaboo Creek, Weary Hut, Frog Level, Shake a Rag, and the Chunky Gal. In eastern Tennessee are No Time settlement and No Business Knob, with creeks known as Big Soak, Suee, Go Forth, and How Come You. Georgia has produced Scataway, Too Nigh, Long Nose, Dug Down, Silly Cook, Turkey Trot, Broke Jug Creek, and Tear Breeches Ridge.

Allowing some license for the mountaineer's irreverence, his whimsical fancies, and his scorn of sentimentalism, it must be said that his descriptive terms are usually apposite and sometimes felicitous. Often he is poetically imaginative, occasionally romantic, and generally picturesque. Roan Mountain, Grandfather, the Lone Bald, Craggy Dome, the Black Brothers, Hairy Bear, the Balsam Cone, Sunset Mountain, the Little Snowbird, are names that linger lovingly in one's memory.

The writer recalls with pleasure not only the features but the mere titles of that superb landscape that he shared with the wild creatures and a few woodsmen when living far up on the divide of the Great Smoky Mountains. Immediately below his cabin were the Defeat and Desolation branches of Bone Valley, with Hazel Creek meandering to the Little Tennessee. Cheoah, Tululah, Santeetlah, the Tuckaseegee, and the Nantahala (Valley of the Noonday Sun) flowed through gorges overlooked by the Wauchecha, the Yalaka and the Cowee ranges, Tellico, Wahyah, the Standing Indian and the Tusquitee.* Sonorous names, these, which our pioneers had the good sense to adopt from the aborigines.

To the east were Cold Spring Knob, the Miry

---

* Pronounced Chee-o-ah, Chil-*how*-ee, Cow-*ee*, Cul-lo-*whee*, High-*wah*-see, Nan-tah-*hay*-lah, O-*ko*-na *Luf*-ty, San-*teet*-lah, *Tel*-li-co, Tuck-a-*lee*-chee, Tuck-a-*see*-gee, Tuh-*loo*-lah, Tus-*quit*-ee, Wah-*yah* (explosively on last syllable), *Wau*-ke-chah, Yah-*lah*-kah (commonly Ah-*lar*-ka or '*Lar*-ky by the settlers), You-*nay*-kah.

Ridge, Siler's Bald, Clingman's Dome, and the great peaks at the head of Okona Lufty. On the west rose Brier Knob, Laurel Top, Thunderhead, Blockhouse, the Fodder-stack, and various "balds" of the Unakas guarding Hiwassee. To the northward were Cade's Cove and the vale of Tuckaleechee, with Chilhowee in the near distance, and the Appalachian Valley stretching beyond our ramparts to where the far Cumberlands marked an ever-blue horizon.

What matter that the plenteous roughs about us were branded with rude or opprobrious names? Rip Shin Thicket, Dog-hobble Ridge, the Rough Arm, Bear-wallow, Woolly Ridge, Roaring Fork, Huggins's Hell, the Devil's Racepath, his Den, his Courthouse, and other playgrounds of Old Nick—they, too, were well and fitly named.

CHAPTER XVII

THE LAW OF THE WILDERNESS

IT is only a town-dreamed allegory that represents Nature as a fond mother suckling her young upon her breast. Those who have lived literally close to wild Nature know her for a tyrant, void of pity and of mercy, from whom nothing can be wrung without toil and the risk of death.

To all pioneer men—to their women and children, too—life has been one long, hard, cruel war against elemental powers. Nothing else than warlike arts, nothing short of warlike hazards, could have subdued the beasts and savages, felled the forests and made our land habitable for those teeming millions who can exist only in a state of mutual dependence and cultivation. The first lesson of pioneering was self-reliance. " Provide with thine own arm," said the Wilderness, " against frost and famine and skulking foes, or thou shalt surely die! "

But there were compensations. As the school of the woods was harsh and stern, so it brought up sons and daughters of lion heart. And its reward to those who endured was the most outright independence to be had on earth. No king was so irresponsible as the pioneer, no czar so absolute as he. It needed no martyr spirit in him to sing:

> "I am the master of my fate,
> I am the captain of my soul."

We have seen that the Appalachian region was peculiar in this: that good bottom lands were few and far between. So our mountain farmers were cut off more from the world and from each other, were thrown still more upon their individual resources, than other pioneers. By compulsion their self-reliance was more complete; hence their independence grew more haughty, their individualism more intense. And these traits, exaggerated as they were by force of environment, remain unweakened among their descendants to the present day.

Here, then, is a key to much that is puzzling in highland character. In the beginning isolation was forced upon the mountaineers; they accepted it as inevitable and bore it with stoical fortitude until in time they came to love solitude for its own sake and to find compensations in it for lack of society.

Says a native writer, Miss Emma Miles, in a clever and illuminating book on *The Spirit of the Mountains*: "We who live so far apart that we rarely see more of one another than the blue smoke of each other's chimneys are never at ease without the feel of the forest on every side—room to breathe, to expand, to develop, as well as to hunt and to wander at will. The nature of the mountaineer demands that he have solitude for the unhampered growth of his personality, wing-room for his eagle heart."

Such feeling, such longing, most of us have experienced in passing moods; but in the highlander it is a permanent state of mind, sustaining him from the cradle to the grave. To enjoy freedom and air and elbow-room he cheerfully puts aside all that society can offer, and stints himself and bears adversity with a calm and steadfast soul. To be free, unbeholden, lord of himself and his surroundings—that is the wine of life to a mountaineer.

Such a man cannot stand it to be bossed around. If he works for another, it must be on a footing of equality. Poverty may oblige him to take a turn on some "public works" (by which he means any job where many men work together, such as lumbering or railroad building), but he must be handled with more

respect than is shown common laborers elsewhere. At a sharp order or a curse from the
foreman he will flare back: " That's enough
out o' you! " and immediately he will drop his
tools. Generally he will stay on a job just long
enough to earn money for immediate needs;
then back to the farm he goes.

Bear in mind that in the mountains every
person is accorded the consideration that his
own qualities entitle him to, and no whit more.
It has always been so. Our highlanders have
neither memory nor tradition of ever having
been herded together, lorded over, persecuted
or denied the privileges of freemen. So, even
within their clans, there is no servility nor any
headship by right of birth. Leaders arise, when
needed, only by virtue of acknowledged ability
and efficiency. In this respect there is no analogy whatever to the clan system of ancient Scotland, to which the loose social structure of our
own highlanders has been compared.

We might expect such fiery individualism to
cool gradually as population grew denser; but,
oddly enough, crowding only intensifies it in
the shy backwoodsman. Neighborliness has not
grown in the mountains—it is on the wane.
There are to-day fewer log-rollings and house-
raisings, fewer husking bees and quilting parties

than in former times; *and no new social gatherings have taken their place.* Our mountain farmer, seeing all arable land taken up, and the free range ever narrowing, has grown jealous and distrustful, resenting the encroachment of too many sharers in what once he felt was his own unfenced domain. And so it has come about that the very quality that is his strength and charm as a man—his staunch individualism —is proving his weakness and reproach as a neighbor and citizen. The virtue of a time outworn has become the vice of an age new-born.

The mountaineers are non-social. As they stand to-day, each man "fighting for his own hand, with his back against the wall," they recognize no social compact. Each one is suspicious of the other. Except as kinsmen or partisans they cannot pull together. Speak to them of community of interests, try to show them the advantages of co-operation, and you might as well be proffering advice to the North Star. They will not work together zealously even to improve their neighborhood roads, each mistrusting that the other may gain some trifling advantage over himself or turn fewer shovelfuls of earth. Labor chiefs fail to organize unions or granges among them because they simply will not stick together.

Miss Miles says of her people (the italics are my own) : " There is no such thing as a community of mountaineers. They are knit together, man to man, as friends, but not as a body of men. . . . Our men are almost incapable of concerted action unless they are needed by the Government. . . . Between blood-relationship and the Federal Government no relations of master and servant, rich and poor, learned and ignorant, employer and employee, are interposed to bind society into a whole. . . . *The mountaineers must awake to a consciousness of themselves as a people.* For although throughout the highlands of Kentucky, Tennessee and the Carolinas our nature is one, our hopes, our loves, our daily life the same, we are yet a people asleep, *a race without knowledge of its own existence.* This condition is due . . . to the isolation that separates the mountaineer from all the world but his own blood and kin, and to the consequent utter simplicity of social relations. When they shall have established a unity of thought corresponding to their homogeneity of character, then their love of country will assume a practical form, and then, indeed, America, with all her peoples, can boast no stronger sons than these same moun taineers."

Let the women do the work

To the highlanders of four States here mentioned should be added all those of Old Virginia, West Virginia, Georgia, and Alabama, making an aggregate to-day of close on four million souls. Together they constitute a distinct people. Not only are they all closely akin in blood, in speech, in ideas, in manners, in ways of living; but their needs, their problems are identical throughout this vast domain. There is no other ethnic group in America so unmixed as these mountaineers and so segregated from all others.

And the strange thing is that they do not know it. Their isolation is so complete that they have no race consciousness at all. In this respect I can think of no other people on the face of the earth to which they may be likened.

As compensation for the peculiar weakness of their social structure, the highlanders display an undying devotion to family and kindred. Mountaineers everywhere are passionately attached to their homes. Tear away from his native rock your Switzer, your Tyrolean, your Basque, your Montenegrin, and all alike are stricken with homesickness beyond speech or cure. At the first chance they will return, and thenceforth will cling to their patrimonies, however poor these be.

So, too, our man of the Appalachians.—" I went down into the valley, wunst, and I declar I nigh sultered! 'Pears like there ain't breath enough to go round, with all them people. And the water don't do a body no good; an' you cain't eat hearty, nor sleep good o' nights. Course they pay big money down thar; but I'd a heap-sight ruther ketch me a big old 'coon fer his hide. Boys, I did hone fer my dog Fiddler, an' the times we'd have a-huntin', and the trout-fishin', an' the smell o' the woods, and nobody bossin' and jowerin' at all. I'm a hill-billy, all right, and they needn't to glory their old flat lands to me!"

Domestic affection is seldom expressed by the mountaineers—not even by motherly or sisterly kisses—but it is very deep and real for all that. In fact, the ties of kinship are stronger with them, and extend to remoter degrees of consanguinity, than with any other Americans that I know. Here again we see working the old feudal idea, an anachronism, but often a beautiful one, in this bustling commercial age. Our hived and promiscuous life in cities is breaking down the old fealty of kith and kin. " God gives us our relatives," sighs the modern, "but, thank God, we can choose our friends!" Such words would strike a mountaineer deep with horror. Rather would he go the limit of Stevenson's Saint Ives: " If it is a question of going to hell, go to hell like a gentleman, with your ancestors!"

When the wilderness came to be settled by white men, courts were feeble to puerility, and every man was a law unto himself. Many hard characters came in with the pioneers — bad neighbors, arrogant, thievish, bold. As society was not organized for mutual protection, it was inevitable that cousin should look to cousin for help in time of trouble. So arose the clan, the family league, and, as things change very slowly in the mountains, we still have clan loyalty outside of and superior to the law. " My family *right or wrong!*" is a slogan to which every highlander will rise, with money or arms in hand, and for it he will lay down his last dollar, the last drop of his blood. There is scarce any limit to which this fealty will not go. Your brother or cousin may have committed a crime that shocks you as it does all other decent citizens; but will you give him up to the officers and testify against him? Not if you are a mountaineer. You will hide him out in the laurel, carry him food, keep him posted, help him to break jail, perjure yourself for him in court— anything, everything, to get him clear.

We see here a survival, very real and widespread, in this twentieth-century Appalachia, of a condition that was general throughout the Scotch Highlands in the far past. " The great virtue of the Highlander," says Lecky, " was his fidelity to his chief and to his clan. It took the place of patriotism and of loyalty to his sovereign. . . . In the reign of James V., an insurrection of Clan Chattan having been suppressed by Murray, two hundred of the insurgents were condemned to death. Each one as he was led to the gallows was offered a pardon if he would reveal the hiding-place of his chief, but they all answered that, were they acquainted with it, no sort of punishment could induce them to be guilty of treachery to their leader. . . . In 1745 the house of Macpherson of Cluny was burnt to the ground by the King's troops. A reward of £1,000 was offered for his apprehension. A large body of soldiers was stationed in the district and a step of promotion was promised to any officer who should secure him. Yet for nine years the chief was able to live concealed on his own property in a cave which his clansmen dug for him during the night, and, though upwards of one hundred persons knew of his place of retreat, no bribe or menace could extort the secret."

The same chivalrous, self-sacrificing fidelity to family and to clan leader is still shown by our own highlanders, as scores of feuds and hundreds of criminal trials attest. All this is openly and unblushingly " above the law "; but let us remember that the law itself, in many of these localities, is but a feeble, dilatory thing that offers practically no protection to those who would obey its letter. So, in an imperfectly organized society, it is good to have blood-ties that are faithful unto death. And none knows it better than he who has missed it—he who has lived strange and alone in some wild, lawless region where everyone else had a clan to back him.

So far as primitive society is concerned, we may admit with the Scotch historian Henderson that " the clan system of government was in its way an ideally perfect one—probably the only perfect one that has ever existed. . . . The clansman was not the subject—a term implying some sort of conquest—but the kinsman of his chief. . . . Obedience became rather a privilege than a task, and no possible bribery or menace could shake his fidelity. Towards the Sassenach or the members of clans at feud with him he might act meanly, treacherously, and cruelly without check and without compunction, for there he recognized no moral obligations whatever. But as a clansman to his clan he was courteous, truthful, virtuous, benevolent, with notions of honor as punctilious as those of the ancient knight."

The trouble with clan government was, as this same writer has pointed out, that " it was the very thoroughness of its adaptation to early needs that made it so hard to adjust to new necessities. In its principles and motives it was essentially opposed to the bent of modern influences. Its appeal was to sentiment rather than to law or even reason: it was a system not of the letter but of the spirit. . . . The clan system was efficient only within a narrow area; it gave rise to interminable feuds; and it was inapplic- able to the circumstances created by the rise of modern industry and trade."

Everywhere throughout Highland Dixie to- day we can observe how clan loyalty interferes with the administration of justice. When a case involving some strong family comes up in the courts, immediately a cloud of false witnesses arises, men who should testify on the other side are bribed or run out of the country before subpoenas can be served, and every juror knows that his peace and prosperity in future depend largely upon which side he espouses.

To what lengths the hostility of a clan may go in defying justice was shown recently in the massacre of almost a whole court by the Allen clan at Hillsville, Virginia. The news of that atrocity swept like wildfire throughout all Appalachia, its history is being reviewed to-day in thousands of mountain cabins, and it is deeply significant that, away out here in western Carolina, where no Allen blood relationship prejudices men's minds, the prevailing judgment of our backwoodsmen is that the State of Virginia did wrong in executing any of the offenders. "There was something back of it—you mark my words," say the country folk. And the drummers, cattle-buyers, and others who pass this way from southwestern Virginia tell us, "Everybody up our way sympathizes with the Allens."

In some measure this morbid sentiment is due to the spectacular features of the Hillsville tragedy. If there be one human quality that the mountaineer admires above all others, it is "nerve." And what greater display of nerve has been made in this generation than for a few clansmen to shoot down a judge at the bench, the public prosecutor, the sheriff, the clerk of the court, and two jurymen, then take to the mountain laurel like Corsicans to the *maquis,* and defy the armed power of the country? The cause does not matter, to a mountaineer. Our highlanders are anything but robbers, for instance, and yet the only outsider who has ballads sung in his memory throughout Appalachia is Jesse James!—unless Jack Donohue was one—I do not know.—

> Come all ye bold undaunted men
> And outlaws of the day,
> Who'd rather wear the ball and chain
> Than work in slavery!
>
> .　.　.　.　.
>
> Said Donohue to his comrades,
> " If you'll prove true to me,
> This day I'll fight with all my might,
> I'll fight for liberty;
> Be of good courage, be bold and strong,
> Be galliant and be true;
> This day I'll fight with all my might,"
> Says bold Jack Donohue.
>
> .　.　.　.　.
>
> Six policemen he shot down
> Before the fatal ball
> Pierced the heart of Donohue
> And 'casioned him to fall;
> And then he closed his struggling eyes,
> And bid this world adieu.
> Come all ye boys that fear no noise,
> And pray for Donohue!

No doubt the mountain minstrels are already composing ballads in honor of the Allens; for it is a fact we cannot blink at that the outlaw is the popular hero of Appalachia to-day, as Rob Roy and Robin Hood were in the Britain of long ago. This is not due to any ingrained hostility to law and order as such, but simply to admiration for any men who fight desperately against overwhelming odds. There is a glamour about bold and lawless adventure that fascinates mature men and women who have never outgrown youthful habits of mind. Whoever has the reputation of being a dangerous man to cross —the " marked " man, who carries his life upon his sleeve, but bears himself as a smiling cavalier—he is the only true aristocrat among a valorous but primitive people.

But this is only half an explanation. The statement that our highlanders are not hostile to law and order must be qualified to this extent: they have a profound distrust of the courts. The mountaineer is not only a born fighter but he is also litigious by nature and tradition. A stranger will be surprised to find how deeply the average backwoodsman is versed in the petty subtleties of legal practice. It comes from experience. " Court-week " draws bigger crowds than a circus. The mountaineer who has never

served as juror, witness, or principal in a law-
suit is a curiosity. And this familiarity has
bred secret contempt. I violate no confidence
in saying that many a mountaineer would hold
up one hand to testify his respect for the law
while the other hand hovered over his pistol.

Why so?

Just because his experience has taught him
(rightly or wrongly—but he firmly believes it)
that courts are swayed by sinister influences
when important matters are at stake. Those
influences are clan money and clan votes.
Hence, if he or a kinsman be involved in
" lawin' " with a member of some rival tribe,
he does not look for impartial treatment, but
prepares to fight cunning with cunning, local
influence with local influence. There are no
moral obligations here. " All's fair in love and
war "—and this is one form of war.

If the reader will take down his *David Balfour* and read the intrigues, plots, and counter-
plots of David's attorneys and those of the
Crown, he will grasp our own highlanders'
viewpoint.

That mountain courts are often impotent is
due in part to the limitations under which their
officers are obliged to serve. For example, in
the judicial district where I reside, the solicitor

(State's attorney) receives nothing but fees, and then only *in case of conviction*. It might seem that this would stir him to extra zeal, and per- haps it does; but he has a large circuit, there are no local officials specially interested in se- curing evidence for him while the case is white- hot, everything spurs the defendant to get rid of dangerous witnesses before the solicitor can get at them, public opinion is extremely lenient toward homicides, and man-slayers so often get off scot-free after the most faithful and labori- ous efforts of the solicitor, that he becomes dis- couraged.

The sheriff, too, serves without salary, getting only fees and a percentage of tax collections. How this works, in securing witnesses, may be shown by an anecdote.—

I looked up from my work, one day, to see a neighbor striding swiftly along the trail that passed my cabin.

" You seem in a hurry, John. Woods afire? "

" No: I'm dodgin' the sheriff."

" Whose pig was it? "

" Aw! He wants me as witness in a concealed weepon case."

" One of your boys? "

" Huk-uh: nobody as I'm keerin' fer."

" Then why don't you go? "

" I cain't afford to. I'd haffter walk nineteen miles out to the railroad, pay seventy cents the round-trip to the county-site, pay my board thar fer mebbe a week, and then a witness don't git no fee at all onless they convict."

"What does the sheriff get for coming away up here?"

"Thirty cents for each witness he cotches. He won't git me, Mister Man; not if I know these woods since yistiddy."

Verily the law of Swain is hard on the solicitor, hard on the sheriff, and hard on the witness, too!

Mountaineers place a low valuation on human life. I need not go outside my own habitat for illustrations. In our judicial district, which comprises the westernmost seven counties of North Carolina, the present yearly toll of homicides varies, according to counties, from about one in 1,000 to one in 2,500 of the population. And ours is not a feud district, nor are there any negroes to speak of. Compare these figures with the rate of homicide in the United States at large, about one to 16,000 population; of Italy, one to 66,000; Great Britain, one to 111,000; Germany, one to 200,000.

And the worst of it is that no Black Hand conspirators or ward gun-men or other professional criminals figure in these killings. Practically all of them are committed by representative citizens, mostly farmers. Take that fact home, and think what it means. Remember, too, that most of these murderers either escape with light penal sentences or none at all. The only capital sentence imposed in our district within the past ten years was upon an Indian who had assaulted and murdered a white girl (there was no red tape or procrastination about *that* trial, the courthouse being filled with men who were ready to lynch him under the judge's nose if the sentence were not satisfactory).

I said at the very outset of this book that "Our mountain folk still live in the eighteenth century. The progress of mankind from that age to this is no heritage of theirs. . . . And so, in order to be fair and just with these our backward kinsmen, we must, for the time, decivilize ourselves to the extent of *going back* and getting an eighteenth century point of view."

As regards the valuation of human life, what was that point of view?

The late Professor Shaler of Harvard, himself a Southerner, one time explained the prevalence of manslaughter among southern gentlemen. His remarks apply with equal truth to our mountaineers, for they, however poor they may be in worldly goods, are by no means " poor white trash," but rather patricians, like the ragged but lofty chiefs and clansmen of old Scotland.—

" Nothing so surprises the northern people as the fact that southern men of good estate will, for what seems to the distant onlooker trifling matters of dispute, proceed to slay each other. Nothing so gravely offends the character-istic southern man as the incapacity of his brethren of north-ern societies to perceive that such action is natural and con-sistent with the rules of gentlemanly behavior. The only way to understand these differences of opinion is by a proper consideration of the history of the moral growth of these diverse peoples.

" The Southerner has retained and fostered—in a certain way reinstated—the medieval estimate as to the value of life. In the opinion of those ages it was but lightly es-teemed; it was not a supreme good for which almost all else was to be sacrificed, but something to be taken in hand and put in risk in the pursuit of manly ideals.

" Modernism has worked to intensify the passion for exist-ence until those who are the most under its dominion can-not well conceive how a man, except for some supreme duty to which he is pledged by altruistic motives, can give up his own life or take that of his neighbor. If these people of to-day will but perceive that the characteristic Southerner has preserved the motives of two centuries ago, if they will but inform themselves as to the state of mind on this subject which prevailed in the epoch when those motives were shaped in men, they will see that their judgment is harsh and unreasonable. It is much as if they judged the actions of

Englishmen of the seventeenth century by the changed standards of to-day.

"Nor will it be altogether reasonable to condemn the lack of regard of life which we find in the southern gentleman as compared with his northern contemporary. We must, of course, reprobate in every way the evil consequences of this state of mind; but the question as to the propriety of that extreme devotion to continued mundane existence which is so manifest in our modern civilization is certainly open to debate. Irrational and brutal as are the ways in which the old-fashioned gentleman of the South shows that his regard for his own honor or that of his household outweighs his love of life, it must be remembered that the same condition existed in the richest ages of our race—those which gave proportionally the largest share of ability and nobility to its history.

"As long as men are more keenly sensitive to the opinions of their fellows than they are to the other goods which existence brings them, as long as this opinion makes personal valor and truthfulness the jewels of their lives, we must expect now and then to have degradation of the essentially noble motives. It is, undoubtedly, a dangerous state of mind, but not one that is degraded."—(*North American Review,* October, 1890.)

"The motives of two centuries ago" are the motives of present-day Appalachia. Here the right of private war is not questioned, outside of a judge's charge from the bench, which everybody takes as a mere formality, a convention that is not to be taken seriously. The argument is this: that when Society, as represented, by the State, cannot protect a man or secure him his dues, then he is not only justified but in duty bound to defend himself or seize what is his own. And in the mountains Society with the big *S* is often powerless against the Clan with a bigger *C*.

In the Valley. (Near Bryson, N. C.)

CHAPTER XVIII

THE BLOOD-FEUD

I N Corsica, when a man is wronged by another, public sentiment requires that he redress his own grievance, and that his family and friends shall share the consequences.

" Before the law made us citizens, great Nature made us men."

"When one has an enemy, one must choose between the three S's — *schiopetto, stiletto, strada*: the rifle, the dagger, or flight."

" There are two presents to be made to an enemy—*palla calda o ferro freddo*: hot shot or cold steel."

The Corsican code of honor does not require that vengeance be taken in fair fight. Rather should there be a sudden thrust of the knife, or a pistol fired point-blank into the enemy's breast, or a rifle-shot from some ambush picked in advance.

The assassin is not conscious of any cowardice in such act. If the trouble between him and his foe had been strictly a personal matter, to be settled forever by one man's fall, then he might have welcomed a duel with all the punctilios. But his blood is not his alone—it belongs to his clan. Whenever a Corsican is slain his family takes up the feud. A vendetta ensues—a war of extermination by clan against clan.

Now, the chief object of war, as all strategists agree, is to inflict the greatest loss upon the enemy with the least loss to one's own side. Hence we have hostilities without declaration of war; we have the ambush, the night attack, masked batteries, mines and submarines. Thus we murder hundreds asleep or unshriven. This is war.

Moreover, while a soldier must be brave in any extremity, it is no less his duty to save himself unharmed as long as he can, so that he may help his own side and kill more and more of the enemy. Therefore it is proper and military for him to "snipe" his foes by deliberate sharp-shooting from behind any lurking-place that he can find. This is war.

And the vendetta, says our Corsican, is nothing else than war.

When Matteo has been slain by an enemy, his friends carry his body home and swear vengeance over the corpse, while his wife soaks her handkerchief in his wounds to keep as a token whereby she will incite her children, as they grow up, to war against all kinsmen of their father's murderer.

Then a son or brother of Matteo slips forth into the night, full-armed to slay like a dog any member of the rival faction whom he may find at a disadvantage. The deed done, he flies to the *maquis,* the mountain thicket, and there he will hide, dodging the gendarmes, fighting off his enemies—an outlaw with a price upon his head, but pitied or admired by all Corsicans outside the feud, and succored by his clan.

It is a far cry from the Mediterranean to our own Appalachia: so why this prelude? Our mountaineers never heard of Corsica. Not a drop of South European blood flows in their veins. Few of them ever heard one word of a foreign tongue. True. And yet we shall mark some strange analogies between Corsican vendettas and Appalachian feuds, Corsican clannishness and Appalachian clannishness, Corsican women and our mountain women—before this chapter ends.

Long, long ago, in the mountains of eastern Kentucky, Dr. Abner Baker married a Miss White. Daniel Bates married Baker's sister, but separated from her in 1844. Baker charged Bates with undue intimacy with his wife, and killed him. The Whites, defending their kins-woman, prosecuted the Doctor, but he was acquitted, and moved to Cuba.

Afterwards Baker returned. In flat violation of the Constitution of the United States, he was tried a second time for the murder of Bates, was convicted, and was hanged. Thenceforth there was " bad blood " between the Bakers and the Whites, involving the Garrards on one side and the Howards on the other, as allies to the re-spective clans.

In 1898, Tom Baker, reputed to be the best shot in the Kentucky mountains, bought a note given by A. B. Howard, for whom he was cut-ting timber. Howard became furious, a fight ensued, one of the Howard boys and Burt Stores were killed from ambush, and the elder Howard was wounded.

Thereupon Jim Howard, son of the clan chief, sought out Tom Baker's father, who was county attorney, compelled the unarmed old man to fall upon his knees, shot him twenty-five times with careful aim to avoid a vital spot, and so killed him by inches. Howard was tried and convicted of murder, but it is said that a pardon was offered him if he would go to the State Capitol at Frankfort and assassinate Governor Goebel, which he is charged with having done.

In Clay County, where this feud waged, the judge, clerk, sheriff, and jailer were of the White clan. Tom Baker killed a brother of the sheriff and took to the hills rather than give himself up to a court ruled by his foemen. Then Albert Garrard was fired upon from ambush while riding with his wife to a religious meeting. He removed to Pineville, in another county, under guard of two armed men, both of whom were shot dead " from the bresh."

Governor Bradley sent State troops into Clay County, and Tom Baker surrendered to them. Baker was tried in the Knox Circuit Court, on a change of venue, and was sentenced to the penitentiary for life. On appeal his attorneys secured a reversal of the verdict, and Baker was released on bail. The new trial was set for June, 1899. Governor Bradley again sent a company of State militia, with a Gatling gun, to Manchester where the trial was to be held. Baker was put in a guard-tent surrounded by a squad of soldiers. A hundred yards or so from this tent stood the unoccupied residence of the sheriff, at the foot of a wooded mountain. An assassin hidden in this house spied upon the guard-tent, and, when Baker appeared, shot him dead with a rifle, then took to the woods and escaped.

I quote now from a history of this feud published in *Munsey's Magazine* of November, 1903.—

"Captain John Bryan, of the 2d Kentucky, said to the widow of the murdered Tom Baker, after they returned from the funeral:

"'Mrs. Baker, why don't you leave this miserable country and escape from these terrible feuds? Move away, and teach your children to forget.'

"'Captain Bryan,' said the widow, and she spoke evenly and quietly, 'I have twelve sons. It will be the chief aim of my life to bring them up to avenge their father's death. Each day I shall show my boys *the handkerchief stained with his blood,* and tell them who murdered him.'"

Corsican vendetta or Kentucky feud—what are language and race against age-long isolation and an environment that keeps humanity feral to the core?

Shortly after Baker's death, four Griffins, of the White-Howard faction, ambushed Big John Philpotts and his cousin, wounding the former severely and the latter mortally. Big John fought them from behind a log and killed all four.

On July 17, 1899, four of the Philpotts were attacked by four Morrises, of the Howard side. Three men were killed, three mortally wounded, and the other two were severely injured. No arrests were made.

Finally, in 1901, the two clans fought a pitched battle in front of the court-house in Manchester. At its conclusion they formally signed a truce.

This is a mere scenario of a feud in the wealthiest and best-schooled county of eastern Kentucky. Two of the families involved were of distinguished lineage, counting in their ranks a governor, three generals, a member of Congress, and a prohibition candidate for the Presidency.

In reviewing this feud, Governor Bradley stated:

"The whole fault in Clay County is a vitiated public sentiment and a failure of the civil authorities to do their duty. The laws are insufficient for the Governor to apply a remedy. Such feuds have been in progress more or less for years, and no Governor of the State has ever been able to quell them. They have terminated only when their force was spent by one side or the other being killed or moving out of the country."

"The laws are insufficient for the Governor to apply a remedy." One naturally asks, " How so? " The answer is that the Governor cannot send troops into a county except upon request of the civil authorities, and they must go as a posse to civil officers. In most feuds these officers are partisans (in fact, it is a favorite ruse for one clan to win or usurp the county offices before making war). Hence the State troops would only serve as a reinforcement to one of the contending factions. To show how this works out, we will sketch briefly the course of another feud.—

In Rowan County, Kentucky, in 1884, there was an election quarrel between two members of the Martin and Toliver families. The Logans sided with the Martins and the Youngs with the Tolivers. The Logan-Martin faction elected their candidate for sheriff by a margin of twelve votes. Then there was an affray in which one Logan was killed and three were wounded.

As usual, in feuds, no immediate redress was attempted, but the injured clan plotted its vengeance with deadly deliberation. After five months, Dick Martin killed Floyd Toliver. His own people worked the trick of arresting him themselves and sent him to Winchester for safe-keeping. The Tolivers succeeded in having him brought back on a forged order and killed him when he was bound and helpless.

The leader of the Young-Toliver faction was a notorious bravo named Craig Toliver. To strengthen his power he became candidate for town marshal of Morehead, and he won the office by intimidation at the polls. Then, for two years, a bushwhacking war went on. Three times the Governor sent troops into Rowan County, but each time they found nothing but creeks and thickets to fight. Then he prevailed upon the clans to sign a truce and expatriate their chiefs for one year in distant States. Craig Toliver obeyed the order by going to Missouri, but returned several months before the expiration of his term, *resumed office,* and renewed his atrocities. In the warfare that ensued all the county officers were involved, from the judge down.

In 1887, Proctor Knott, Governor of Kentucky, said in his message, of the Logan-Toliver feud:

"Though composed of only a small portion of the community, these factions have succeeded by their violence in overawing and silencing the voice of the peaceful element, and in intimidating the officers of the law. Having their origin partly in party rancor, they have ceased to have any political significance, and have become contests of personal ambition and revenge; each party seeking apparently to possess itself of the machinery of justice in order that it may, under the forms of law, seek the gratification of personal animosities.

"During the present year the local leader of one of these

factions came in possession of the office of police judge of the town of Morehead. Under color of the authority of that office, and sustained by an armed band of adherents, he exercised despotic sway over the town and its vicinage. He banished citizens who were obnoxious to him; and, in one instance, after arresting two citizens who seem to have been guilty of no offense, he and his party, attended by a deputy sheriff of the county, murdered them in cold blood.

"This act of atrocity fully aroused the community. A posse acting under the authority of a warrant from the county judge attacked the police judge and his adherents on the 22d of June last, killed several of their number, and put the rest to flight, and temporarily restored something like tranquility to the community.

"The proceedings of the Circuit Court, which was held in August, were not calculated to inspire the citizens with confidence in securing justice. The report of the Adjutant General on this subject shows, from information derived 'from representative men without reference to party affiliations,' that the judge of the Circuit Court seems so far under the influence of the reputed leader of one of the factions as to permit such an organization of the grand juries as will effectually prevent the indictment of members of that faction for the most flagrant crimes."

The posse here mentioned was organized by Daniel Boone Logan, a cousin of the two young men who had been murdered, a college graduate, and a lawyer of good standing. With the assent of the Governor, he gathered fifty to seventy-five picked men and armed them with the best modern rifles and revolvers. Some of the men were of his own clan; others he hired. His plan was to end the war by exterminating the Tolivers.

The posse, led by Logan and the sheriff, suddenly surrounded the town of Morehead. Everybody gave in except Craig Toliver, Jay Toliver, Bud Toliver, and Hiram Cook, who barricaded themselves in the railroad station, where all of them were shot dead by the posse.

Boone Logan was indicted for murder. At the trial he admitted the killings; but he showed that the feud had cost the lives of not less than twenty-three men, that not one person had been legally punished for these murders, and that he had acted for the good of the public in ending this infamous struggle. The court accepted this view of the case, the community sustained it, and the " war " was closed.

A feud, in the restricted sense here used, is an armed conflict between families, each endeavoring to exterminate or drive out the other. It spreads swiftly not only to blood-kin and relatives by marriage, but to friends and retainers as well. It may lie dormant for a time, perhaps for a generation, and then burst forth with recruited strength long after its original cause has ceased to interest anyone, or maybe after it has been forgotten.

Such feuds are by no means prevalent throughout the length and breadth of Appalachia, but are restricted mostly to certain well defined districts, of which the chief, in extent of territory as well as in the number and ferocity of its "wars," is the country round the upper waters of the Kentucky, Licking, Big Sandy, Tug, and Cumberland rivers, embracing many of the mountain counties of eastern Kentucky and adjoining parts of West Virginia, Old Virginia, and Tennessee. In this thinly settled region probably five hundred men have been slain in feuds since our centennial year, and only three of the murderers, so far as I know, have been executed by law.

The active feudists, as a rule, include only a small part of the community; but public sentiment, in feud districts, approves or at least tolerates the vendetta, just as it does in Corsica or the Balkans. Those citizens who are not directly implicated take pains to hear little and see less. They keep their mouths shut. They can neither be persuaded, bribed, nor coerced into informing or testifying against either side, but, on the contrary, will throw dust in the eyes of an investigator or try to stare him down. A jury composed of such men will not convict anybody.

When a feud is raging, nobody outside the
warring clans is in any danger at all. A stranger
is safer in the heart of Feuddom than he would
be in Chicago or New York, so long as he at-
tends strictly to his own business, asks no questions, and tells no " tales." If, on the contrary,
he should express horror or curiosity, he is regarded as a busybody or suspected as a spy, and
is likely to be run out of the country or even
" laywayed " and silenced forever.

What causes feuds?

Some of them start in mere drunken rows or
in a dispute over a game of cards; others in
quarrels over land boundaries or other property.
The Hatfield-McCoy feud started because Randolph McCoy penned up two wild hogs that
were claimed by Floyd Hatfield. The spite
over these hogs broke out two years later, and
one partisan was killed from ambush. The feud
itself began in 1882 over a debt of $1.75, with
the hogs and the bushwhacking brought up in
recrimination. Love of women is the primary
cause, or the secondary aggravation, of many a
feud. Some of the most widespread and deadliest vendettas have originated in political strifes.

It should be understood that national and
state politics cut little or no figure in these
"wars." Local politics in most of the mountain

counties is merely a factional fight, in which family matters and business interests are involved, and the contest becomes bitterly personal on that account. This explains most of the collusion or partisanship of county officers and their remissness in enforcing the law in murder cases. Family ties or political alliances override even the oath of office.

Within the past year I have heard a deputy sheriff admit nonchalantly, on the stand, that when a homicide was committed near him, and he was the only officer in the vicinity, he advised the slayer to take to the mountains and "hide out." The judge questioned him sharply on this point, was reassured by the witness that it was so, and then—offered no comment at all. Within the same period, in another but not distant court, a desperado from the Shelton Laurel, on trial for murder, admitted that he had shot six men since he moved over from Tennessee to North Carolina, and swore that while he was being held in jail pending trial for this last offense the sheriff permitted him to "keep a gun in his cell, drink whiskey in the jail, and eat at table with the family of the sheriff."

Feuds spread not only through clan fealty but also because they offer excellent chances to pay off old scores. The mountaineer has a long memory. The average highlander is fiery and combative by nature, but at the same time cunning and vindictive. If publicly insulted he will strike at once, but if he feels wronged by some act that does not demand instant retaliation he will brood over it and plot patiently to get his enemy at a disadvantage. Some moun, taineers always fight fair; but many of them prefer to wait and watch quietly until the foe gets drunk and unwary, or until he is engaged in some illegal or scandalous act, or until he is known to be carrying a concealed weapon, whereupon he can be shot down unexpectedly and his assailant can " prove " by friendly witnesses that he acted in self-defense. So, if a man be involved in feud, he may be assassinated from ambush by someone who is not concerned in the clan trouble, but who has hated him for years on another account, and who knows that his death now will be charged up to the opposing faction.

From the earliest times it has been customary for our highlanders to go armed most of the time. This was a necessity in the old Indian-fighting days, and throughout the kukluxing and white-capping era following the Civil War. Such a habit, once formed, is hard to eradicate. Even to-day, in all parts of Appalachia that I am familiar with, most of the young men, I judge, and many of the older ones, carry concealed weapons.

Among them I have never seen a stand-up and knock-down fight according to the rules of the ring. They have many rough-and-tumble brawls, in which they slug, wrestle, kick, bite, strangle, until one gets the other down, whereat the one on top continues to maul his victim until he cries "Enough!" Oftener a club or stone will be used in mad endeavor to knock the opponent senseless at a blow. There is no compunction about striking foul and very little about "double-teaming." Let us pause long enough to admit that this was the British and American way of man-handling, universal among the common people, until well into the nineteenth century—and the mountaineers are still ignorant of any other, except fighting with weapons.

Many of the young men carry home-made billies or "brass knucks." Every man and boy has at least a pocket-knife with serviceable blade. Fights with such crude weapons are frequent. There are few spectacles. more sickening than two powerful but awkward men slashing each other with common jack-knives, though the fatalities are much less frequent than in gun-fighting. I have known two old mountain preachers to draw knives on each other at the close of a sermon.

The typical highland bravo always carries a revolver or an automatic pistol. This is likely to be a weapon of large bore and good stopping-power that is worn in a shoulder-holster concealed under the coat or vest or shirt. Most mountaineers are good shots with such arms, though not so deadly quick as the frontiersmen of our old-time West—in fact, they cannot be so quick without wearing the weapon exposed. When a highlander has time, he prefers to hold his pistol in both hands (left clasped over right) and aims it as he would a rifle. To a Westerner such gun practice looks absurd; but it is accurate, beyond question. Few mountain gun-fights fail to score at least one victim.

The average mountain woman is as combative in spirit as her menfolk. She would despise any man who took insult or injury without showing fight. In fact, the woman, in many cases, deliberately stirs up trouble out of vanity, or for the sheer excitement of it. Some of the older women display the ferocity of she-wolves. The mother of a large family said in my presence, with the calm earnestness of one fully experienced: "If a feller 'd treated me the way ———— did ———— I'd git me a forty-some-odd and shoot enough meat off o' his bones to feed a hound-dog a week." Three of this woman's brothers had been shot dead in frays. One of them killed the first husband of her sister, who married again, and whose second husband was killed by a man with whom she then tried a third matrimonial venture. Such matters may not be interesting in themselves, but they give one pause when he learns, in addition, that these people are received as friends and on a footing of equality by everybody in their community.

That the mountaineers are fierce and relentless in their feuds is beyond denial. A warfare of bushwhacking and assassination knows no refinements. Quarter is neither given nor expected. Property, however, is not violated, and women are not often injured. There have been some atrocious exceptions. In the Hatfield-McCoy feud, Cap Hatfield and Tom Wallace attacked the latter's wife and her mother at night, dragged both women from bed, and Cap beat the old woman with a cow's tail that he had clipped off " jes' to see 'er jump." He broke two of the woman's ribs, leaving her injured for life, while Tom beat his wife. Later, on New Year's night, 1888, a gang of the Hatfields surrounded the home of Randolph McCoy, killed the eldest daughter, Allaphare. broke her mother's ribs and knocked her senseless with their guns, and killed a son, Calvin. In several instances women who fought in defense of their homes have been killed, as in the case of Mrs. Charles Daniels and her 16-year-old daughter, in Pike County, Kentucky, in November, 1909.

The mountain women do not shrink from feuds, but on the contrary excite and cheer their men to desperate deeds, and sometimes fight by their side. In the French-Eversole feud, a woman, learning that her unarmed husband was besieged by his foes, seized his rifle, filled her apron with cartridges, rushed past the firing-line, and stood by her " old man " until he beat his assailants off. When men are "hiding out " in the laurel, it is the women's part, which they never shirk, to carry them food and information.

In every feud each clan has a leader, a man of prominence either on account of his wealth or his political influence or his shrewdness or his physical prowess. This leader's orders are obeyed, while hostilities last, with the same unquestioning loyalty that the old Scotch retainer showed to his chieftain. Either the leader or someone acting for him supplies the men with food, with weapons if they need them, with ammunition, and with money. Sometimes mercenaries are hired. Mr. Fox says that " In one local war, I remember, four dollars per day were the wages of the fighting man, and the leader on one occasion, while besieging his enemies—in the county court-house—tried to purchase a cannon, and from no other place than the State arsenal, and from no other personage than the Governor himself." In some of the feuds professional bravos have been employed who would assassinate, for a few dollars, anybody who was pointed out to them, provided he was alien to their own clans.

The character of the highland bravo is precisely that of the western " bad man " as pictured by Jed Parker in Stewart Edward White's *Arizona Nights:*

" ' There's a good deal of romance been written about the " bad man," and there's about the same amount of nonsense. The bad man is just a plain murderer, neither more nor less. He never does get into a real, good, plain, stand-up gun-fight if he can possibly help it. His killin's are done from behind a door, or when he's got his man dead to rights. There's Sam Cook. You've all heard of him. He had nerve, of course, and when he was backed into a corner he made good; and he was sure sudden death with a gun. But when he went out for a man deliberate, he didn't take no special chances. . . .

" ' The point is that these yere bad men are a low-down, miserable proposition, and plain, cold-blooded murderers, willin' to wait for a sure thing, and without no compunctions whatever. The bad man takes you unawares, when you're sleepin', or talkin', or drinkin', or lookin' to see what for a day it's goin' to be, anyway. He don't give you no show, and sooner or later he's goin' to get you in the safest and easiest way for himself. There ain't no romance about that.' "

And there is no romance about a real mountain feud. It is marked by suave treachery, " double-teaming," " laywaying," " blind-shooting," and general heartlessness and brutality. If one side refuses to assassinate but seeks open, honorable combat, as has happened in several feuds, it is sure to be beaten. Whoever appeals to the law is sure to be beaten. In either case he is considered a fool or a coward by most of the countryside. Our highlander, untouched by the culture of the world about him, has never been taught the meaning of fair play. Magnanimity to a fallen foe he would regard as sure proof of an addled brain. The motive of one who forgives his enemy is utterly beyond his comprehension. As for bushwhacking, " Hit's as fa'r for one as 'tis for t'other. You can't fight a man fa'r and squar who'll shoot you in the back. A pore man can't fight money in the courts." In this he is simply his ancient Scotch or English ancestor born over again. Such was the code of Jacobite Scotland and Tudor England. And *back there* is where our mountaineer belongs in the scale of human evolution.

The feud, as Miss Miles puts it, is an outbreak of *perverted* family affection. Its mainspring is an honorable clan loyalty. It is a direct consequence of the clan organization that our mountaineers preserve as it was handed down to them by their forefathers. The implacability of their vengeance, the treacheries they practice, the murders from ambush, are invariable features of clan warfare wherever and by whomsoever it is waged. They are not vices or crimes peculiar to the Kentuckian or the Corsican or the Sicilian or the Albanian or the Arab, but natural results of clan government, which in turn is a result of isolation, of physical environment, of geographical position unfavorable to free intercourse and commerce with the world at large.

The most hideous feature of the feud is the shooting down of unarmed or unwarned men. Assassination, in our modern eyes, is the last and lowest infamy of a coward. Such it truly is, when committed in the civilized society of our day. But in studying primitive races, or in going back along the line of our own ancestry to the civilized society of two centuries ago, we must face and acknowledge the strange paradox of a valorous and honorable people (according to their lights) who, in certain cases, practiced assassination without compunction and, in fact, with pride. History is red with it in those very " richest ages of our race " that Professor Shaler cited. Until a century or two ago, throughout Christendom, the secret murder of enemies was committed unblushingly by nobles and kings and prelates, often with a pious " Thus sayeth the Lord! " It was practiced by men valiant in open battle, and by those wise in the counsels of the realm. Take Scotland, for example, as pictured by a native writer.—

" No tenet nor practice, no influence nor power nor principality in the Scotland of the past has outvied assassination in ascendancy or in moment. Not theoretically, indeed, but practically, it occupied for centuries a distinct, almost a supreme, place in her political constitution—was, in fact, the understood if not recognized expedient always in reserve should other milder and more hallowed methods fail of accomplishing the desired political or, it might be, religious consummation. . . .

" For centuries such justice as was exercised was haphazard and rude, and practically there was no law but the will of the stronger. Few, if any, of the great families but had their special feud; and feuds once originated survived for ages; to forget them would have been treason to the dead, and wild purposes of revenge were handed down from generation to generation as a sacred legacy.

"To take an enemy at a disadvantage was not deemed mean and contemptible, but—

'Of all the arts in which the wise excel
Nature's chief masterpiece.'

To do it boldly and adroitly was to win a peculiar halo of renown; and thus assassination ceased to be the weapon of the avowed desperado, and came to be wielded unblushingly not only by so-called men of honor, but by the so-called religious as well. A noble did not scruple to use it against his king, and the king himself felt no dishonor in resorting to it against a dangerous noble. James I. was hacked to death in the night by Sir Robert Graham; and James II. rid himself of the imperious and intriguing Douglas by suddenly stabbing him while within his own royal palace under protection of a safe conduct.

"The leaders of the Reformation discerned in assassination (that of their enemies) the special 'work and judgment of God.' . . . When the assassination of Cardinal Beaton took place in 1546, all the savage details of it were set down by Knox with unbridled gusto. 'These things we wreat mearlie,' is his own ingenuous comment on his performance.

"The burden of George Buchanan's *De Jure Regni apud Scotos* is the lawfulness or righteousness of the removal—by assassination or any other fitting or convenient means—of incompetent kings, whether heinously wicked and tyrannical or merely unwise and weak of purpose; and he cites as a case in point and an 'example in time coming,' the murder of James III., which, if it were only on account of the assassin's hideous travesty of the last offices of the Church, would deserve to be held in unique and everlasting detestation."—(Henderson, *Old-world Scotland,* 182-186.)

Yet the Scots have always been a notably warlike and fearless race. So, too, are our southern mountaineers: in the Civil War and the Spanish War they sent a larger proportion of their men into the service than almost any other section of our country.

Let us not overlook the fact that it demands courage of a high order for one to stay in a feud-infested district, conscious of being marked for slaughter—stay there month in and month out, year in and year out, not knowing at what moment he may be beset by overpowering numbers, from what laurel thicket he may be shot, or at what hour of the night he may be called to his door and struck dead before his family. On the credit side of their valor, then, be it entered that few mountaineers will shrink from such ordeal when, even from no fault of their own, it is thrust upon them.

The blood-feud is simply a horrible survival of medievalism. It is the highlander's misfortune to be stranded far out of the course of civilization. He is no worse than that bygone age that he really belongs to. In some ways he is better. He is far less cruel than his ancestors were—than our ancestors were. He does not torture with the tumbril, the stocks, the ducking-stool, the pillory, the branding-irons, the ear-pruners and nostril-shears and tongue-branks that were in everyday use under the old criminal code. He does not tie a woman to the cart's tail and publicly lash her bare back until it streams with blood, nor does he hang a man for picking somebody's pocket of twelve pence and a farthing. He does not go slumming in bedlam, paying tuppence for the sport of mocking the maniacs until they rattle their chains in rage or horror. He does not turn executions of criminals into public festivals. He never has been known to burn a condemned one at the stake. If he hangs a man, he does not first draw his entrails and burn them before his eyes, with a mob crowding about to jeer the poor devil's flinching or to compliment him on his " nerve." Yet all these pleasantries were proper and legal in Christian Britain two centuries ago.

This isolated and belated people who still carry on the blood-feud are not half so much to blame for such a savage survival as the rich, powerful, educated, twentieth-century nation that abandons them as if they were hopelessly derelict or wrecked. It took but a few decades to civilize Scotland. How much swifter and surer and easier are our means of enlightenment to-day ! Let us not forget that these highlanders are blood of our blood and bone of our bone; for they are old-time Americans to a man, proud of their nationality, and passionately loyal to the flag that they, more than any other of us, according to their strength, have fought and suffered for.

CHAPTER XIX

WHO ARE THE MOUNTAINEERS?

THE Southern Appalachian Mountains happen to be parceled out among eight different States, and for that reason they are seldom considered as a geographical unit. In the same way their inhabitants are thought of as Kentucky mountaineers or Carolina mountaineers, and so on, but not often as a body of Appalachian mountaineers. And yet these inhabitants are as distinct an ethnographic group as the mountains themselves are a geographic group.

The mountaineers are homogeneous so far as speech and manners and experiences and ideals can make them. In the aggregate they are nearly twice as numerous and cover twice as much territory as any one of the States among which they have been distributed; but in each of these States they occupy only the backyard, and generally take back seats in the councils of the commonwealth. They have been fenced off from each other by political boundaries, and have no such coherence among themselves as would come from common leadership or a sense of common origin and mutual dependence.

And they are a people without annals. Back of their grandfathers they have neither screed nor hearsay. " Borned in the kentry and ain't never been out o' hit " is all that most of them can say for themselves. Here and there one will assert, "My foreparents war principally Scotch," or " Us Bumgyarners [Baumgartners] was Dutch," but such traditions of a far-back foreign origin are uncommon.

Who are these southern mountaineers? Whence came they? What is the secret of their belatedness and isolation?

Before the Civil War they were seldom heard of in the outside world. Vaguely it was understood that the Appalachian highlands were occupied by a peculiar people called " mountain whites." This odd name was given them not to distinguish them from mountain negroes, for there were, practically, no mountain negroes; but to indicate their similarity, in social condition and economic status, to the " poor whites " of the southern lowlands. It was assumed, on no historical basis whatever, that the highlanders came from the more venturesome or desperate element of the " poor whites," and differed from these only to the extent that environment had shaped them.

Since this theory still prevails throughout the South, and is accepted generally elsewhere on its face value, it deserves just enough consideration to refute it.

The unfortunate class known as poor whites in the South is descended mainly from the convicts and indentured servants with which England supplied labor to the southern plantations before slavery days. The Cavaliers who founded and dominated southern society came from the conservative, the feudal element of England. Their character and training were essentially aristocratic and military. They were not town-dwellers, but masters of plantations. Their chief crop and article of export was tobacco. The culture of tobacco required an abundance of cheap and servile labor.

On the plantations there was little demand for skilled labor, small room anywhere for a middle class of manufacturers and merchants, no inducement for independent farmers who would till with their own hands. Outside of the planters and a small professional class there was little employment offered save what was menial and degrading. Consequently the South was shunned, from the beginning, by British yeomanry and by the thrifty Teutons such as flocked into the northern provinces. The demand for menials on the plantations was met, then, by importing bond-servants from Great Britain. These were obtained in three ways.—

1. Convicted criminals were deported to serve out their terms on the plantations. Some of these had been charged only with political offenses, and had the making of good citizens.; but the greater number were rogues of the shiftless and petty delinquent order, such as were too lazy to work but not desperate enough to have incurred capital sentences.

2. Boys and girls, chiefly from the slums of British seaports, were kidnapped and sold into temporary slavery on the plantations.

3. Impoverished people who wished to emigrate, but could not pay for their passage, voluntarily sold their services for a term of years in return for transportation.

Thus a considerable proportion of the white laborers of the South, in the seventeenth century, were criminals or ne'er-do-wells from the start. A large number of the others came from the dregs of society. As for the remainder, the companionships into which they were thrust, the brutalities to which they were subjected, their impotence before the law, the contempt in which they were held by the ruling caste, and the wretchedness of their prospect when released, were enough to undermine all but the strongest characters. Few ever succeeded in rising to respectable positions.

Then came a vast social change. At a time when the laboring classes of Europe had achieved emancipation from serfdom, and feudalism was overthrown, African slavery in our own Southland laid the foundation for a new feudalism. Southern society reverted to a type that the rest of the civilized world had outgrown.

The effect upon white labor was deplorable. The former bond-servants were now freedmen, it is true, but freedmen shorn of such opportunities as they were fitted to use. Sprung from a more or less degraded stock, still branded by caste, untrained to any career demanding skill and intelligence, devitalized by evil habits of life, densely ignorant of the world around them, these, the naturally shiftless, were now turned out into the backwoods to shift for themselves. It was inevitable that most of them should degenerate even below the level of their former estate, for they were no longer forced into steady industry.

The white freedmen generally became squatters on such land as was unfit for tobacco, cotton, and other crops profitable to slave-owners. As the plantations expanded, these freedmen were pushed further and further back upon more and more sterile soil. They became " pine-landers " or " piney-woods-people," " sand-hillers," " knob-people," " corn-crackers " or " crackers," gaining a bare subsistence from corn planted and " tended " chiefly by the women and children, from hogs running wild in the forest, and from desultory hunting and fishing. As a class, such whites lapsed into sloth and apathy. Even the institution of slavery they regarded with cynical tolerance, doubtless realizing that if it were not for the blacks they would be slaves themselves.

Now these poor whites had nothing to do with settling the mountains. There was then, and still is, plenty of wild land for them in their native lowlands. They had neither the initiative nor the courage to seek a promised land far away among the unexplored and savage peaks of the western country. They were a brave enough folk in facing familiar dangers, but they had a terror of the unknown, being densely ignorant and superstitious. The mountains, to those who ever heard of them, suggested nothing but laborious climbing amid mysterious and por-

tentous perils. The poor whites were not highlanders by descent, nor had they a whit of the
bold, self-reliant spirit of our western pioneers.
They never entered Appalachia until after it
had been won and settled by a far manlier race,
and even then they went only in driblets. The
theory that the southern mountains were peo-
pled mainly by outcasts or refugees from old
settlements in the lowlands rests on no other
basis than imagination.

How the mountains actually were settled is
another and a very different story.—

The first frontiersmen of the Appalachians
were those Swiss and Palatine Germans who
began flocking into Pennsylvania about 1682.
They settled westward of the Quakers in the
fertile limestone belts at the foot of the Blue
Ridge and the Alleghanies. Here they formed
the Quakers' buffer against the Indians, and,
for some time, theirs were the westernmost settlements of British subjects in America. These
Germans were of the Reformed or Lutheran
faith. They were strongly democratic in a social sense, and detested slavery. They were
model farmers and many of them were skilled
workmen at trades.

Shortly after the tide of German immigration set into Pennsylvania, another and quite

different class of foreigners began to arrive in this province, attracted hither by the same lodestones that drew the Germans, namely, democratic institutions and religious liberty. These newcomers were the Scotch-Irish, or Ulstermen of Ireland.

When James I., in 1607, confiscated the estates of the native Irish in six counties of Ulster, he planted them with Scotch and English Presbyterians. These outsiders came to be known as Scotch-Irish, because they were chiefly of Scotch blood and had settled in Ireland. The native Irish, to whom they were alien both by blood and by religion, detested them as usurpers, and fought them many a bloody battle.

In time, as their leases in Ulster began to expire, the Scotch-Irish themselves came in conflict with the Crown, by whom they were persecuted and evicted. Then the Ulstermen began immigrating in large numbers to Pennsylvania. As Froude says, "In the two years that followed the Antrim evictions, thirty thousand Protestants left Ulster for a land where there was no legal robbery, and where those who sowed the seed could reap the harvest."

So it was that these people became, in their turn, our westernmost frontiersmen, taking up land just outside the German settlements. Immediately they began to clash with the Indians, and there followed a long series of border wars, waged with extreme ferocity, in which sometimes it is hard to say which side was most to blame. One thing, however, is certain: if any race was ordained to exterminate the Indians that race was the Scotch-Irish.

They were a brave but hot-headed folk, as might be expected of a people who for a century had been planted amid hostile Hibernians. Justin Winsor describes them as having " all that excitable character which goes with a keen-minded adherence to original sin, total depravity, predestination, and election," and as seeing " no use in an Indian but to be a target for their bullets." They were quick-witted as well as quick-tempered, rather visionary, imperious and aggressive.

Being by tradition and habit a border people the Scotch-Irish pushed to the extreme western fringe of settlement amid the Alleghanies. They were not over-solicitous about the quality of soil. When Arthur Lee, of Virginia, was telling Doctor Samuel Johnson, in London, of a colony of Scotch who had settled upon a particularly sterile tract in western Virginia and had expressed his wonder that they should

do so, Johnson replied, " Why, sir, all barren-
ness is comparative: the Scotch will never know
that it is barren."

West of the Susquehanna, however, the land
was so rocky and poor that even the Scotch shied
at it, and so, when eastern Pennsylvania became
crowded, the overflow of settlers passed not
westward but southwestward, along the Cumberland Valley, into western Maryland, and
then into the Shenandoah and those other long,
narrow, parallel valleys of western Virginia
that we noted in our first chapter. This western region still lay unoccupied and scarcely
known by the Virginians themselves. Its fertile lands were discovered by Pennsylvania
Dutchmen. The first house in western Virginia
was erected by one of them, Joist Hite, and he
established a colony of his people near the future site of Winchester. A majority of those
who settled in the eastern part of the Shenandoah Valley were Pennsylvania Dutch, while
the Scotch-Irish, following in their train,
pushed a little to the west of them and occupied
more exposed positions. There were representatives of other races along the border: English,
Irish, French Huguenots, and so on; but everywhere the Scotch-Irish and Germans predomi-
nated.

And the southwestward movement, once started, never stopped. So there went on a gradual but sure progress of northern peoples across the Potomac, up the Shenandoah, across the Staunton, the Dan, the Yadkin, until the western piedmont and foot-hill region of Carolina was similarly settled, chiefly by Pennsylvanians.

The archivist of North Carolina, the late William L. Saunders, Secretary of State, said in one of his historical sketches that " to Lancaster and York counties, in Pennsylvania, North Carolina owes more of her population than to any other known part of the world." He called attention to the interesting fact that when the North Carolina boys of Scotch-Irish and Pennsylvania Dutch descent followed Lee into Pennsylvania in the Gettysburg campaign, they were returning to the homes of their an-· cestors, by precisely the same route that those ancestors had taken in going south.

Among those who made the long trek from Pennsylvania southward in the eighteenth century, were Daniel Boone and the ancestors of David Crockett, Samuel Houston, John C. Calhoun, "Stonewall" Jackson, and Abraham Lincoln. Boone and the Lincolns, although English themselves, had been neighbors in

WHO ARE THE MOUNTAINEERS? 439

Berks County, one of the most German parts
of all eastern Pennsylvania.

So the western piedmont and the mountains
were settled neither by Cavaliers nor by poor
whites, but by a radically distinct and even
antagonistic people who are appropriately
called the Roundheads of the South. These
Roundheads had little or nothing to do with
slavery, detested the state church, loathed tithes,
and distrusted all authority save that of conspicuous merit and natural justice. The first characteristic that these pioneers developed was an
intense individualism. The strong and even
violent independence that made them forsake
all the comforts of civilization and prefer the
wild freedom of the border was fanned at times
into turbulence and riot; but it blazed forth at
a happy time for this country when our liberties
were imperilled.

Daniel Boone first appears in history when,
from his new home on the Yadkin, he crossed
the Blue Ridge and the Unakas into that part
of western Carolina which is now eastern Tennessee. He was exploring the Watauga region
as early as 1760. Both British and French Indian traders and soldiers had been in this region
before him, but had left few marks of their
wanderings. In 1761 a party of hunters from

Pennsylvania and contiguous counties of Virginia, piloted by Boone, began to use this region as a hunting-ground, on account of the great abundance of game. From them, and especially from Boone, the fame of its attractions spread to the settlements on the eastern slope of the mountains, and in the winter of 1768-69 the first permanent occupation of eastern Tennessee was made by a few families from North Carolina.

About this time there broke out in Carolina a struggle between the independent settlers of the piedmont and the rich trading and official class of the coast. The former rose in bodies under the name of Regulators and a battle followed in which they were defeated. To escape from the persecutions of the aristocracy, many of the Regulators and their friends crossed the Appalachian Mountains and built their cabins in the Watauga region. Here, in 1772, there was established by these " rebels " the first republic in America, based upon a written constitution " the first ever adopted by a community of American-born freemen." Of these pioneers in " The Winning of the West," Theodore Roosevelt says: " As in western Virginia the first settlers came, for the most part, from Pennsylvania, so, in turn, in what was then western

North Carolina, and is now eastern Tennessee, the first settlers came mainly from Virginia, and indeed, in great part, from this same Pennsylvania stock."

Boone first visited Kentucky, on a hunting trip, in 1769. Six years later he began to colonize it, in flat defiance of the British government, and in the face of a menacing proclamation from the royal governor of North Carolina. On the Kentucky River, three days after the battle of Lexington, the flag of the new colony of Transylvania was run up on his fort at Boonesborough. It was not until the following August that these "rebels of Kentuck" heard of the signing of the Declaration of Independence, and celebrated it with shrill warwhoops around a bonfire in the center of their stockade.

Such was the stuff of which the Appalachian frontiersmen were made. They were the first Americans to cut loose entirely from the seaboard and fall back upon their own resources. They were the first to establish governments of their own, in defiance of king and aristocracy. Says John Fiske:

"Jefferson is often called the father of modern American democracy; in a certain sense the Shenandoah Valley and adjacent Appalachian regions may be called its cradle. In that rude frontier society, life assumed many new aspects.

old customs were forgotten, old distinctions abolished, social equality acquired even more importance than unchecked individualism. The notions, sometimes crude and noxious, sometimes just and wholesome, which characterized Jeffersonian democracy, flourished greatly on the frontier and have thence been propagated eastward through the older communities, affecting their legislation and their politics more or less according to frequency of contact and intercourse. Massachusetts, relatively remote and relatively ancient, has been perhaps least affected by this group of ideas, but all parts of the United States have felt its influence powerfully. This phase of democracy, which is destined to continue so long as frontier life retains any importance, can nowhere be so well studied in its beginnings as among the Presbyterian population of the Appalachian region in the 18th century."

During the Revolution, the Appalachian frontier was held by a double line of the men whom we have been considering: one line east of the mountains, and the other west of them. The mountain region itself remained almost uninhabited by whites, because the pioneers who crossed it were seeking better hunting grounds and farmsteads than the mountains afforded. It was not until the buffalo and elk and beaver had been driven out of Tennessee and Kentucky, and those rolling savannahs were being fenced and tilled, that much attention was given to the mountains proper. Then small companies of hunters and trappers from both east and west began to move into the highlands and settle there.

These explorers, pushing outward from the cross-mountain trails in every direction, found many interesting things that had been over-looked in the scurry of migration westward. They discovered fair river valleys and rich coves, adapted to tillage, which soon attracted settlers of a better class; and so, gradually, the mountain solitudes began to echo with the ring of axes and the lowing of herds. By 1830 about a million permanent settlers occupied the south-ern Appalachians. Naturally, most of them came from adjoining regions—from the foot of the Blue Ridge on one side and from the foot of the Unakas or of the Cumberlands on the other, and hence they were chiefly of the same frontier stock that we have been describing. No colonies of farmers from a distance ever have been imported into the mountains, down to our own day.

Deterioration of the mountain people began as soon as population began to press upon the limits of subsistence. At first, naturally, the best people among the mountaineers were at-tracted to the best lands. And there to-day, in the generous river valleys, we find a class of citizens superior to the average mountaineers that we have been considering in this book. But the number and extent of such valleys was narrowly limited. The United States topographers report that in Appalachia, as a whole, the mountain slopes occupy 90 per cent. of the total area, and that 85 per cent. of the land has a steeper slope than one foot in five. So, as the years passed, a larger and larger proportion of the highlanders was forced back along the creek branches and up along the steep hillsides to "scrabble" for a living.

It will be asked, Why did not this overplus do as other crowded Americans did: move west?

First, because they were so immured in the mountains, so utterly cut off from communication with the outer world, that they did not know anything about the opportunities offered new settlers in far-away lands. Moving "west" to them would have meant merely going a few days' wagon-travel down into the lowlands of Kentucky or Tennessee, which already were thickly settled by a people of very different social class. Here they could not hope to be anything but tenants or menials, ruled over by proprietors or bosses—and they would die rather than endure such treatment. As for the new lands of the farther West, there was scarce a peasant in Ireland or in Scandinavia but knew more about them than did the southern mountaineers.

Second, because they were passionately attached to their homes and kindred, to their own old-fashioned ways. The mountaineer shrinks from lowland society as he does from the water and the climate of such regions. He is never at ease until back with his home-folks, foot-loose and free.

Third, because there was nothing in his environment to arouse ambition. The hard, hopeless life of the mountain farm, sustained only by a meager and ill-cooked diet, begat laziness and shiftless unconcern.

Finally, the poverty of the hillside farmers and branch-water people was so extreme that they could not gather funds to emigrate with. There were no industries to which a man might turn and earn ready money, no markets in which he could sell a surplus from the farm.

So, while the transmontane settlers grew rapidly in wealth and culture, their kinsfolk back in the mountains either stood still or retrograded, and the contrast was due not nearly so much to any difference of capacity as to a law of Nature that dooms an isolated and impoverished people to deterioration.

Beyond this, it is not to be overlooked that the mountains were cursed with a considerable incubus of naturally weak or depraved characters, not lowland " poor whites," but a miscellaneous flotsam from all quarters, which, after more or less circling round and round, was drawn into the stagnant eddy of highland society as derelicts drift into the Sargasso Sea. In the train of western immigration there were some feeble souls who never got across the mountains. These have been described tersely as the men who lost heart on account of a broken axle.

The anemic element thus introduced is less noticeable in Kentucky than in Virginia and the States farther south—for the reason, no doubt, that it took at least two axles to reach Kentucky—but it exists in all parts of Appalachia. Moreover, the vast roughs of the mountain region offered harborage for outlaws, desperadoes of the border, and here many of them settled and propagated their kind. In the backwoods one cannot choose his neighbors. All are on equal footing. Hence the contagion of crime and shiftlessness spreads to decent families and tends to undermine them.

We can understand, then, how it happened in many cases that highland families founded

by well-informed and thrifty pioneers deteri-
orated into illiterate and idle triflers, all run
down at heels. Lincoln's family is an apt illus-
tration. His grandfather sold his Virginia
farms for seventeen thousand dollars and
bought large tracts of land in Kentucky. But
Abraham Lincoln's father set up housekeeping
in a shed, later built a log hut of one room
without doors or windows (although he was a
carpenter by trade), then moved to another
cabin a little better, tired of it, moved over into
Indiana, and made his family spend the winter
in a half-faced camp, where they were saved
from freezing by keeping up a great log fire
in front of the lean-to through days and nights
when the temperature was far below zero. The
Lincolns were not mountaineers, but they were
of the same stock, and were subjected to much
the same vicissitudes.

So the southern highlanders languished in
isolation, sunk in a Rip Van Winkle sleep,
until aroused by the thunder-crash of the Civil
War. Let John Fox tell the extraordinary
result of that awakening.—

"The American mountaineer was discovered, I say, at
the beginning of the war, when the Confederate leaders
were counting on the presumption that Mason and Dixon's

Line was the dividing line between the North and South, and formed, therefore, the plan of marching an army from Wheeling, in West Virginia, to some point on the Lakes, and thus dissevering the North at one blow.

"The plan seemed so feasible that it is said to have materially aided the sale of Confederate bonds in England. But when Captain Garnett, a West Point graduate, started to carry it out, he got no farther than Harper's Ferry. When he struck the mountains, he struck enemies who shot at his men from ambush, cut down bridges before him, carried the news of his march to the Federals, and Garnett himself fell with a bullet from a mountaineer's squirrel rifle at Harper's Ferry.

"Then the South began to realize what a long, lean, powerful arm of the Union it was that the southern mountaineer stretched through its very vitals; for that arm helped hold Kentucky in the Union by giving preponderance to the Union sympathizers in the Blue-grass; it kept the east Tennesseans loyal to the man; it made West Virginia, as the phrase goes, 'secede from secession'; it drew out a horde of one hundred thousand volunteers, when Lincoln called for troops, depleting Jackson County, Kentucky, for instance, of every male under sixty years of age and over fifteen; and it raised a hostile barrier between the armies of the coast and the armies of the Mississippi. The North has never realized, perhaps, what it owes for its victory to this non-slaveholding southern mountaineer."

President Frost, of Berea College, says:

"The loyalty of this region in the Civil War was a surprise to both northern and southern statesmen. The mountain people owned land but did not own slaves, and the national feeling of the revolutionary period had not spent its force among them. Their services in West Virginia and east Tennessee are perhaps generally known. But very few know or remember that the whole mountain region was loyal [except where conscripted]. General Carl Schurz had soldiers enlisted in the mountains of Alabama, and the writer has recently seen a letter written by the Confederate Governor of South Carolina in which he relates to General Hardee the troubles caused by Union sentiment in the mountain counties.

"It is pathetic to know how these mountain regiments disbanded with no poet or historian or monument to perpetuate the memory of their valor. The very flag that was first on Lookout Mountain and 'waved above the clouds' was lost to fame in an obscure mountain home until Berea discovered and rescued it from oblivion and destruction."

It may be added that no other part of our country suffered longer or more severely from the aftermath of war. Throughout that struggle the mountain region was a nest for bushwhackers and bandits that preyed upon the aged and defenseless who were left at home, and thus there was left an evil legacy of neighborhood wrongs and private grudges. Most of the mountain counties had incurred the bitter hostility of their own States by standing loyal to the Union. After Appomattox they were cast back into a worse isolation than they had ever known. Most unfortunately, too, the Federal

Government, at this juncture, instead of interposing to restore law and order in the highlands, turned the loyalty of the mountaineers into outlawry, as in 1794, by imposing a prohibitive excise tax upon their chief merchantable commodity.

Left, then, to their own devices, unchecked by any stronger arm, inflamed by a multitude of personal wrongs, habituated to the shedding of human blood, contemptuous of State laws that did not reach them, enraged by Federal acts that impugned, as they thought, an inalienable right of man, it was inevitable that this fiery and vindictive race should fall speedily into warring among themselves. Old scores were now to be wiped out in a reign of terror. The open combat of bannered war was turned into the secret ferocity of family feuds.

But the mountaineers of to-day are face to face with a mighty change. The feud epoch has ceased throughout the greater part of Appalachia. A new era dawns. Everywhere the highways of civilization are pushing into remote mountain fastnesses. Vast enterprises are being installed. The timber and the minerals are being garnered. The mighty waterpower that has been running to waste since these mountains rose from the primal sea is now about to be harnessed in the service of man. Along with this economic revolution will come, inevitably, good schools, newspapers, a finer and more liberal social life   The highlander. at last, is to be caught up in the current of human progress.

CHAPTER XX

THE southern mountaineers are pre-eminently a rural folk. When the twentieth century opened, only four per cent. of them dwelt in cities of 8,000 inhabitants and upwards. There were but seven such cities in all Appalachia—a region larger than England and Scotland combined—and these owed their development to outside influences. Only 77 out of 186 mountain counties had towns of 1,000 and upwards.

Our highlanders are the most homogeneous people in the United States. In 1900, out of a total population of 3,039,835, there were only 18,617 of foreign birth. This includes the cities and industrial camps. Back in the mountains, a man using any other tongue than English, or speaking broken English, was regarded as a freak. Nine mountain counties of Virginia, four of West Virginia, fifteen of Kentucky, ten of Tennessee, nine of North Carolina, eight of

452

Georgia, two of Alabama, and one of South Carolina had less than ten foreign-born residents each. Three of them had none at all.

Compare the North Atlantic states. In this same census year, 57 per cent. of their people lived in cities of 8,000 and upwards. As for foreigners—the one city of Fall River, Mass., with 104,863 inhabitants, had 50,042 of foreign birth.

The mountains proper are free not only from foreigners but from negroes as well. There are many blacks in the larger valleys and towns, but throughout most of Appalachia the population is almost exclusively white. In 1900, Jackson County, Ky. (the same that sent every one of its sons into the Union army who could bear arms), had only nineteen negroes among 10,542 whites; Johnson County, Ky., only one black resident among 13,729 whites; Dickenson County, Va., not a single negro within its borders.

In many mountain settlements negroes are not allowed to tarry. It has been assumed that this prejudice against colored folk had its origin far back in the time when " poor whites " found themselves thrust aside by competition with slave labor. This is an error. Our mountaineers never had to compete with slavery. Few of them knew anything about it except from hearsay. Their dislike of negroes is simply an instinctive racial antipathy, plus a contempt for anyone who submits to servile conditions. A neighbor in the Smokies said to me: " I b'lieve in treatin' niggers squar. The Bible says they're human—leastways some says it does—and so there'd orter be a place for them. But it's *some place else*—not around me! " That is the whole thing in a nutshell.

Here, then, is Appalachia: one of the great land-locked areas of the globe, more English in speech than Britain itself, more American by blood than any other part of America, encompassed by a high-tensioned civilization, yet less affected to-day by modern ideas, less cognizant of modern progress, than any other part of the English-speaking world.

Of course, such an anomaly cannot continue. Commercialism has discovered the mountains at last, and no sentiment, however honest, however hallowed, can keep it out. The transformation is swift. Suddenly the mountaineer is awakened from his eighteenth-century bed by the blare of steam whistles and the boom of dynamite. He sees his forests leveled and whisked away; his rivers dammed by concrete walls and shot into turbines that outpower all the horses in Appalachia. He is dazed by elec-

tric lights, nonplussed by speaking wires, awed
by vast transfers of property, incensed by rude
demands. Aroused, now, and wide-eyed, he
realizes with sinking heart that here is a sudden
end of that Old Dispensation under which he
and his ancestors were born, the beginning of
a New Order that heeds him and his neighbors
not a whit.

All this insults his conservatism. The old
way was the established order of the universe:
to change it is fairly impious. What is the good
of all this fuss and fury? That fifty-story building they tell about, in their big city—what is it
but another Tower of Babel? And these silly,
stuck-up strangers who brag and brag about
" modern improvements "—what are they, under
their fine manners and fine clothes? Hirelings
all. Shrewdly he observes them in their relations to each other.—

> " Each man is some man's servant; every soul
>   Is by some other's presence quite discrowned."

Proudly he contrasts his ragged self: he who
never has acknowledged a superior, never has
taken an order from living man, save as a patriot
in time of war. And he turns upon his heel.

Yet, before he can fairly credit it as a reality,

the lands around his own home are bought up by corporations. All about him, slash, crash, go the devastating forces. His old neighbors vanish. New and unwelcome ones swarm in. He is crowded, but ignored. His hard-earned patrimony is robbed of all that made it precious: its home-like seclusion, independence, dignity. He sells out, and moves away to some uninvaded place where he " will not be bothered."

"I don't like these improve*ments*," said an old mountaineer to me. "Some calls them 'progress,' and says they put money to circulatin'. So they do; but *who gits it?*"

There is a class of highlanders more sanguine, more adaptable, that welcomes all outsiders who come with skill and capital to develop their country. Many of these are shrewd traders in merchandise or in real estate, or they are capable foremen who can handle native labor much better than any strangers could. Such men naturally profit by the change.

Others, deluded by what seems easy money, sell their little homesteads for just enough cash to set them up as laborers in town or camp. Being untrained to any trade, they can get only the lowest wages, which are quickly dissipated in rent and in foods that formerly they raised for themselves. Unused to continuous labor,

they irk under its discipline, drop out, and fall
into desultory habits. Meantime false ambitions
arise, especially among the womenfolk. Store
credit soon runs such a family in debt.

"When I was a young man," said one of my
neighbors, "the traders never thought of bring-
in' meal in here. If a man run out of meal, why,
he was *out,* and he had to live on 'taters or somethin' else. Nowadays we dress better, and live
better, but some other feller allers has his hands
in our pockets."

Then it is "good-by" to the old independence that made such characters manly. Enmeshed in obligations that they cannot meet,
they struggle vainly, brood hopelessly, and lose
that dearest of all possessions, their self-respect.
Servility is literal hell to a mountaineer, and
when it is forced upon him he turns into a mean,
underhanded, slinking fellow, easily tempted
into crime.

The curse of our invading civilization is that
its vanguard is composed of men who care nothing for the welfare of the people they dispossess.
A northern lumberman admitted to me, with
frankness unusual in his class, that "All we
want here is to get the most we can out of this
country, as quick as we can, and then get out."
This is all we can expect of those who exploit

458 OUR SOUTHERN HIGHLANDERS

raw materials, or of manufactures that employ
only cheap labor. Until we have industries that
demand skilled workmen, and until manual
training schools are established in the mountains, we may look for deterioration, rather than
betterment, of those highlanders who leave their
farms.

All who know the mountaineers intimately
have observed that the sudden inroad of commercialism has a bad effect upon them. As
President Frost says, "Ruthless change is
knocking at the door of every mountain cabin.
The jackals of civlization have already abused
the confidence of many a highland home. The
lumber, coal, and mineral wealth of the mountains is to be possessed, and the unprincipled
vanguard of commercialism can easily debauch
a simple people. The question is whether the
mountain people can be enlightened and guided
so that they can have a part in the development
of their own country, or whether they must give
place to foreigners and melt away like so many
Indians."

It is easy to say that the fittest will survive.
But the fittest for what? Miss Miles answers:
"I have heard it said that civilization, when it
touches the people of the backwoods, acts as a
useful precipitant in thus sending the dregs to

the bottom. As a matter of fact, it is only the shrewder and more determined, not the truly fit, that survive the struggle. Among these very submerged ones, reduced to dependence on an alien people, there are thousands who inherit the skill of their forefathers who fashioned their own locks, musical instruments, and guns. And these very women who are breaking their health and spirit over a thankless tub of suds ought surely to turn their talents to better account, ought to be designing and weaving coverlets and Roman-striped rugs, or 'piecing' the quilt patterns now so popular. Need these razors be used to cut grindstones? Must this free folk who are in many ways the truest Americans of America be brought under the yoke of caste division, to the degradation of all their finer qualities, merely for lack of the right work to do?"

There are some who would have it so; who would calmly write for these our own kindred, as for the Indians, *fuerunt*—their day is past. In a History of Southern Literature, written not long ago by a professor in the University of Virginia, a sketch of Miss Murfree's work closes with these words: "There [at Beersheba Springs, Tenn.] it was that she first studied the curious type of humanity, the Tennessee mountaineer, a people so ignorant, so superstitious, so far behind the world of to-day as to excite wonder and even pity in all who see them. . . . [She] is telling the story of a people who, in these opening years of the 20th century, wander on through their limited range of life much as their ancestors for generations have wandered. They, too, will some time vanish—the sooner the better."

One cannot read such a sentiment without wonder and even pity for the ignorance of history and of human nature that it discloses. Is the case of our mountaineers so much worse than that of the Scotch highlanders of two centuries ago? We know that those Scotchmen did not "vanish—the quicker the better." What were they before civilization reached them? Let us open the ready pages of Macaulay.—

"It is not easy for a modern Englishman . . . to believe that, in the time of his great-grandfathers, Saint James's Street had as little connection with the Grampians as with the Andes. Yet so it was. In the south of our island scarcely anything was known about the Celtic part of Scotland; and what was known excited no feeling but contempt and loathing. . . .

"It is not strange that the Wild Scotch, as they were sometimes called, should, in the 17th century, have been considered by the Saxons as mere savages. But it is surely strange that, considered as savages, they should not have been objects of interest and curiosity. The English were then abundantly inquisitive about the manners of rude nations separated from our island by great continents and oceans. Numerous books were printed describing the laws, the superstitions, the cabins, the repasts, the dresses, the marriages, the funerals of Laplanders and Hottentots, Mohawks and Malays. The plays and poems of that age are full of allusions to the usages of the black men of Africa and the red men of America. The only barbarian about whom there was no wish to have any information was the Highlander. . . .

" While the old Gaelic institutions were in full vigor, no account of them was given by any observer qualified to judge of them fairly. Had such an observer studied the character of the Highlanders, he would doubtless have found in it closely intermingled the good and the bad qualities of an uncivilized nation. He would have found that the people had no love for their country or for their king, that they had no attachment to any commonwealth larger than the clan, or to any magistrate superior to the chief. He would have found that life was governed by a code of morality and honor widely different from that which is established in peaceful and prosperous societies. He would have learned that a stab in the back, or a shot from behind a fragment of rock, were approved modes of taking satisfaction for insults. He would have heard men relate boastfully how they or their fathers had wracked on hereditary enemies in a neighboring valley such vengeance as would have made old soldiers of the Thirty Years' War shudder.

" He would have found that robbery was held to be a

calling not merely innocent but honorable. He would have seen, wherever he turned, that dislike of steady industry, and that disposition to throw on the weaker sex the heaviest part of manual labor, which are characteristic of savages. He would have been struck by the spectacle of athletic men basking in the sun, angling for salmon, or taking aim at grouse, while their aged mothers, their pregnant wives, their tender daughters, were reaping the scanty harvest of oats. Nor did the women repine at their hard lot. In their view it was quite fit that a man, especially if he assumed the aristocratic title of Duinhe Wassel and adorned his bonnet with the eagle's feather, should take his ease, except when he was fighting, hunting, or marauding. To mention the name of such a man in connection with commerce or with any mechanical art was an insult. Agriculture was indeed less despised. Yet a highborn warrior was much more becomingly employed in plundering the land of others than in tilling his own.

"The religion of the greater part of the Highlands was a rude mixture of Popery and Paganism. The symbol of redemption was associated with heathen sacrifices and incantations. Baptised men poured libations of ale on one Dæmon, and set out drink offerings of milk for another. Seers wrapped themselves up in bulls' hides, and awaited, in that vesture, the inspiration which was to reveal the future. Even among those minstrels and genealogists whose hereditary vocation was to preserve the memory of past events, an enquirer would have found very few who could read. In truth, he might easily have journeyed from sea to sea without discovering a page of Gaelic printed or written.

"The price which he would have had to pay for his

knowledge of the country would have been heavy. He would have had to endure hardships as great as if he had sojourned among the Esquimaux or the Samoyeds. Here and there, indeed, at the castle of some great lord who had a seat in the Parliament and Privy Council, and who was accustomed to pass a large part of his life in the cities of the South, might have been found wigs and embroidered coats, plate and fine linen, lace and jewels, French dishes and French wines. But, in general, the traveler would have been forced to content himself with very different quarters. In many dwellings the furniture, the food, the clothing, nay, the very hair and skin of his hosts, would have put his philosophy to the proof. His lodging would sometimes have been in a hut of which every nook would have swarmed with vermin. He would have inhaled an atmosphere thick with peat smoke, and foul with a hundred exhalations. At supper grain fit only for horses would have been set before him, accompanied with a cake of blood drawn from living cows. Some of the company with whom he would have feasted would have been covered with cutaneous eruptions, and others would have been smeared with tar like sheep. His couch would have been the bare earth, dry or wet as the weather might be; and from that couch he would have risen half poisoned with stench, half blind with the reek of turf, and half mad with the itch.

This is not an attractive picture. And yet an enlightened and dispassionate observer would have found in the character and manners of this rude people something which might well excite admiration and a good hope. Their courage was what great exploits achieved in all the four quarters of the globe have since proved it to be. Their intense attachment to their own tribe and to their own patriarch, though politically a great evil, partook of the nature of virtue. The sentiment was misdirected and ill regulated; but still it was heroic. There must be some elevation of soul in a man who loves the society of which he is a member and the leader whom he follows with a love stronger than the love of life. It was true that the Highlander had few scruples about shedding the blood of an enemy; but it was not less true that he had high notions of the duty of observing faith to allies and hospitality to guests. It was true that his predatory habits were most pernicious to the commonwealth. Yet those erred greatly who imagined that he bore any resemblance to villains who, in rich and well governed communities, live by stealing. When he drove before him the herds of Lowland farmers up the pass which led to his native glen, he no more considered himself as a thief than the Raleighs and Drakes considered themselves as thieves when they divided the cargoes of Spanish galleons. He was a warrior seizing lawful prize of war, of war never once intermitted during the thirty-five generations which had passed away since the Teutonic invaders had driven the children of the soil to the mountains. . . .

" His inordinate pride of birth and his contempt for labor and trade were indeed great weaknesses, and had done far more than the inclemency of the air and the sterility of the soil to keep his country poor and rude. Yet even here there was some compensation. It must in fairness be acknowledged that the patrician virtues were not less widely diffused among the population of the Highlands than the patrician vices. As there was no other part of the island where men, sordidly clothed, lodged, and fed, indulged themselves to such a degree in the idle, sauntering habits of an aristocracy, so there was no other part of the island where such men had in such a degree the better qualities of an aristocracy, grace and dignity of manner, self-respect, and that noble sensibility which makes dishonor more terrible than death. A gentleman of Skye or Lochaber, whose clothes were begrimed with the accumulated filth of years, and whose hovel smelt worse than an English hogstye, would often do the honors of that hovel with a lofty courtesy worthy of the splendid circle of Versailles. Though he had as little book-learning as the most stupid plough-boys of England, it would have been a great error to put him in the same intellectual rank with such ploughboys. It is indeed only by reading that men can become profoundly acquainted with any science. But the arts of poetry and rhetoric may be carried near to absolute perfection, and may exercise a mighty influence on the public mind, in an age in which books are wholly or almost wholly unknown."

So, too, in the rudest communities of Appalachia, among the most trifling and unmoral natives of this region, among the illiterate and hide-bound, there still is much to excite admiration and good hope. I have not shrunk from telling the truth about these people, even when it was far from pleasant; but I would have preserved strict silence had I not seen in the most backward of them certain sterling qualities of manliness that our nation can ill afford to waste. It is a truth as old as the human race that savageries may co-exist with admirable qualities of head and heart. The only people who can consistently despair of the future for even the lowest of our mountaineers are those who deny evolution and who believe, with Archbishop Usher, that man was created *perfect* at 9 A. M. on the 21st of October, in the year B. C. 4004.

Let us remember, Sir and Madam, that we ourselves are descended from white barbarians. From William the Conqueror, you? Very well; how many other ancestors of yours were walking about England and elsewhere at the time of William? Untold thousands of them were just such people as you can find to-day brawling in some mountain still-house (unless there has been a deal of incest somewhere along your line), and you have infinitely more of their blood in your veins than you have of the Conqueror's—who, by the way, could he be re-incarnated, would not be tolerated in your drawing-room for half an hour. I may have made the point too brutally plain; but if it sinks through the smug self-complacency of those who " do not belong to the masses," who act as though civilization and morals and good manners were entailed to them through a mere dozen or so of selected ancestors, I remain unrepentant and unashamed. Let us thank whatever gods there be that it is not merely thou and I, our few friends and next of kin, but all humanity, that scientific faith embraces and will sustain.

" People who have been among the southern mountaineers testify," says Mr. Fox, " that, as a race, they are proud, sensitive, hospitable, kindly, obliging in an unreckoning way that is almost pathetic, honest, loyal, in spite of their common ignorance, poverty, and isolation; that they are naturally capable, eager to learn, easy to uplift. Americans to the core, they make the southern mountains a storehouse of patriotism; in themselves they are an important offset to the Old World outcasts whom we have welcomed to our shores; and they surely deserve as much consideration from the nation as the negroes, or as the heathen, to whom we give millions."

President Frost, of Berea College, who has worked among these people for nearly a lifetime, and has helped to educate their young folks by thousands, says: " It does one's heart good to help a young Lincoln who comes walking in perhaps a three-days' journey on foot, with a few hard-earned dollars in his pocket and a great eagerness for the education he can so faintly comprehend. (Scores of our young people see their first railroad train at Berea.) And it is a joy to welcome the mountain girl who comes back after having taught her first school, bringing the money to pay her debts and buy her first comfortable outfit—including rubbers and suitable underclothing—and perhaps bringing with her a younger sister. Such a girl exerts a great influence in her school and mountain home. An enthusiastic mountaineer described an example in this wise: ' I tell yeou hit teks a moughty reso*lute* gal ter do what that thar gal has done. She got, I reckon, about the toughest deestric' in the ceounty, which is sayin' a good deal. An' then fer boardin'-place—well, there warn't much choice. There was one house, with one room. But she kep right on, an' yeou would hev thought she was havin' the finest kind of a time, ter look at her. An' then the last day, when they was sayin' their pieces and sich, some sorry fellers come in thar full o' moonshine an' shot their revolvers. I'm a-tellin' ye hit takes a moughty reso*lute* gal."

The great need of our mountaineers to-day is trained leaders of their own. The future of Appalachia lies mostly in the hands of those resolute native boys and girls who win the education fitting them for such leadership. Here is where the nation at large is summoned by a solemn duty. And it should act quickly, because commercialism exploits and debauches quickly. But the schools needed here are not ordinary graded schools. They should be vocational schools that will turn out good farmers, good mechanics, good housewives. Meantime let a model farm be established in every mountain county showing how to get the most out of mountain land. Such object lessons would speedily work an economic revolution. It is an economic problem, fundamentally, that the mountaineer has to face.